GUIDANCE

Compiled by
Martin H. Manser

HarperCollins*Publishers*

HarperCollins Publishers
P.O. Box, Glasgow G4 0NB

First published in 1988 by Marshall Pickering,
an imprint of HarperCollins Publishers

This edition first published 1995

Reprint 10 9 8 7 6 5 4 3 2 1 0

ISBN 0 00 470833 4

Scripture quotations in this publication are from the Holy Bible, New
International Version. Copyright © 1973, 1978, 1984 International Bible
Society. Published by Hodder & Stoughton.

Acknowledgement is due for permission to reproduce the following copyright
hymns in this book.

F. Houghton, *Facing a Task Unfinished* (words). Copyright © OMF
T. Harris, *Who Can Cheer the Heart*. Copyright © Nazarene Publishing House
T. Dudley-Smith, *Tell Out my Soul*. Copyright © T. Dudley-Smith
K.A.M. Kelly, *Give Me A Sight*. Copyright © Young Life
T.O. Chisholm, *Great is thy Faithfulness*. Copyright © Hope Publishing Co.
R.B. Hoyle (translation), *Thine be the Glory*. Copyright © The World Student
  Christian Federation
P. Dearmer (translation), *Unto us a Boy*. Copyright © Oxford University Press

Printed in Great Britain by
HarperCollins Manufacturing, Glasgow

PREFACE

These readings from the Bible have been compiled with the aim of providing a source of daily encouragement and guidance for Christians. The extracts have been specially chosen from the New International Version of the Bible to give inspiration – and at times challenge – to believers. The readings are accompanied by extracts from hymns, which can be used to make a personal response to God and his word.

The Bible portions and hymns in this book could perhaps best be complemented by following a plan of reading through the whole Bible. In this way a personal devotional time with God becomes a daily opportunity to 'seek the Lord's face' (Psalm 27:8) as God speaks to us about our lives 'face to face, as a man speaks with his friend' (Exodus 33:11).

Martin H. Manser
February 1995

Where to find help when you're feeling ...

The perfect guidance of God

I will instruct and teach you in the way you should go;
I will counsel you and watch over you.

Psalm 32:8

'If you spend yourselves on behalf of the hungry and
satisfy the needs of the oppressed, then your light will
rise in the darkness, and your night will become like
the noonday. The Lord will guide you always; he will
satisfy your needs in a sun-scorched land and will
strengthen your frame. You will be like a well-watered
garden, like a spring whose waters never fail.'

Isaiah 58:10–11

Jesus answered, 'I am the way and the truth and the
life. No-one comes to the Father except through me.'

John 14:6

> All the way my Saviour leads me:
>   What have I to ask beside?
> Can I doubt His tender mercy
>   Who through life has been my Guide?
> Heavenly peace, divinest comfort,
>   Here by faith in Him to dwell!
> For I know whate'er befall me,
>   Jesus doeth all things well.
>
> All the way my Saviour leads me;
>   O the fulness of His love!
> Perfect rest to me is promised
>   In my Father's house above.
> When my spirit, clothed immortal,
>   Wings its flight to realms of day,
> This, my song through endless ages,
>   Jesus led me all the way.

Frances Jane Van Alstyne, 1820–1915

The good shepherd

The Lord is my shepherd, I shall not be in want. He makes me lie down in green pastures, he leads me beside quiet waters, he restores my soul. He guides me in paths of righteousness for his name's sake. Even though I walk through the valley of the shadow of death, I will fear no evil, for you are with me; your rod and your staff, they comfort me.

You prepare a table before me in the presence of my enemies. You anoint my head with oil; my cup overflows. Surely goodness and love will follow me all the days of my life, and I will dwell in the house of the Lord for ever.

Psalm 23:1–6

'I am the good shepherd. The good shepherd lays down his life for the sheep. I am the good shepherd; I know my sheep and my sheep know me – just as the Father knows me and I know the Father – and I lay down my life for the sheep.' 'My sheep listen to my voice; I know them, and they follow me.'

John 10:11, 14–15, 27

> Green pastures are before me
> Which yet I have not seen;
> Bright skies will soon be o'er me,
> Where the dark clouds have been:
> My hope I cannot measure,
> My path to life is free;
> My Saviour has my treasure,
> And He will walk with me.

Anna Laetitia Waring, 1820–1910

Knowing Jesus

'All things have been committed to me by my Father. No-one knows the Son except the Father, and no-one knows the Father except the Son and those to whom the Son chooses to reveal him.'

Matthew 11:27

'Now this is eternal life, that they may know you, the only true God, and Jesus Christ, whom you have sent.'
John 17:3

I keep asking that the God of our Lord Jesus, the glorious Father, may give you the Spirit of wisdom and revelation, so that you may know him better.

Ephesians 1:17

I want to know Christ and the power of his resurrection and the fellowship of sharing in his sufferings, becoming like him in his death, and so, somehow, to attain to the resurrection from the dead.

Philippians 3:10

More about Jesus would I know,
More of His grace to others show,
More of His saving fulness see,
More of His love – who died for me.

More, more about Jesus,
More, more about Jesus;
More of His saving fulness see,
More of His love who died for me.

Eliza Edmunds Hewitt, 1851–1920

Bearing fruit

Blessed is the man who does not walk in the counsel of the wicked or stand in the way of sinners or sit in the seat of mockers. But his delight is in the law of the Lord, and on his law he meditates day and night. He is like a tree planted by streams of water, which yields its fruit in season and whose leaf does not wither. Whatever he does prospers.

Psalm 1:1–3

The fruit of the righteous is a tree of life, and he who wins souls is wise.

Proverbs 11:30

'I am the vine; you are the branches. If a man remains in me and I in him, he will bear much fruit; apart from me you can do nothing. If anyone does not remain in me, he is like a branch that is thrown away and withers; such branches are picked up, thrown into the fire and burned. If you remain in me and my words remain in you, ask whatever you wish, and it will be given you. This is to my Father's glory, that you bear much fruit, showing yourselves to be my disciples.'

John 15:5–8

> Forth in Thy Name, O Lord, I go,
>   My daily labour to pursue,
> Thee only Thee, resolved to know
>   In all I think, or speak, or do.
>
> The task Thy wisdom hath assigned
>   O let me cheerfully fulfil,
> In all my works Thy presence find,
>   And prove Thy good and perfect will.

Charles Wesley, 1707–88

God, the Creator

In the beginning God created the heavens and the earth.

Genesis 1:1

Then God said, 'Let us make man in our image, in our likeness, and let them rule over the fish of the sea and the birds of the air, over the livestock, over all the earth, and over all the creatures that move along the ground.' So God created man in his own image, in the image of God he created him; male and female he created them.

Genesis 1:26–27

In the beginning was the Word, and the Word was with God, and the Word was God. He was with God in the beginning. Through him all things were made; without him nothing was made that has been made.

John 1:1–3

Praise to the Lord, the Almighty,
    the King of creation;
O my soul, praise Him, for He is
    thy health and salvation;
  All ye who hear,
  Brothers and sisters, draw near,
Praise Him in glad adoration.

Praise to the Lord, Who doth prosper
    thy work and defend thee;
Surely His goodness and mercy
    here daily attend thee:
  Ponder anew
  What the Almighty can do,
If with His love He befriend thee.

Joachim Neander, 1650–80
tr. Catherine Winkworth, 1829–78, and others

JANUARY 6

Depending upon God

Why do you say, O Jacob, and complain, O Israel, 'My way is hidden from the Lord; my cause is disregarded by my God'? Do you not know? Have you not heard? The Lord is the everlasting God, the Creator of the ends of the earth. He will not grow tired or weary, and his understanding no-one can fathom. He gives strength to the weary and increases the power of the weak. Even youths grow tired and weary, and young men stumble and fall; but those who hope in the Lord will renew their strength. They will soar on wings like eagles; they will run and not grow weary, they will walk and not be faint.

Isaiah 40:27–31

Happy the man whose hopes rely
On Israel's God! He made the sky,
   And earth, and sea, with all their train:
His truth for ever stands secure;
He saves the oppressed, He feeds the poor,
   And none shall find His promise vain.

I'll praise Him while he lends me breath;
And when my voice is lost in death,
   Praise shall employ my nobler powers:
My days of praise shall ne'er be past,
While life, and thought, and being last,
   Or immortality endures.

Isaac Watts, 1674–1748

The blood of Christ

In him we have redemption through his blood, the forgiveness of sins, in accordance with the riches of God's grace.

Ephesians 1:7

Therefore, brothers, since we have confidence to enter the Most Holy Place by the blood of Jesus, by a new and living way opened for us through the curtain, that is, his body, and since we have a great priest over the house of God, let us draw near to God with a sincere heart in full assurance of faith, having our hearts sprinkled to cleanse us from a guilty conscience and having our bodies washed with pure water.

Hebrews 10:19–22

> 'Man of Sorrows!' what a name
> For the Son of God, Who came
> Ruined sinners to reclaim!
>   Hallelujah! what a Saviour!
>
> Bearing shame and scoffing rude,
> In my place condemned He stood;
> Sealed my pardon with His blood:
>   Hallelujah what a Saviour!

Philipp Paul Bliss, 1838–76

God's perfect peace

How great is your goodness, which you have stored up for those who fear you, which you bestow in the sight of men on those who take refuge in you.

Psalm 31:19

'Surely God is my salvation; I will trust and not be afraid. The Lord, the Lord, is my strength and my song; he has become my salvation.' With joy you will draw water from the wells of salvation.

Isaiah 12:2–3

You will keep in perfect peace him whose mind is steadfast, because he trusts in you. Trust in the Lord for ever, for the Lord, the Lord, is the Rock eternal.

Isaiah 26:3–4

> Like a river glorious
> Is God's perfect peace,
> Over all victorious
> In its bright increase;
>
> Perfect, yet it floweth
> Fuller every day;
> Perfect, yet it groweth
> Deeper all the way.
>
> *Stayed upon Jehovah*
> *Hearts are fully blest,*
> *Finding, as He promised,*
> *Perfect peace and rest.*

Frances Ridley Havergal, 1836–79

Submitting to our Father

Endure hardship as discipline; God is treating you as sons. For what son is not disciplined by his father? If you are not disciplined (and everyone undergoes discipline), then you are illegitimate children and not true sons. Moreover, we have all had human fathers who disciplined us and we respected them for it. How much more should we submit to the Father of our spirits and live! Our fathers disciplined us for a little while as they thought best; but God disciplines us for our good, that we may share in his holiness. No discipline seems pleasant at the time, but painful. Later on, however, it produces a harvest of righteousness and peace for those who have been trained by it.

Hebrews 12:7–11

Submit yourselves, then, to God. Resist the devil, and he will flee from you.

James 4:7

Search me, O God, and know my heart; test me and know my anxious thoughts. See if there is any offensive way in me, and lead me in the way everlasting.

Psalm 139:23–24

Have Thine own way, Lord, have Thine own way;
Thou art the potter, I am the clay.
Mould me and make me after thy will,
While I am waiting yielded and still.

Adelaide Addison Pollard, 1862–1934

The Christian's priority

'Blessed are the meek, for they will inherit the earth.
Blessed are those who hunger and thirst for righteousness, for they will be filled. Blessed are the merciful, for
they will be shown mercy. Blessed are the pure in heart,
for they will see God.'

Matthew 5:5–8

'But seek first his kingdom and his righteousness, and
all these things will be given to you as well.'

Matthew 6:33

> Seek ye first, not earthly pleasure,
> Fading joy and failing treasure;
> But the love that knows no measure
>   Seek ye first.
>
> Seek this first: be pure and holy,
> Like the Master, meek and lowly,
> Yielded to His service wholly:
>   Seek this first.

Georgianna Mary Taylor, 1848–1915

God's holy word

Oh, how I love your law! I meditate on it all day long.
Your commands make me wiser than my enemies, for
they are ever with me. I have more insight than all my
teachers, for I meditate on your statutes. I have more
understanding than the elders, for I obey your precepts.
Your word is a lamp to my feet and a light for my path.

Psalm 119:97–100, 105

The holy Scriptures . . . which are able to make you wise
for salvation through faith in Christ Jesus. All Scripture
is God-breathed and is useful for teaching, rebuking,
correcting and training in righteousness, so that the
man of God may be thoroughly equipped for every good
work.

2 Timothy 3:15–17

> Lord, Thy Word abideth,
> And our footsteps guideth;
> Who its truth believeth
> Light and joy receiveth.
>
> O that we, discerning
> Its most holy learning,
> Lord, may love and fear Thee,
> Evermore be near Thee!

Henry Williams Baker, 1821–77

——————— **JANUARY 12** ———————

Worshipping Jesus

While he [Jesus] was in Bethany, reclining at the table in the home of a man known as Simon the Leper, a woman came with an alabaster jar of very expensive perfume, made of pure nard. She broke the jar and poured the perfume on his head.

Some of those present were saying indignantly to one another, 'Why this waste of perfume? It could have been sold for more than a year's wages and the money given to the poor.' And they rebuked her harshly.

'Leave her alone,' said Jesus. 'Why are you bothering her? She has done a beautiful thing to me. The poor you will always have with you, and you can help them any time you want. But you will not always have me. She did what she could. She poured perfume on my body beforehand to prepare for my burial. I tell you the truth, wherever the gospel is preached throughout the world, what she has done will also be told, in memory of her.'
Mark 14:3–9

How sweet the Name of Jesus sounds
   In a believer's ear!
It soothes his sorrows, heals his wounds,
   And drives away his fear.

Jesus! my Shepherd, Brother, Friend,
   My Prophet, Priest and King,
My Lord, my Life, my Way, my End,
   Accept the praise I bring.

John Newton, 1725–1807

A life of praise

But you are a chosen people, a royal priesthood, a holy nation, a people belonging to God, that you may declare the praises of him who called you out of darkness into his wonderful light. Once you were not a people, but now you are the people of God; once you had not received mercy, but now you have received mercy.

1 Peter 2:9–10

Through Jesus, therefore, let us continually offer to God a sacrifice of praise – the fruit of lips that confess his name. And do not forget to do good and to share with others, for with such sacrifices God is pleased.

Hebrews 13:15–16

Fill Thou my life, O Lord my God,
In every part with praise,
That my whole being may proclaim
Thy being and Thy ways.

Horatius Bonar, 1808–89

Christ, our rock

I waited patiently for the Lord; he turned to me and heard my cry. He lifted me out of the slimy pit, out of the mud and mire; he set my feet on a rock and gave me a firm place to stand. He put a new song in my mouth, a hymn of praise to our God. Many will see and fear and put their trust in the Lord.

Blessed is the man who makes the Lord his trust, who does not look to the proud, to those who turn aside to false gods.

Psalm 40:1–4

But now a righteousness from God, apart from law, has been made known, to which the Law and the Prophets testify. This righteousness from God comes through faith in Jesus Christ to all who believe. There is no difference, for all have sinned and fall short of the glory of God, and are justified freely by his grace through the redemption that came by Christ Jesus. God presented him as a sacrifice of atonement, through faith in his blood.

Romans 3:21–25

My hope is built on nothing less
Than Jesus' blood and righteousness;
I dare not trust the sweetest frame,
But wholly lean on Jesus' Name.

On Christ, the solid Rock, I stand;
All other ground is sinking sand.

Edward Mote, 1797–1874

'Come to me'

Faith comes from hearing the message, and the message is heard through the word of Christ.

Romans 10:17

'Listen, listen to me, and eat what is good, and your soul will delight in the richest of fare. Give ear and come to me; hear me, that your soul may live. I will make an everlasting covenant with you, my faithful love promised to David.'

Isaiah 55:2–3

'Come to me, all you who are weary and burdened, and I will give you rest. Take my yoke upon you and learn from me, for I am gentle and humble in heart, and you will find rest for your souls. For my yoke is easy and my burden is light.'

Matthew 11:28–30

> I heard the voice of Jesus say,
> 'Come unto Me and rest;
> Lay down, thou weary one, lay down
> Thy head upon My breast!'
> I came to Jesus as I was,
> Weary, and worn, and sad;
> I found in Him a resting-place,
> And He has made me glad.

Horatius Bonar, 1808–89

God, the compassionate one

He will not always accuse, nor will he harbour his anger
for ever; he does not treat us as our sins deserve or repay
us according to our iniquities. For as high as the heavens
are above the earth, so great is his love for those who
fear him; as far as the east is from the west, so far has
he removed our transgressions from us. As a father has
compassion on his children, so the Lord has compassion
on those who fear him; for he knows how we are formed,
he remembers that we are dust.

Psalm 103:9–14

Who is a God like you, who pardons sin and forgives the
transgression of the remnant of his inheritance? You do
not stay angry for ever but delight to show mercy. You
will again have compassion on us; you will tread our
sins underfoot and hurl all our iniquities into the depths
of the sea.

Micah 7:18–19

> Great God of wonders! all Thy ways
> Are matchless, godlike, and divine;
> But the fair glories of Thy grace,
> More godlike and unrivalled shine:
>
> *Who is a pardoning God like Thee?*
> *Or who has grace so rich and free?*

Samuel Davies, 1723–61

Christ is risen!

I declare to you, brothers, that flesh and blood cannot inherit the kingdom of God, nor does the perishable inherit the imperishable. Listen, I tell you a mystery: We will not all sleep, but we will all be changed – in a flash, in the twinkling of an eye, at the last trumpet. For the trumpet will sound, the dead will be raised imperishable, and we will be changed. For the perishable must clothe itself with the imperishable, and the mortal with immortality. When the perishable has been clothed with the imperishable, and the mortal with immortality, then the saying that is written will come true: 'Death has been swallowed up in victory.' 'Where, O death, is your victory? Where, O death, is your sting?' The sting of death is sin, and the power of sin is the law. But thanks be to God! He gives us the victory through our Lord Jesus Christ. Therefore, my dear brothers, stand firm. Let nothing move you. Always give yourselves fully to the work of the Lord, because you know that your labour in the Lord is not in vain.

1 Corinthians 15:50–58

Christ is risen! Hallelujah!
  Risen our victorious Head!
Sing His praises! Hallelujah!
  Christ is risen from the dead.
Gratefully our hearts adore Him
  As His light once more appears,
Bowing down in joy before Him,
  Rising up from grief and tears.

Christ is risen! Hallelujah!
  Risen our victorious Head!
Sing His praises! Hallelujah!
  Christ is risen from the dead.

John Samuel Bewley Monsell, 1811–75

Amazing grace!

From the fulness of his grace we have all received one blessing after another. For the law was given through Moses; grace and truth came through Jesus Christ.

John 1:16–17

As for you, you were dead in your transgressions and sins, in which you used to live when you followed the ways of this world and of the ruler of the kingdom of the air, the spirit who is now at work in those who are disobedient. All of us also lived among them at one time, gratifying the cravings of our sinful nature and following its desires and thoughts. Like the rest, we were by nature objects of wrath. But because of his great love for us, God, who is rich in mercy, made us alive with Christ even when we were dead in transgressions – it is by grace you have been saved. And God raised us up with Christ and seated us with him in the heavenly realms in Christ Jesus, in order that in the coming ages he might show the incomparable riches of his grace, expressed in his kindness to us in Christ Jesus. For it is by grace you have been saved, through faith – and this not from yourselves, it is the gift of God – not by works, so that no-one can boast.

Ephesians 2:1–9

Amazing grace! how sweet the sound
  That saved a wretch like me;
I once was lost, but now am found;
  Was blind, but now I see.

'Twas grace that taught my heart to fear,
  And grace my fears relieved;
How precious did that grace appear,
  The hour I first believed!

John Newton, 1725–1807

The law of the Lord

The law of the Lord is perfect, reviving the soul. The statutes of the Lord are trustworthy, making wise the simple. The precepts of the Lord are right, giving joy to the heart. The commands of the Lord are radiant, giving light to the eyes. The fear of the Lord is pure, enduring for ever. The ordinances of the Lord are sure and altogether righteous. They are more precious than gold, than much pure gold; they are sweeter than honey, than honey from the comb. By them is your servant warned; in keeping them there is great reward.

May the words of my mouth and the meditation of my heart be pleasing in your sight, O Lord, my Rock and my Redeemer.

Psalm 19:7–11, 14

Jesus, I can trust Thee,
    Trust Thy written Word,
Though Thy voice of pity
    I have never heard:
When Thy Spirit teacheth,
    To my taste how sweet!
Only may I hearken,
    Sitting at Thy feet.

Mary Jane Walker, 1816–78

The coming of the Spirit

'When the Counsellor comes, whom I will send to you from the Father, the Spirit of truth who goes out from the Father, he will testify about me. And you also must testify, for you have been with me from the beginning.'

John 15:26–27

Jesus said, 'Peace be with you! As the Father has sent me, I am sending you.' And with that he breathed on them and said, 'Receive the Holy Spirit. If you forgive anyone his sins, they are forgiven; if you do not forgive them, they are not forgiven.'

John 20:21–23

'But you will receive power when the Holy Spirit comes on you; and you will be my witnesses in Jerusalem, and in all Judea and Samaria, and to the ends of the earth.'

Acts 1:8

> Breathe on me, Breath of God,
>   Fill me with life anew;
> That I may love what Thou dost love
>   And do what Thou wouldst do.
>
> Breathe on me, Breath of God,
>   Till I am wholly Thine;
> Until this earthly part of me
>   Glows with Thy fire divine.

Edwin Hatch, 1835–89

True obedience

Then the Pharisees went out and laid plans to trap him in his words. They sent their disciples to him along with the Herodians. 'Teacher,' they said, 'we know you are a man of integrity and that you teach the way of God in accordance with the truth. You aren't swayed by men, because you pay no attention to who they are. Tell us then, what is your opinion? Is it right to pay taxes to Caesar or not?'

But Jesus, knowing their evil intent, said, 'You hypocrites, why are you trying to trap me? Show me the coin used for paying the tax.' They brought him a denarius, and he asked them, 'Whose portrait is this? And whose inscription?'

'Caesar's,' they replied.

Then he said to them, 'Give to Caesar what is Caesar's, and to God what is God's.'

Matthew 22:15–21

Everyone must submit himself to the governing authorities, for there is no authority except that which God has established. The authorities that exist have been established by God.

Romans 13:1

> So let our lips and lives express
> The holy gospel we profess;
> So let our works and virtues shine,
> To prove the doctrine all divine.

Isaac Watts, 1674–1748

The strength of Christ in us

To keep me from becoming conceited because of these surpassingly great revelations, there was given me a thorn in my flesh, a messenger of Satan, to torment me. Three times I pleaded with the Lord to take it away from me. But he said to me, 'My grace is sufficient for you, for my power is made perfect in weakness.' Therefore I will boast all the more gladly about my weaknesses, so that Christ's power may rest on me. That is why, for Christ's sake, I delight in weaknesses, in insults, in hardships, in persecutions, in difficulties. For when I am weak, then I am strong.

2 Corinthians 12:7–10

I have learned to be content whatever the circumstances. I know what it is to be in need, and I know what it is to have plenty. I have learned the secret of being content in any and every situation, whether well fed or hungry, whether living in plenty or in want. I can do everything through him who gives me strength.

Philippians 4:11–13

> Jesus, my strength, my hope,
>   On Thee I cast my care,
> With humble confidence look up,
>   And know Thou hear'st my prayer.
> Give me on Thee to wait,
>   Till I can all things do,
> On Thee, almighty to create,
>   Almighty to renew.

Charles Wesley, 1707–88

Our life in Christ

For you died, and your life is now hidden with Christ in God.

Colossians 3:3

Now the Lord is the Spirit, and where the Spirit of the Lord is, there is freedom. And we, who with unveiled faces all reflect the Lord's glory, are being transformed into his likeness with ever-increasing glory, which comes from the Lord, who is the Spirit.

2 Corinthians 3:17–18

Dear friends, now we are children of God, and what we will be has not yet been made known. But we know that when he appears, we shall be like him, for we shall see him as he is. Everyone who has this hope in him purifies himself, just as he is pure.

1 John 3:2–3

> Our life is hid with Christ,
>   With Christ in God above;
> Upward our hearts would go to Him,
>   Whom, seeing not, we love.
>
> When He who is our life
>   In glory shall appear,
> We too shall be revealed with Him,
>   And His bright raiment wear.
>
> In Him we then shall be
>   Transformed and glorified,
> For we shall see Him as He is,
>   And in His light abide.

Horatius Bonar, 1808–89

Listening to the Lord

As Jesus and his disciples were on their way, he came to a village where a woman named Martha opened her home to him. She had a sister called Mary, who sat at the Lord's feet listening to what he said. But Martha was distracted by all the preparations that had to be made. She came to him and asked, 'Lord, don't you care that my sister has left me to do the work by myself? Tell her to help me!'

'Martha, Martha,' the Lord answered, 'you are worried and upset about many things, but only one thing is needed. Mary has chosen what is better, and it will not be taken away from her.'

Luke 10:38–42

'Therefore do not worry about tomorrow, for tomorrow will worry about itself. Each day has enough trouble of its own.'

Matthew 6:34

> O that I could for ever sit
> With Mary at the Master's feet!
>   Be this my happy choice:
> My only care, delight, and bliss,
> My joy, my heaven on earth, be this –
>   To hear the Bridegroom's voice!

Charles Wesley, 1707–88

Following Jesus

As Jesus walked beside the Sea of Galilee, he saw Simon and his brother Andrew casting a net into the lake, for they were fishermen. 'Come, follow me,' Jesus said, 'and I will make you fishers of men.' At once they left their nets and followed him. When he had gone a little father, he saw James son of Zebedee and his brother John in a boat, preparing their nets. Without delay he called them, and they left their father Zebedee in the boat with the hired men and followed him.

Mark 1:16–20

As they were walking along the road, a man said to him, 'I will follow you wherever you go.' Jesus replied, 'Foxes have holes and birds of the air have nests, but the Son of Man has nowhere to lay his head.' He said to another man, 'Follow me.' But the man replied, 'Lord, first let me go and bury my father.' Jesus said to him, 'Let the dead bury their own dead, but you go and proclaim the kingdom of God.'

Still another said, 'I will follow you, Lord; but first let me go back and say good-bye to my family.' Jesus replied, 'No-one who puts his hand to the plough and looks back is fit for service in the kingdom of God.'

Luke 9:57–62

> Jesus calls us! O'er the tumult
> Of our life's wild restless sea,
> Day by day His sweet voice soundeth,
> Saying, 'Christian, follow Me':
>
> Jesus calls us! By Thy mercies,
> Saviour, make us hear Thy call,
> Give our hearts to Thy obedience,
> Serve and love Thee best of all.

Cecil Frances Alexander, 1818–95

Our help on life's journey

While Samuel was sacrificing the burnt offering, the Philistines drew near to engage Israel in battle. But that day the Lord thundered with loud thunder against the Philistines and threw them into such a panic that they were routed before the Israelites. The men of Israel rushed out of Mizpah and pursued the Philistines, slaughtering them along the way to a point below Beth Car.

Then Samuel took a stone and set it up between Mizpah and Shen. He named it Ebenezer, saying, 'Thus far has the Lord helped us.'

1 Samuel 7:10–12

Yet you are enthroned as the Holy One; you are the praise of Israel. In you our fathers put their trust; they trusted and you delivered them. They cried to you and were saved; in you they trusted and were not disappointed.

Psalm 22:3–5

> Here I raise my Ebenezer,
> Hither by Thy help I'm come,
> And I hope by Thy good pleasure
> Safely to arrive at home.
> Jesus sought me when a stranger,
> Wandering from the fold of God;
> He, to rescue me from danger,
> Interposed His precious blood.

Robert Robinson, 1735–90

Christ's second coming

At that time the sign of the Son of Man will appear in the sky, and all the nations of the earth will mourn. They will see the Son of Man coming on the clouds of the sky, with power and great glory.

Matthew 24:30

The Lord himself will come down from heaven, with a loud command, with the voice of the archangel and with the trumpet call of God, and the dead in Christ will rise first. After that, we who are still alive and are left will be caught up together with them in the clouds to meet the Lord in the air. And so we will be with the Lord for ever. Therefore encourage each other with these words.

1 Thessalonians 4:16–18

Look, he is coming with the clouds, and every eye will see him, even those who pierced him; and all the peoples of the earth will mourn because of him. So shall it be! Amen.

Revelation 1:7

Lo! He comes with clouds descending,
　　Once for favoured sinners slain;
Thousand thousand saints attending
　　Swell the triumph of His train:
　　　　Hallelujah!
　　God appears on earth to reign.

Every eye shall now behold Him
　　Robed in dreadful majesty;
Those who set at nought and sold Him,
　　Pierced and nailed Him to the tree,
　　　　Deeply wailing,
　　Shall the true Messiah see.

John Cennick, 1718–55
and Charles Wesley, 1707–88

The Light of the world

When Jesus spoke again to the people, he said, 'I am the light of the world. Whoever follows me will never walk in darkness, but will have the light of life.'

John 8:12

In him was life, and that life was the light of men. The light shines in the darkness, but the darkness has not understood it.

There came a man who was sent from God; his name was John. He came as a witness to testify concerning that light, so that through him all men might believe. He himself was not the light; he came only as a witness to the light. The true light that gives light to every man was coming into the world.

John 1:4–9

'This is the verdict: Light has come into the world, but men loved darkness instead of light because their deeds were evil. Everyone who does evil hates the light, and will not come into the light for fear that his deeds will be exposed. But whoever lives by the truth comes into the light, so that it may be seen plainly that what he has done has been done through God.'

John 3:19–21

> I heard the voice of Jesus say,
>   'I am this dark world's Light;
> Look unto Me, thy morn shall rise,
>   And all thy day be bright.'
> I looked to Jesus, and I found
>   In Him my Star, my Sun;
> And in that light of life I'll walk
>   Till travelling days are done.

Horatius Bonar, 1808–89

The precious blood of Christ

But if we walk in the light, as he is in the light, we have
fellowship with one another, and the blood of Jesus, his
Son, purifies us from all sin.

1 John 1:7

'Whoever wants to be first must be slave of all. For even
the Son of Man did not come to be served, but to serve,
and to give his life as a ransom for many.'

Mark 10:44—45

For you know that it was not with perishable things
such as silver or gold that you were redeemed from the
empty way of life handed down to you from your forefathers, but with the precious blood of Christ, a lamb
without blemish or defect. He was chosen before the
creation of the world, but was revealed in these last
times for your sake. Through him you believe in God,
who raised him from the dead and glorified him, and so
your faith and hope are in God.

1 Peter 1:18—21

Just as I am without one plea
But that Thy blood was shed for me,
And that Thou bidd'st me come to Thee,
   O Lamb of God, I come.

Just as I am, Thou wilt receive,
Wilt welcome, pardon, cleanse, relieve;
Because Thy promise I believe,
   O Lamb of God, I come.

Just as I am, of that free love
The breadth, length, depth, and height to prove,
Here for a season, then above,
   O Lamb of God, I come.

Charlotte Elliott, 1789–1871

The children of God

Because those who are led by the Spirit of God are sons of God. For you did not receive a spirit that makes you a slave again to fear, but you received the Spirit of sonship. And by him we cry, '*Abba*, Father.' The Spirit himself testifies with our spirit that we are God's children. Now if we are children, then we are heirs – heirs of God and co-heirs with Christ, if indeed we share in his sufferings in order that we may also share in his glory.

Romans 8:14–17

How great is the love the Father has lavished on us, that we should be called children of God! And that is what we are! The reason the world does not know us is that it did not know him.

1 John 3:1

> Behold, what wondrous grace
>   The Father hath bestowed
> On sinners of a mortal race
>   To call them sons of God.
>
> Nor doth it yet appear
>   How great we must be made;
> But when we see our Saviour here,
>   We shall be like our Head.

Isaac Watts, 1674–1748

Spiritual power

' "Not by might nor by power, but by my Spirit," says the Lord Almighty.'

Zechariah 4:6

A woman was there who had been subject to bleeding for twelve years. She had suffered a great deal under the care of many doctors and had spent all she had, yet instead of getting better she grew worse. When she heard about Jesus, she came up behind him in the crowd and touched his cloak, because she thought, 'If I just touch his clothes, I will be healed.' Immediately her bleeding stopped and she felt in her body that she was freed from her suffering.

At once Jesus realized that power had gone out from him.

Mark 5:25–30

But we have this treasure in jars of clay to show that this all-surpassing power is from God and not from us.

2 Corinthians 4:7

> Holy Spirit, power divine,
> Fill and nerve this will of mine;
> By Thee may I strongly live,
> Bravely bear, and nobly strive.

Samuel Longfellow, 1819–92

God gave us his Son

'For God so loved the world that he gave his one and only Son, that whoever believes in him shall not perish but have eternal life.'

John 3:16

You see, at just the right time, when we were still powerless, Christ died for the ungodly. Very rarely will anyone die for a righteous man, though for a good man someone might possibly dare to die. But God demonstrates his own love for us in this: While we were still sinners, Christ died for us.

Romans 5:6–8

For what I received I passed on to you as of first importance: that Christ died for our sins according to the Scriptures, that he was buried, that he was raised on the third day according to the Scriptures, and that he appeared to Peter, and then to the Twelve.

1 Corinthians 15:3–5

> To God be the glory! great things He hath done!
> So loved He the world that He gave us His Son;
> Who yielded His life an atonement for sin,
> And opened the life-gate that all may go in.

Praise the Lord! praise the Lord! Let the earth hear His voice!
Praise the Lord, praise the Lord! Let the people rejoice!
O come to the Father through Jesus the Son:
And give Him the glory! great things He hath done!

Frances Jane Van Alstyne, 1820–1915

FEBRUARY 2

The name of Jesus

Your attitude should be the same as that of Christ Jesus:
Who, being in very nature God, did not consider equality
with God something to be grasped, but made himself
nothing, taking the very nature of a servant, being made
in human likeness. And being found in appearance as
a man, he humbled himself and became obedient to
death – even death on a cross! Therefore God exalted
him to the highest place and gave him the name that is
above every name, that at the name of Jesus every knee
should bow, in heaven and on earth and under the earth,
and every tongue confess that Jesus Christ is Lord, to
the glory of God the Father.

Philippians 2:5–11

Jesus! the Name high over all,
    In hell, or earth, or sky;
Angels and men before it fall,
    And devils fear and fly.

O that the world might taste and see
    The riches of His grace;
The arms of love that compass me
    Would all mankind embrace.

Charles Wesley, 1707–88

The peace of Christ

Remember that at that time you were separate from Christ, excluded from citizenship in Israel and foreigners to the covenants of the promise, without hope and without God in the world. But now in Christ Jesus you who once were far away have been brought near through the blood of Christ.

For he himself is our peace, who has made the two one and has destroyed the barrier, the dividing wall of hostility, by abolishing in his flesh the law with its commandments and regulations. His purpose was to create in himself one new man out of the two, thus making peace, and in this one body to reconcile both of them to God through the cross, by which he put to death their hostility. He came and preached peace to you who were far away and peace to those who were near. For through him we both have access to the Father by one Spirit.

Ephesians 2:12–18

Making peace through his blood, shed on the cross.
Colossians 1:20

Peace, perfect peace, in this dark world of sin?
The blood of Jesus whispers peace within.

Peace, perfect peace, by thronging duties pressed?
To do the will of Jesus, this is rest.

Peace, perfect peace, our future all unknown?
Jesus we know, and He is on the throne.

Edward Henry Bickersteth, 1825–1906

Come to my heart, Lord Jesus

He was in the world, and though the world was made
through him, the world did not recognise him. He came
to that which was his own, but his own did not receive
him. Yet to all who received him, to those who believed
in his name, he gave the right to become children of
God – children born not of natural descent, nor of human
decision or a husband's will, but born of God.

John 1:10–13

Praise be to the God and Father of our Lord Jesus Christ,
who has blessed us in the heavenly realms with every
spiritual blessing in Christ. For he chose us in him
before the creation of the world to be holy and blameless
in his sight. In love he predestined us to be adopted as
his sons through Jesus Christ, in accordance with his
pleasure and will.

Ephesians 1:3–5

> Thou didst leave Thy throne
> And Thy kingly crown,
>   When Thou camest to earth for me;
> But in Bethlehem's home
> Was there found no room
>   For Thy holy nativity:
> O come to my heart, Lord Jesus!
> There is room in my heart for Thee.

Emily Elizabeth Steele Elliott, 1836–97

Christ, the living water

'Come, all you who are thirsty, come to the waters; and you who have no money, come, buy and eat! Come, buy wine and milk without money and without cost.'

Isaiah 55:1

On the last and greatest day of the Feast, Jesus stood and said in a loud voice, 'If anyone is thirsty, let him come to me and drink. Whoever believes in me, as the Scripture has said, streams of living water will flow from within him.' By this he meant the Spirit, whom those who believed in him were later to receive. Up to that time the Spirit had not been given, since Jesus had not yet been glorified.

John 7:37–39

I heard the voice of Jesus say,
'Behold, I freely give
The living water – thirsty one,
Stoop down, and drink, and live!'

I came to Jesus, and I drank
Of that life-giving stream;
My thirst was quenched, my soul revived,
And now I live in Him.

Horatius Bonar, 1808–89

Preaching the gospel

I remind you to fan into flame the gift of God, which is in you through the laying on of my hands. For God did not give us a spirit of timidity, but a spirit of power, of love and of self-discipline.

So do not be ashamed to testify about our Lord, or ashamed of me his prisoner. But join with me in suffering for the gospel, by the power of God, who has saved us and called us to a holy life – not because of anything we have done but because of his own purpose and grace. This grace was given us in Christ Jesus before the beginning of time, but it has now been revealed through the appearing of our Saviour, Christ Jesus, who has destroyed death and has brought life and immortality to light through the gospel.

2 Timothy 1:6–10

Yet when I preach the gospel, I cannot boast, for I am compelled to preach. Woe to me if I do not preach the gospel!

1 Corinthians 9:16

O Thou who camest from above
  The pure celestial fire to impart,
Kindle a flame of sacred love
  On the mean altar of my heart!

Jesus, confirm my heart's desire
  To work and speak and think for Thee;
Still let me guard the holy fire,
  And still stir up Thy gift in me.

Charles Wesley, 1707–88

Who is on the Lord's side?

'Now fear the Lord and serve him with all faithfulness.
Throw away the gods your forefathers worshipped
beyond the River and in Egypt, and serve the Lord....
choose for yourselves this day whom you will serve,
whether the gods your forefathers served beyond the
River, or the gods of the Amorites, in whose land you
are living. But as for me and my household, we will
serve the Lord.'

Joshua 24:14–15

Elijah went before the people and said, 'How long will
you waver between two opinions? If the Lord is God,
follow him; but if Baal is God, follow him.'

1 Kings 18:21

'My sheep listen to my voice; I know them, and they
follow me. I give them eternal life, and they shall never
perish; no-one can snatch them out of my hand. My
Father, who has given them to me, is greater than all;
no-one can snatch them out of my Father's hand. I and
the Father are one.'

John 10:27–30

Who is on the Lord's side?
    Who will serve the King?
Who will be His helpers
    Other lives to bring?
Who will leave the world's side?
    Who will face the foe?
Who is on the Lord's side?
    Who for Him will go?
By Thy call of mercy,
    By Thy grace divine,
We are on the Lord's side;
    Saviour, we are Thine.

Frances Ridley Havergal, 1836–79

Eternal security

Who will bring any charge against those whom God has chosen? It is God who justifies. Who is he that condemns? Christ Jesus, who died – more than that, who was raised to life – is at the right hand of God and is also interceding for us. Who shall separate us from the love of Christ? Shall trouble or hardship or persecution or famine or nakedness or danger or sword? As it is written:

'For your sake we face death all day long; we are considered as sheep to be slaughtered.'

No, in all these things we are more than conquerors through him who loved us. For I am convinced that neither death nor life, neither angels nor demons, neither the present nor the future, nor any powers, neither height nor depth, nor anything else in all creation, will be able to separate us from the love of God that is in Christ Jesus our Lord.

Romans 8:33 – 39

The soul that on Jesus has leaned for repose
He will not, He will not, desert to its foes;
That soul, though all hell should endeavour to shake,
He'll never, no never, no never forsake.

'K' in Rippon's *Selection*, 1787

True joy in God

Let the righteous rejoice in the Lord and take refuge in him; let all the upright in heart praise him!

Psalm 64:10

They will see the glory of the Lord, the splendour of our God. And a highway will be there; it will be called the Way of Holiness. The unclean will not journey on it. And the ransomed of the Lord will return. They will enter Zion with singing; everlasting joy will crown their heads. Gladness and joy will overtake them, and sorrow and sighing will flee away.

Isaiah 35:2, 8, 10

> Come, we that love the Lord,
>   And let our joys be known;
> Join in a song with sweet accord,
>   And thus surround the throne.

Isaac Watts, 1674–1748

Seeing the glory of God

'I pray also for those who will believe in me through their message, that all of them may be one, Father, just as you are in me and I am in you. May they also be in us so that the world may believe that you have sent me. I have given them the glory that you gave me, that they may be one as we are one: I in them and you in me. May they be brought to complete unity to let the world know that you sent me and have loved them even as you have loved me.

'Father, I want those you have given me to be with me where I am, and to see my glory, the glory you have given me because you loved me before the creation of the world.'

John 17:20–24

> More of Thyself, O show me hour by hour,
> More of Thy glory, O my God and Lord;
> More of Thyself, in all Thy grace and power;
> More of Thy love and truth, incarnate Word!

Horatius Bonar, 1808–89

The word of God

'The grass withers and the flowers fall, because the breath of the Lord blows on them. Surely the people are grass. The grass withers and the flowers fall, but the word of our God stands for ever.'

Isaiah 40:7–8

All your words are true; all your righteous laws are eternal.

Psalm 119:160

The word of God is living and active. Sharper than any double-edged sword, it penetrates even to dividing soul and spirit, joints and marrow; it judges the thoughts and attitudes of the heart. Nothing in all creation is hidden from God's sight. Everything is uncovered and laid bare before the eyes of him to whom we must give account.

Hebrews 4:12–13

How firm a foundation, ye saints of the Lord.
Is laid for your faith in His excellent word;
What more can He say than to you He hath said.
You who unto Jesus for refuge have fled?

'K' in Rippon's *Selection*, 1787

Thy way, O Lord

Give ear to my words, O Lord, consider my sighing. Listen to my cry for help, my King and my God, for to you I pray. In the morning, O Lord, you hear my voice; in the morning I lay my requests before you and wait in expectation.

You are not a God who takes pleasure in evil; with you the wicked cannot dwell. The arrogant cannot stand in your presence; you hate all who do wrong.

You destroy those who tell lies, bloodthirsty and deceitful men the Lord abhors.

But I, by your great mercy, will come into your house; in reverence will I bow down towards your holy temple. Lead me, O Lord, in your righteousness because of my enemies – make straight your way before me.

Psalm 5:1–8

Thy way, not mine, O Lord,
  However dark it be!
Lead me by Thine own hand,
  Choose out the path for me.

Smooth let it be, or rough,
  It will be still the best;
Winding, or straight, it leads
  Right onward to Thy rest.

Horatius Bonar, 1808–89

True worship

Ezra opened the book. All the people could see him because he was standing above them; and as he opened it, the people all stood up. Ezra praised the Lord, the great God; and all the people lifted their hands and responded, 'Amen! Amen!' Then they bowed down and worshipped the Lord with their faces to the ground.

Nehemiah 8:5–6

After this I looked and there before me was a great multitude that no-one could count, from every nation, tribe, people and language, standing before the throne and in front of the Lamb. They were wearing white robes and were holding palm branches in their hands. And they cried out in a loud voice: 'Salvation belongs to our God, who sits on the throne, and to the Lamb.' All the angels were standing round the throne and around the elders and the four living creatures. They fell down on their faces before the throne and worshipped God, saying: 'Amen! Praise and glory and wisdom and thanks and honour and power and strength be to our God for ever and ever. Amen!'

Revelation 7:9–12

Stand up, and bless the Lord,
Ye people of His choice:
Stand up, and bless the Lord your God
With heart and soul and voice.

Though high above all praise,
Above all blessing high,
Who would not fear His holy Name,
And laud and magnify?

James Montgomery, 1717–1854

A new responsive heart

' "For I will take you out of the nations; I will gather you from all the countries. . . . I will sprinkle clean water on you, and you will be clean; I will cleanse you from all your impurities and from all your idols. I will give you a new heart and put a new spirit in you; I will remove from you your heart of stone and give you a heart of flesh. And I will put my Spirit in you and move you to follow my decrees and be careful to keep my laws. You will live in the land I gave your forefathers; you will be my people, and I will be your God." '

Ezekiel 36:24–28

God has poured out his love into our hearts by the Holy Spirit, whom he has given us.

Romans 5:5

When the kindness and love of God our Saviour appeared, he saved us, not because of righteous things we had done, but because of his mercy. He saved us through the washing of rebirth and renewal by the Holy Spirit, whom he poured out on us generously through Jesus Christ our Saviour, so that, having been justified by his grace, we might become heirs having the hope of eternal life.

Titus 3:4–7

> O for a heart to praise my God,
>   A heart from sin set free;
> A heart that always feels Thy blood
>   So freely shed for me;
>
> A heart resigned, submissive, meek,
>   My great Redeemer's throne,
> Where only Christ is heard to speak,
>   Where Jesus reigns alone.

Charles Wesley, 1707–88

The path of commitment

My son, do not forget my teaching, but keep my commands in your heart, for they will prolong your life many years and bring you prosperity.

Let love and faithfulness never leave you; bind them around your neck, write them on the tablet of your heart. Then you will win favour and a good name in the sight of God and man.

Trust in the Lord with all your heart and lean not on your own understanding; in all your ways acknowledge him, and he will make your paths straight.

Do not be wise in your own eyes; fear the Lord and shun evil. This will bring health to your body and nourishment to your bones.

Proverbs 3:1–8

I am trusting Thee, Lord Jesus,
　　Trusting only Thee,
Trusting Thee for full salvation,
　　Great and free.

I am trusting Thee to guide me:
　　Thou alone shalt lead,
Every day and hour supplying
　　All my need.

Frances Ridley Havergal, 1836–79

Seeing Jesus

One thing I ask of the Lord, this is what I seek: that I may dwell in the house of the Lord all the days of my life, to gaze upon the beauty of the Lord and to seek him in his temple. For in the day of trouble he will keep me safe in his dwelling; he will hide me in the shelter of his tabernacle and set me high upon a rock. Then my head will be exalted above the enemies who surround me; at his tabernacle will I sacrifice with shouts of joy; I will sing and make music to the Lord.

Hear my voice when I call, O Lord; be merciful to me and answer me. My heart says of you, 'Seek his face!' Your face, Lord, I will seek.

Psalm 27:4–8

One thing I do: Forgetting what is behind and straining towards what is ahead, I press on towards the goal to win the prize for which God has called me heavenwards in Christ Jesus.

Philippians 3:13–14

> May I run the race before me,
>   Strong and brave to face the foe,
> Looking only unto Jesus
>   As I onward go.
>
> May His beauty rest upon me
>   As I seek the lost to win,
> And may they forget the channel,
>   Seeing only Him.

Katie Barclay Wilkinson, 1859–1928

Go and make disciples of all nations

Ask of me, and I will make the nations your inheritance, the ends of the earth your possession. . . . Serve the Lord with fear and rejoice with trembling. Kiss the Son, lest he be angry and you be destroyed in your way, for his wrath can flare up in a moment. Blessed are all who take refuge in him.

Psalm 2:8, 11–12

Then the eleven disciples went to Galilee, to the mountain where Jesus had told them to go. When they saw him, they worshipped him; but some doubted. Then Jesus came to them and said, 'All authority in heaven and on earth has been given to me. Therefore go and make disciples of all nations, baptising them in the name of the Father and of the Son and of the Holy Spirit, and teaching them to obey everything I have commanded you. And surely I am with you always, to the very end of the age.'

Matthew 28:16–20

Facing a task unfinished,
That drives us to our knees,
A need that, undiminished,
Rebukes our slothful ease,
We who rejoice to know Thee,
Renew before Thy throne
The solemn pledge we owe Thee,
To go and make Thee known.

Frank Houghton, 1894–1972

Enjoying God

It is good to praise the Lord and make music to your name, O Most High, to proclaim your love in the morning and your faithfulness at night, to the music of the ten-stringed lyre and the melody of the harp.

For you make me glad by your deeds, O Lord; I sing for joy at the work of your hands. How great are your work, O Lord, how profound your thoughts! The senseless man does not know, fools do not understand, that though the wicked spring up like grass and all evildoers flourish, they will be for ever destroyed.

But you, O Lord, are exalted for ever.

Psalm 92:1–8

Sweet is the work, my God, my King,
To praise Thy Name, give thanks and sing;
To show Thy love by morning light,
And talk of all Thy truth at night.

My heart shall triumph in the Lord,
And bless His works and bless His Word;
Thy works of grace, how bright they shine,
How deep Thy counsels, how divine!

Isaac Watts, 1674–1748

The way of peace

As a prisoner for the Lord, then, I urge you to live a life worthy of the calling you have received. Be completely humble and gentle; be patient, bearing with one another in love. Make every effort to keep the unity of the Spirit through the bond of peace. There is one body and one Spirit – just as you were called to one hope when you were called – one Lord, one faith, one baptism; one God and Father of all, who is over all and through all and in all.

Ephesians 4:1–6

All of you, clothe yourselves with humility towards one another, because, 'God opposes the proud but gives grace to the humble.' Humble yourselves, therefore, under God's mighty hand, that he may lift you up in due time.

I Peter 5:5–6

> May the mind of Christ my Saviour
>   Live in me from day to day,
> By His love and power controlling
>   All I do and say.
>
> May the peace of God my Father
>   Rule my life in everything,
> That I may be calm to comfort
>   Sick and sorrowing.
>
> May the love of Jesus fill me
>   As the waters fill the sea;
> Him exalting, self abasing,
>   This is victory.

Katie Barclay Wilkinson, 1859–1928

Confidence in Christ

Therefore, there is now no condemnation for those who are in Christ Jesus.

Romans 8:1

Since we have a great high priest who has gone through the heavens, Jesus the Son of God, let us hold firmly to the faith we profess. For we do not have a high priest who is unable to sympathise with our weaknesses, but we have one who has been tempted in every way, just as we are – yet was without sin. Let us then approach the throne of grace with confidence, so that we may receive mercy and find grace to help us in our time of need.

Hebrews 4:14–16

> No condemnation now I dread;
>   Jesus, and all in Him, is mine!
> Alive in Him, my living Head,
>   And clothed in righteousness divine,
> Bold I approach the eternal throne,
> And claim the crown, through Christ my own.

Charles Wesley, 1707–88

Watch and pray

Then Jesus went with his disciples to a place called Gethsemane, and he said to them, 'Sit here while I go over there and pray.' He took Peter and the two sons of Zebedee along with him, and he began to be sorrowful and troubled. Then he said to them, 'My soul is overwhelmed with sorrow to the point of death. Stay here and keep watch with me.'

Going a little farther, he fell with his face to the ground and prayed, 'My Father, if it is possible, may this cup be taken from me. Yet not as I will, but as you will.'

Then he returned to his disciples and found them sleeping. 'Could you men not keep watch with me for one hour?' he asked Peter. 'Watch and pray so that you will not fall into temptation. The spirit is willing, but the body is weak.'

Matthew 26:36–41

' "Forgive us our sins, for we also forgive everyone who sins against us. And lead us not into temptation." '

Luke 11:4

> Christian, seek not yet repose;
>   Cast thy dreams of ease away;
> Thou art in the midst of foes:
>   Watch and pray.
>
> Watch, as if on that alone
>   Hung the issue of the day;
> Pray, that help may be sent down:
>   Watch and pray.

Charlotte Elliott, 1789–1871

His righteousness

It is we who are the circumcision, we who worship by
the Spirit of God, who glory in Christ Jesus, and who
put no confidence in the flesh – though I myself have
reasons for such confidence.

If anyone else thinks he has reasons to put confidence
in the flesh, I have more: circumcised on the eighth day,
of the people of Israel, of the tribe of Benjamin, a Hebrew
of Hebrews; in regard to the law, a Pharisee; as for zeal,
persecuting the church; as for legalistic righteousness,
faultless.

But whatever was to my profit I now consider loss for
the sake of Christ. What is more, I consider everything
a loss compared to the surpassing greatness of knowing
Christ Jesus my Lord, for whose sake I have lost all
things. I consider them rubbish, that I may gain Christ
and be found in him, not having a righteousness of my
own that comes from the law, but that which is through
faith in Christ – the righteousness that comes from God
and is by faith.

Philippians 3:3–9

Jesus! the Name to sinners dear,
　　The Name to sinners given;
It scatters all their guilty fear,
　　It turns their hell to heaven.

His only righteousness I show,
　　His saving truth proclaim;
'Tis all my business here below
　　To cry, 'Behold the Lamb!'

Charles Wesley, 1707–88

Growing in holiness

Godliness has value for all things, holding promise for both the present life and the life to come.

This is a trustworthy saying that deserves full acceptance (and for this we labour and strive), that we have put our hope in the living God, who is the Saviour of all men, and especially of those who believe.

Command and teach these things. Don't let anyone look down on you because you are young, but set an example for the believers in speech, in life, in love, in faith and in purity. Until I come, devote yourself to the public reading of Scripture, to preaching and to teaching. Do not neglect your gift, which was given you through a prophetic message when the body of elders laid their hands on you.

Be diligent in these matters; give yourself wholly to them, so that everyone may see your progress. Watch your life and doctrine closely. Persevere in them, because if you do, you will save both yourself and your hearers.

1 Timothy 4:8–16

Take time to be holy, speak oft with thy Lord;
Abide in Him always, and feed on His Word,
Make friends of God's children, help those who are
   weak;
Forgetting in nothing His blessing to seek.

Take time to be holy, the world rushes on;
Spend much time in secret with Jesus alone.
By looking to Jesus like Him thou shalt be;
Thy friends, in thy conduct, His likeness shall see.

William Dunn Longstaff, 1822–94

Responding to God

Seek the Lord while he may be found; call on him while he is near. Let the wicked forsake his way and the evil man his thoughts. Let him turn to the Lord, and he will have mercy on him, and to our God, for he will freely pardon.

'For my thoughts are not your thoughts, neither are your ways my ways,' declares the Lord. 'As the heavens are higher than the earth, so are my ways higher than your ways and my thoughts than your thoughts.'

Isaiah 55:6–9

For Christ died for sins once for all, the righteous for the unrighteous, to bring you to God. He was put to death in the body but made alive by the Spirit.

1 Peter 3:18

> Out of my bondage, sorrow and night,
> Jesus, I come; Jesus, I come;
> Into Thy freedom, gladness and light,
> Jesus, I come to Thee.
> Out of my sickness into Thy health,
> Out of my want and into Thy wealth,
> Out of my sin and into Thyself,
> Jesus, I come to Thee.

William True Sleeper, 1840–1920

Giving ourselves to God

Therefore, I urge you, brothers, in view of God's mercy, to offer your bodies as living sacrifices, holy and pleasing to God – this is your spiritual act of worship. Do not conform any longer to the pattern of this world, but be transformed by the renewing of your mind. Then you will be able to test and approve what God's will is – his good, pleasing and perfect will.

For by the grace given me I say to every one of you: Do not think of yourself more highly than you ought, but rather think of yourself with sober judgment, in accordance with the measure of faith God has given you. Just as each of us has one body with many members, and these members do not all have the same function, so in Christ we who are many form one body, and each member belongs to all the others. We have different gifts, according to the grace given us. If a man's gift is prophesying, let him use it in proportion to his faith. If it is serving, let him serve; if it is teaching, let him teach; if it is encouraging, let him encourage; if it is contributing to the needs of others, let him give generously; if it is leadership, let him govern diligently; if it is showing mercy, let him do it cheerfully.

Romans 12:1–8

Take my life, and let it be
Consecrated, Lord, to Thee;
Take my moments and my days,
Let them flow in ceaseless praise.

Take my will, and make it Thine;
It shall be no longer mine:
Take my heart, it is Thine own;
It shall be Thy royal throne.

Take my love; my Lord, I pour
At Thy feet its treasure-store:
Take myself, and I will be
Ever, only, all for Thee!

Frances Ridley Havergal, 1836–79

'I know whom I have believed'

The grace of our Lord was poured out on me abundantly, along with the faith and love that are in Christ Jesus.

Here is a trustworthy saying that deserves full acceptance: Christ Jesus came into the world to save sinners – of whom I am the worst. But for that very reason I was shown mercy so that in me, the worst of sinners, Christ Jesus might display his unlimited patience as an example for those who would believe on him and receive eternal life. Now to the King eternal, immortal, invisible, the only God, be honour and glory for ever and ever. Amen.

1 Timothy 1:14–17

And of this gospel I was appointed a herald and an apostle and a teacher. That is why I am suffering as I am. Yet I am not ashamed, because I know whom I have believed, and am convinced that he is able to guard what I have entrusted to him for that day.

What you heard from me, keep as the pattern of sound teaching, with faith and love in Christ Jesus. Guard the good deposit that was entrusted to you – guard it with the help of the Holy Spirit who lives in us.

2 Timothy 1:11–14

I know not why God's wondrous grace
　　To me has been made known,
Nor why – unworthy as I am –
　　He claimed me for His own.

*But 'I know whom I have believed, and am
persuaded that He is able to keep that which
I've committed unto Him against that day.'*

Daniel Webster Whittle, 1840–1901

Praise the Lord

Praise the Lord.

Praise the Lord from the heavens, praise him in the heights above. Praise him, all his angels, praise him, all his heavenly hosts. Praise him, sun and moon, praise him, all you shining stars. Praise him, you highest heavens and you waters above the skies. Let them praise the name of the Lord, for he commanded and they were created. He set them in place for ever and ever; he gave a decree that will never pass away. He has raised up for his people a horn, the praise of all his saints, of Israel, the people close to his heart.

Praise the Lord.

Psalm 148:1–6, 14

Praise the Lord! ye heavens, adore Him;
  Praise Him, angels in the height;
Sun and moon, rejoice before Him;
  Praise Him, all ye stars and light.

Praise the Lord! for He hath spoken;
  Worlds His mighty voice obeyed;
Laws, that never shall be broken,
  For their guidance He hath made.

Anonymous

Walking with God

Enoch walked with God; then he was no more, because God took him away.

Genesis 5:24

'Come, let us go up to the mountain of the Lord, to the house of the God of Jacob. He will teach us his ways, so that we may walk in his paths.' The law will go out from Zion, the word of the Lord from Jerusalem. He will judge between the nations and will settle disputes for many peoples. They will beat their swords into ploughshares and their spears into pruning hooks. Nation will not take up sword against nation, nor will they train for war any more.

Come, O house of Jacob, let us walk in the light of the Lord.

Isaiah 2:3–5

If we claim to have fellowship with him yet walk in darkness, we lie and do not live by the truth. But if we walk in the light, as he is in the light, we have fellowship with one another, and the blood of Jesus, his Son, purifies us from all sin.

1 John 1:6–7

O for a closer walk with God,
  A calm and heavenly frame,
A light to shine upon the road
  That leads me to the Lamb!

So shall my walk be close with God,
  Calm and serene my frame;
So purer light shall mark the road
  That leads me to the Lamb.

William Cowper, 1731–1800

The Saviour's love for us

As they led him [Jesus] away, they seized Simon from Cyrene, who was on his way in from the country, and put the cross on him and made him carry it behind Jesus. A large number of people followed him, including women who mourned and wailed for him. Jesus turned and said to them, 'Daughters of Jerusalem, do not weep for me; weep for yourselves and for your children.'

Luke 23:26–28

It was now about the sixth hour, and darkness came over the whole land until the ninth hour, for the sun stopped shining. And the curtain of the temple was torn in two. Jesus called out with a loud voice, 'Father, into your hands I commit my spirit.' When he had said this, he breathed his last.

Luke 23:44–46

He himself bore our sins in his body on the tree, so that we might die to sins and live for righteousness; by his wounds you have been healed.

1 Peter 2:24

Give me a sight, O Saviour,
  Of Thy wondrous love to me,
Of the love that brought Thee down to earth,
  To die on Calvary.

O make me understand it,
  Help me to take it in,
What it meant to Thee, the Holy One,
  To bear away my sin.

Katharine Agnes May Kelly, 1869–1942

Great is thy faithfulness

I remember my affliction and my wandering, the bitterness and the gall. I well remember them, and my soul is downcast within me. Yet this I call to mind and therefore I have hope.

Because of the Lord's great love we are not consumed, for his compassions never fail. They are new every morning; great is your faithfulness. I say to myself, 'The Lord is my portion; therefore I will wait for him.'

The Lord is good to those whose hope is in him, to the one who seeks him; it is good to wait quietly for the salvation of the Lord. It is good for a man to bear the yoke while he is young.

Lamentations 3:19–27

Great is Thy faithfulness, O God my Father,
　　There is no shadow of turning with Thee;
Thou changest not, Thy compassions they fail not,
　　As Thou hast been Thou for ever wilt be.

Great is Thy faithfulness!
Great is Thy faithfulness!
　　Morning by morning new mercies I see;
All I have needed Thy hand hath provided, –
　　Great is Thy faithfulness, Lord, unto me!

Summer and winter, and spring-time and harvest,
　　Sun, moon and stars in their courses above,
Join with all nature in manifold witness
　　To Thy great faithfulness, mercy and love.

Thomas O. Chisholm, 1866–1960

Jesus, the Lamb of God

The next day John saw Jesus coming towards him and said, 'Look, the Lamb of God, who takes away the sin of the world! This is the one I meant when I said, "A man who comes after me has surpassed me because he was before me." I myself did not know him, but the reason I came baptising with water was that he might be revealed to Israel.'

Then John gave this testimony: 'I saw the Spirit come down from heaven as a dove and remain on him. I would not have known him, except that the one who sent me to baptise with water told me, "The man on whom you see the Spirit come down and remain is he who will baptise with the Holy Spirit." I have seen and I testify that this is the Son of God.'

The next day John was there again with two of his disciples. When he saw Jesus passing by, he said, 'Look, the Lamb of God!'

When the two disciples heard him say this, they followed Jesus.

John 1:29–37

> Jesus! the prisoner's fetters breaks,
>   And bruises Satan's head;
> Power into strengthless souls it speaks,
>   And life into the dead.
>
> Happy, if with my latest breath
>   I may but gasp His Name;
> Preach Him to all, and cry in death,
>   'Behold, behold the Lamb!'

Charles Wesley, 1707–88

God, our refuge and strength

God is our refuge and strength, an ever-present help in trouble. Therefore we will not fear, though the earth give way and the mountains fall into the heart of the sea, though its waters roar and foam and the mountains quake with their surging.

There is a river whose streams make glad the city of God, the holy place where the Most High dwells. God is within her, she will not fall; God will help her at break of day. Nations are in uproar, kingdoms fall; he lifts his voice, the earth melts.

The Lord Almighty is with us; the God of Jacob is our fortress.

Psalm 46:1–7

A safe stronghold our God is still,
   A trusty shield and weapon;
He'll help us clear from all the ill
   That hath us now o'ertaken.
The ancient prince of hell
Hath risen with purpose fell;

Strong mail of craft and power
He weareth in this hour;
   On earth is not his fellow.

Martin Luther, 1483–1546
tr. Thomas Carlyle, 1795–1881

Becoming like Jesus

Do not let any unwholesome talk come out of your mouths, but only what is helpful for building others up according to their needs, that it may benefit those who listen. And do not grieve the Holy Spirit of God, with whom you were sealed for the day of redemption. Get rid of all bitterness, rage and anger, brawling and slander, along with every form of malice. Be kind and compassionate to one another, forgiving each other, just as in Christ God forgave you.

Be imitators of God, therefore, as dearly loved children and live a life of love, just as Christ loved us and gave himself up for us as a fragrant offering and sacrifice to God.

Ephesians 4:29–5:2

More of Thy glory let me see,
  Thou Holy, Wise, and True!
I would Thy living image be,
  In joy and sorrow too.

Fill me with gladness from above,
  Hold me by strength divine!
Lord, let the glow of Thy great love
  Through my whole being shine.

Johann Caspar Lavater, 1741–1801
tr. Elizabeth Lee Smith, 1817–98

Victory through Christ

'I have told you these things, so that in me you may have peace. In this world you will have trouble. But take heart! I have overcome the world.'

John 16:33

Be self-controlled and alert. Your enemy the devil prowls around like a roaring lion looking for someone to devour. Resist him, standing firm in the faith, because you know that your brothers throughout the world are undergoing the same kind of sufferings.

And the God of all grace, who called you to his eternal glory in Christ, after you have suffered a little while, will himself restore you and make you strong, firm and steadfast. To him be the power for ever and ever. Amen.

I Peter 5:8–11

Yield not to temptation, for yielding is sin;
Each victory will help you some other to win;
Fight manfully onward; dark passions subdue;
Look ever to Jesus, He will carry you through.

Ask the Saviour to help you,
Comfort, strengthen, and keep you;
He is willing to aid you,
He will carry you through.

Horatio Richmond Palmer, 1834–1907

With Christ in glory

'My prayer is not for them [Jesus' disciples] alone. I pray also for those who will believe in me through their message, that all of them may be one, Father, just as you are in me and I am in you. May they also be in us so that the world may believe that you have sent me. I have given them the glory that you gave me, that they may be one as we are one: I in them and you in me. May they be brought to complete unity to let the world know that you sent me and have loved them even as you have loved me.

'Father, I want those you have given me to be with me where I am, and to see my glory, the glory you have given me because you loved me before the creation of the world.

'Righteous Father, though the world does not know you, I know you, and they know that you have sent me. I have made you known to them, and will continue to make you known in order that the love you have for me may be in them and that I myself may be in them.'

John 17:20–26

O Jesus, Thou hast promised,
  To all who follow Thee,
That where Thou art in glory
  There shall Thy servant be;
And, Jesus, I have promised
  To serve Thee to the end:
O give me grace to follow,
  My Master and my Friend.

John Ernest Bode, 1816–74

Faith for life's struggles

A squall came down on the lake, so that the boat was being swamped, and they were in great danger. The disciples went and woke him, saying, 'Master, Master, we're going to drown!' He got up and rebuked the wind and the raging waters; the storm subsided, and all was calm. 'Where is your faith?' he asked his disciples. In fear and amazement they asked one another, 'Who is this? He commands even the winds and the water, and they obey him.'

Luke 8:23–25

They returned to Lystra, Iconium and Antioch, strengthening the disciples and encouraging them to remain true to the faith. 'We must go through many hardships to enter the kingdom of God,' they said.

Acts 14:21–22

> Begone, unbelief;
>   My Saviour is near,
> And for my relief
>   Will surely appear:
> By prayer let me wrestle,
>   And He will perform;
> With Christ in the vessel,
>   I smile at the storm.
>
> Why should I complain
>   Of want or distress,
> Temptation or pain?
>   He told me no less;
> The heirs of salvation,
>   I know from His Word,
> Through much tribulation
>   Must follow their Lord.

John Newton, 1725–1807

The grace of God

The Lord did not set his affection on you and choose you
because you were more numerous than other peoples,
for you were the fewest of all peoples. But it was because
the Lord loved you and kept the oath he swore to your
forefathers that he brought you out with a mighty hand
and redeemed you from the land of slavery, from the
power of Pharaoh king of Egypt.

Deuteronomy 7:7–8

Grace and peace to you from God our Father and the
Lord Jesus Christ, who gave himself for our sins to rescue us from the present evil age, according to the will
of our God and Father, to whom be glory for ever and
ever. Amen.

Galatians 1:3–5

> Come, Thou Fount of every blessing,
>   Tune my heart to sing Thy grace;
> Streams of mercy, never ceasing,
>   Call for songs of loudest praise.
> Teach me some melodious measure,
>   Sung by flaming tongues above;
> O the vast; the boundless treasure
>   Of my Lord's unchanging love!
>
> O to grace how great a debtor
>   Daily I'm constrained to be!
> Let that grace, Lord, like a fetter,
>   Bind my wandering heart to Thee.
> Prone to wander, Lord, I feel it,
>   Prone to leave the God I love;
> Take my heart, O take and seal it,
>   Seal it from Thy courts above!

Robert Robinson, 1735–90

The boundless love of Christ

For this reason I kneel before the Father, from whom his whole family in heaven and on earth derives its name. I pray that out of his glorious riches he may strengthen you with power through his spirit in your inner being, so that Christ may dwell in your hearts through faith. And I pray that you, being rooted and established in love, may have power, together with all the saints, to grasp how wide and long and high and deep is the love of Christ, and to know this love that surpasses knowledge – that you may be filled to the measure of all the fulness of God.

Now to him who is able to do immeasurably more than all we ask or imagine, according to his power that is at work within us, to him be glory in the church and in Christ Jesus throughout all generations, for ever and ever! Amen.

Ephesians 3:14–21

It passeth knowledge, that dear love of Thine,
My Saviour, Jesus, yet this soul of mine
Would of Thy love, in all its breadth and length,
Its height and depth, its everlasting strength,
    Know more and more.

Mary Shekleton, 1827–83

Finding the lost sheep

Now the tax collectors and 'sinners' were all gathering round to hear him. But the Pharisees and the teachers of the law muttered, 'This man welcomes sinners, and eats with them.'

Then Jesus told them this parable: 'Suppose one of you has a hundred sheep and loses one of them. Does he not leave the ninety-nine in the open country and go after the lost sheep until he finds it? And when he finds it, he joyfully puts it on his shoulders and goes home. Then he calls his friends and neighbours together and says, "Rejoice with me; I have found my lost sheep." I tell you that in the same way there will be more rejoicing in heaven over one sinner who repents than over ninety-nine righteous persons who do not need to repent.'

Luke 15:1–7

I will sing the wondrous story
   Of the Christ who died for me;
How He left His home in glory
   For the cross on Calvary.
I was lost: but Jesus found me,
   Found the sheep that went astray;
Threw His loving arms around me
   Drew me back into His way.

Francis Harold Rawley, 1854–1952

Not worthy to be children

'When he [the younger son] came to his senses, he said, "How many of my father's hired men have food to spare, and here I am starving to death! I will set out and go back to my father and say to him: Father, I have sinned against heaven and against you. I am no longer worthy to be called your son; make me like one of your hired men." So he got up and went to his father.

'But while he was still a long way off, his father saw him and was filled with compassion for him; he ran to his son, threw his arms around him and kissed him.

'The son said to him, "Father, I have sinned against heaven and against you. I am no longer worthy to be called your son."

'But the father said to his servants, "Quick! Bring the best robe and put it on him. Put a ring on his finger and sandals on his feet. Bring the fattened calf and kill it. Let's have a feast and celebrate. For this son of mine was dead and is alive again; he was lost and is found." So they began to celebrate.'

Luke 15:17–24

Not worthy, Lord, to gather up the crumbs
 With trembling hand that from Thy table fall,
A weary heavy-laden sinner comes
 To plead Thy promise and obey Thy call.

I am not worthy to be thought Thy child,
 Nor sit the last and lowest at Thy board;
Too long a wanderer, and too oft beguiled,
 I only ask one reconciling word.

Edward Henry Bickersteth, 1825–1906

The power of God's word

How can a young man keep his way pure? By living according to your word. I seek you with all my heart; do not let me stray from your commands. I have hidden your word in my heart that I might not sin against you. Praise be to you, O Lord; teach me your decrees. With my lips I recount all the laws that come from your mouth. I rejoice in following your statutes as one rejoices in great riches. I meditate on your precepts and consider your ways. I delight in your decrees; I will not neglect your word.

Psalm 119:9–16

'I have heard what the prophets say who prophesy lies in my name. They say, "I had a dream! I had a dream!" How long will this continue in the hearts of these lying prophets, who prophesy the delusions of their own minds? They think the dreams they tell one another will make my people forget my name, just as their fathers forgot my name through Baal worship. Let the prophet who has a dream tell his dream, but let the one who has my word speak it faithfully. For what has straw to do with grain?' declares the Lord. 'Is not my word like fire,' declares the Lord, 'and like a hammer that breaks a rock in pieces?'

Jeremiah 23:25–29

Come, O Thou all-victorious Lord,
　　Thy power to us make known;
Strike with the hammer of Thy Word,
　　And break these hearts of stone.

Give us ourselves and Thee to know,
　　In this our gracious day;
Repentance unto life bestow,
　　And take our sins away.

Charles Wesley, 1707–88

The greatness of God

Your love, O Lord, reaches to the heavens, your faithfulness to the skies. Your righteousness is like the mighty mountains, your justice like the great deep. O Lord, you preserve both man and beast. How priceless is your unfailing love! Both high and low among men find refuge in the shadow of your wings. They feast in the abundance of your house; you give them drink from your river of delights. For with you is the fountain of life; in your light we see light.

Continue your love to those who know you, your righteousness to the upright in heart. May the foot of the proud not come against me, nor the hand of the wicked drive me away. See how the evildoers lie fallen – thrown down, not able to rise!

Psalm 36:5–12

Unresting, unhasting, and silent as light,
Nor wanting, nor wasting, Thou rulest in might;
Thy justice like mountains high soaring above,
Thy clouds which are fountains of goodness and love.

To all life Thou givest, to both great and small;
In all life Thou livest, the true life of all;
We blossom and flourish as leaves on the tree,
And wither and perish – but nought changeth Thee.

Immortal, invisible, God only wise,
In light inaccessible hid from our eyes,
Most blessed, most glorious the Ancient of Days,
Almighty, victorious, Thy great Name we praise.

Walter Chalmers Smith, 1824–1908

Teach us to pray

One day Jesus was praying in a certain place. When he finished, one of his disciples said to him, 'Lord, teach us to pray, just as John taught his disciples.'

He said to them, 'When you pray, say: "Father, hallowed be your name, your kingdom come. Give us each day our daily bread. Forgive us our sins, for we also forgive everyone who sins against us. And lead us not into temptation." '

Luke 11:1–4

'Have faith in God,' Jesus answered. 'I tell you the truth, if anyone says to this mountain, "Go, throw yourself into the sea," and does not doubt in his heart but believes that what he says will happen, it will be done for him. Therefore I tell you, whatever you ask for in prayer, believe that you have received it, and it will be yours.'

Mark 11:22–24

> O Thou by whom we come to God,
>   The Life, the Truth, the Way,
> The path of prayer Thyself hast trod;
>   Lord, teach us how to pray.
>
> Prayer is the soul's sincere desire,
>   Uttered or unexpressed;
> The motion of a hidden fire
>   That trembles in the breast.

James Montgomery, 1771–1854

Born of the Spirit

Now there was a man of the Pharisees named Nicodemus, a member of the Jewish ruling council. He came to Jesus at night and said, 'Rabbi, we know you are a teacher who has come from God. For no-one could perform the miraculous signs you are doing if God were not with him.'

In reply Jesus declared, 'I tell you the truth, no-one can see the kingdom of God unless he is born again.'

'How can a man be born when he is old?' Nicodemus asked. 'Surely he cannot enter a second time into his mother's womb to be born!'

Jesus answered, 'I tell you the truth, no-one can enter the kingdom of God unless he is born of water and the Spirit. Flesh gives birth to flesh, but the Spirit gives birth to spirit. You should not be surprised at my saying, 'You must be born again.' The wind blows wherever it pleases. You hear its sound, but you cannot tell where it comes from or where it is going. So it is with everyone born of the Spirit.'

John 3:1–8

Blessed assurance, Jesus is mine:
O what a foretaste of glory divine!
Heir of salvation, purchase of God,
Born of His Spirit, washed in His blood.

This is my story, this is my song,
Praising my Saviour all the day long.

Frances Jane Van Alstyne, 1820–1915

Leaving our cares with Jesus

Rejoice in the Lord always. I will say it again: Rejoice! Let your gentleness be evident to all. The Lord is near. Do not be anxious about anything, but in everything, by prayer and petition, with thanksgiving, present your requests to God. And the peace of God, which transcends all understanding, will guard your hearts and your minds in Christ Jesus.

Philippians 4:4–7

Humble yourselves, therefore, under God's mighty hand, that he may lift you up in due time. Cast all your anxiety on him because he cares for you.

1 Peter 5:6–7

Are we weak and heavy-laden,
    Cumbered with a load of care?
Precious Saviour, still our refuge:
    Take it to the Lord in prayer.

Do thy friends despise, forsake thee?
    Take it to the Lord in prayer;
In His arms He'll take and shield thee,
    Thou wilt find a solace there.

Joseph Medlicott Scriven, 1819–86

The greatest is love

Love is patient, love is kind. It does not envy, it does not boast, it is not proud. It is not rude, it is not self-seeking, it is not easily angered, it keeps no record of wrongs. Love does not delight in evil but rejoices with the truth. It always protects, always trusts, always hopes, always perseveres.

Love never fails. But where there are prophecies, they will cease; where there are tongues, they will be stilled; where there is knowledge, it will pass away. For we know in part and we prophesy in part, but when perfection comes, the imperfect disappears. When I was a child, I talked like a child, I thought like a child, I reasoned like a child. When I became a man, I put childish ways behind me. Now we see but a poor reflection as in a mirror; then we shall see face to face. Now I know in part; then I shall know fully, even as I am fully known.

And now these three remain: faith, hope and love. But the greatest of these is love.

1 Corinthians 13:4–13

God only knows the love of God;
O that it now were shed abroad
  In this poor stony heart!
For love I sigh, for love I pine;
This only portion, Lord, be mine,
  Be mine this better part!

Charles Wesley, 1707–88

Pass me not

As Jesus approached Jericho, a blind man was sitting by the roadside begging. When he heard the crowd going by, he asked what was happening. They told him, 'Jesus, Son of Nazareth is passing by.'

He called out, 'Jesus, Son of David, have mercy on me!'

Those who led the way rebuked him and told him to be quiet, but he shouted all the more, 'Son of David, have mercy on me!'

Jesus stopped and ordered the man to be brought to him. When he came near, Jesus asked him, 'What do you want me to do for you?'

'Lord, I want to see,' he replied.

Jesus said to him, 'Receive your sight; your faith has healed you.' Immediately he received his sight and followed Jesus, praising God. When all the people saw it, they also praised God.

Luke 18:35–43

Pass me not, O gentle Saviour,
Hear my humble cry;
While on others Thou art calling,
Do not pass me by.

Saviour! Saviour!
Hear my humble cry,
And while others Thou art calling,
Do not pass me by.

Frances Jane Van Alstyne, 1820–1915

Knowing forgiveness

Blessed is he whose transgressions are forgiven, whose sins are covered. Blessed is the man whose sin the Lord does not count against him and in whose spirit is no deceit.

When I kept silent, my bones wasted away through my groaning all day long. For day and night your hand was heavy upon me; my strength was sapped as in the heat of summer. Then I acknowledged my sin to you and did not cover up my iniquity. I said, 'I confess my transgressions to the Lord' – and you forgave the guilt of my sin.

Psalm 32:1–5

If we claim to be without sin, we deceive ourselves and the truth is not in us. If we confess our sins, he is faithful and just and will forgive us our sins and purify us from all unrighteousness. If we claim we have not sinned, we make him out to be a liar and his word has no place in our lives.

1 John 1:8–9

> Just as I am, and waiting not
> To rid my soul of one dark blot,
> To Thee, whose blood can cleanse each spot,
>   O Lamb of God, I come.
>
> Just as I am – Thy love unknown
> Has broken every barrier down –
> Now to be Thine, yea, Thine alone,
>   O Lamb of God, I come.

Charlotte Elliott, 1780–1871

Crucify him!

The chief priests and the elders persuaded the crowd to ask for Barabbas and to have Jesus executed. 'Which of the two do you want me to release to you?' asked the governor. 'Barabbas,' they answered. 'What shall I do, then, with Jesus who is called Christ?' Pilate asked. They all answered, 'Crucify him!' 'Why? What crime has he committed?' asked Pilate. But they shouted all the louder, 'Crucify him!' When Pilate saw that he was getting nowhere, but that instead an uproar was starting, he took water and washed his hands in front of the crowd. 'I am innocent of this man's blood,' he said. 'It is your responsibility!' All the people answered, 'Let his blood be on us and on our children!' Then he released Barabbas to them. But he had Jesus flogged, and handled him over to be crucified.

Matthew 27:20–26

My song is love unknown,
　My Saviour's love to me,
Love to the loveless shown,
　That they might lovely be.
　　O who am I,
　　　That for my sake
　　　My Lord should take
　　Frail flesh, and die?

Sometimes they strew His way,
　And His sweet praises sing;
Resounding all the day
　Hosannas to their King.
　　Then 'Crucify!'
　　　Is all their breath,
　　　And for His death
　　They thirst and cry.

Samuel Crossman, 1624–83

Jesus on the cross

As they were going out, they met a man from Cyrene, named Simon, and they forced him to carry the cross. They came to a place called Golgotha (which means The Place of the Skull). There they offered Jesus wine to drink, mixed with gall; but after tasting it, he refused to drink it. When they had crucified him, they divided up his clothes by casting lots. And sitting down, they kept watch over him there. Above his head they placed the written charge against him: THIS IS JESUS, THE KING OF THE JEWS. Two robbers were crucified with him, one on his right and one on his left. Those who passed by hurled insults at him, shaking their heads and saying, 'You who are going to destroy the temple and build it in three days, save yourself! Come down from the cross, if you are the Son of God!'

Matthew 27:32–40

There is a green hill far away,
    Outside a city wall,
Where the dear Lord was crucified
    Who died to save us all.

We may not know, we cannot tell
    What pains He had to bear;
But we believe it was for us
    He hung and suffered there.

O dearly, dearly has He loved,
    And we must love Him too,
And trust in His redeeming blood,
    And try His works to do.

Cecil Frances Alexander, 1818–95

Forgiveness from the cross

Two other men, both criminals, were also led out with him to be executed. When they came to the place called the Skull, there they crucified him, along with the criminals – one on his right, the other on his left. Jesus said, 'Father, forgive them, for they do not know what they are doing.' And they divided up his clothes by casting lots.

The people stood watching, and the rulers even sneered at him. They said, 'He saved others; let him save himself if he is the Christ of God, the Chosen One.'

Luke 23:32–35

'Is it nothing to you, all you who pass by? Look around and see. Is any suffering like my suffering that was inflicted on me, that the Lord brought on me in the day of his fierce anger?'

Lamentations 1:12

All ye that pass by,
To Jesus draw nigh;
To you is it nothing that Jesus should die?
Your ransom and peace,
Your surety He is,
Come, see if there ever was sorrow like His.

He dies to atone
For sins not His own;
Your debt He hath paid, and your work he hath done.
Ye all may receive
The peace He did leave,
Who made intercession, 'My Father, forgive!'

Charles Wesley, 1707–88

The Prince of glory dies

From the sixth hour until the ninth hour darkness came over all the land. About the ninth hour Jesus cried out in a loud voice, *'Eloi, Eloi, lama sabachthani?'* – which means, 'My God, my God, why have you forsaken me?'

When some of those standing there heard this, they said, 'He's calling Elijah.'

Immediately one of them ran and got a sponge. He filled it with wine vinegar, put it on a stick, and offered it to Jesus to drink. The rest said, 'Now leave him alone. Let's see if Elijah comes to save him.'

And when Jesus had cried out again in a loud voice, he gave up his spirit.

Matthew 27:45–50

When I survey the wondrous cross,
    On which the Prince of glory died,
My richest gain I count but loss,
    And pour contempt on all my pride.

See, from His head, His hands, His feet,
    Sorrow and love flow mingled down;
Did e'er such love and sorrow meet,
    Or thorns compose so rich a crown?

Were the whole realm of nature mine,
    That were an offering far too small;
Love so amazing, so divine,
    Demands my soul, my life, my all.

Isaac Watts, 1674–1748

'It is finished'

Near the cross of Jesus stood his mother, his mother's sister, Mary the wife of Clopas, and Mary Magdalene. When Jesus saw his mother there, and the disciple whom he loved standing near by, he said to his mother, 'Dear woman, here is your son,' and to the disciple, 'Here is your mother.' From that time on, this disciple took her into his home.

Later, knowing that all was now completed, and so that the Scripture would be fulfilled, Jesus said, 'I am thirsty.' A jar of wine vinegar was there, so they soaked a sponge in it, put the sponge on a stalk of the hyssop plant, and lifted it to Jesus' lips. When he had received the drink, Jesus said, 'It is finished.' With that, he bowed his head and gave up his spirit.

John 19:25–30

> Lifted up was He to die,
> 'It is finished!' was His cry;
> Now in heaven exalted high:
>   Hallelujah! what a Saviour!
>
> When He comes, our glorious King,
> All his ransomed home to bring,
> Then anew this song we'll sing:
>   Hallelujah! what a Saviour!

Philipp Paul Bliss, 1838–76

The piercing of Jesus' side

Now it was the day of Preparation, and the next day was to be a special Sabbath. Because the Jews did not want the bodies left on the crosses during the Sabbath, they asked Pilate to have the legs broken and the bodies taken down. The soldiers therefore came and broke the legs of the first man who had been crucified with Jesus, and then those of the other. But when they came to Jesus and found that he was already dead, they did not break his legs. Instead, one of the soldiers pierced Jesus' side with a spear, bringing a sudden flow of blood and water. The man who saw it has given testimony, and his testimony is true. He knows that he tells the truth, and he testifies so that you also may believe. These things happened so that the scripture would be fulfilled: 'Not one of his bones will be broken,' and, as another scripture says, 'They will look on the one they have pierced.'

John 19:31–37

Rock of Ages, cleft for me,
Let me hide myself in Thee;
Let the water and the blood,
From Thy riven side which flowed,
Be of sin the double cure,
Cleanse me from its guilt and power.

Nothing in my hand I bring,
Simply to Thy cross I cling;
Naked, come to Thee for dress;
Helpless, look to Thee for grace;
Foul, I to the fountain fly;
Wash me, Saviour, or I die.

Augustus Montague Toplady, 1740–78

He has risen!

On the first day of the week, very early in the morning,
the women took the spices they had prepared and went
to the tomb. They found the stone rolled away from the
tomb, but when they entered, they did not find the body
of the Lord Jesus. While they were wondering about
this, suddenly two men in clothes that gleamed like
lightning stood beside them. In their fright the women
bowed down with their faces to the ground, but the men
said to them, 'Why do you look for the living among the
dead? He is not here; he has risen! Remember how he
told you, while he was still with you in Galilee: "The
Son of Man must be delivered into the hands of sinful
men, be crucified and on the third day be raised again."'
Then they remembered his words.

Luke 24:1–8

Low in the grave He lay,
  Jesus, my Saviour!
Waiting the coming day,
  Jesus, my Lord!

Up from the grave He arose,
With a mighty triumph o'er His foes;
He arose a Victor from the dark domain,
And He lives for ever with His saints to reign;
He arose! He arose!
Hallelujah! Christ arose!

Robert Lowry, 1826–99

Meeting the risen Jesus

The angel said to the women, 'Do not be afraid, for I know that you are looking for Jesus, who was crucified. He is not here; he has risen, just as he said. Come and see the place where he lay. Then go quickly and tell his disciples: "He has risen from the dead and is going ahead of you into Galilee. There you will see him." Now I have told you.'

So the women hurried away from the tomb, afraid yet filled with joy, and ran to tell his disciples. Suddenly Jesus met them. 'Greetings,' he said. They came to him, clasped his feet and worshipped him. Then Jesus said to them, 'Do not be afraid. Go and tell my brothers to go to Galilee; there they will see me.'

Matthew 28:5–10

Lo! Jesus meets us, risen from the tomb;
Lovingly He greets us, scatters fear and gloom;
Let the Church with gladness hymns of triumph
    sing,
For her Lord now liveth, death hath lost its sting.

Thine be the glory, risen, conquering Son,
Endless is the victory Thou o'er death hast won.

Edmond Louis Budry, 1854–1932
tr. Richard Birch Hoyle, 1875–1939

Sadness turns to joy

Then the disciples went back to their homes, but Mary stood outside the tomb crying. As she wept, she bent over to look into the tomb and saw two angels in white, seated where Jesus body had been, one at the head and the other at the foot. They asked her, 'Woman, why are you crying?' 'They have taken my Lord away,' she said, 'and I don't know where they have put him.' At this, she turned round and saw Jesus standing there, but she did not realize that it was Jesus. 'Woman,' he said, 'why are you crying? Who is it you are looking for?' Thinking he was the gardener, she said, 'Sir, if you have carried him away, tell me where you have put him, and I will get him.' Jesus said to her, 'Mary.' She turned towards him and cried out in Aramaic, 'Rabboni!' (which means Teacher). Jesus said, 'Do not hold on to me, for I have not yet returned to the Father. Go instead to my brothers and tell them, "I am returning to my Father and your Father, to my God and your God."' Mary Magdalene went to the disciples with the news: 'I have seen the Lord!' And she told them that he had said these things to her.

John 20:10–18

Christ, the Lord, is risen today,
Hallelujah!
Sons of men and angels say:
Raise your joys and triumphs high;
Sing, ye heavens, and earth reply.

Vain the stone, the watch, the seal;
Christ hath burst the gates of hell;
Death in vain forbids Him rise;
Christ hath opened paradise.

Charles Wesley, 1707–88

Victory over death

But if it is preached that Christ has been raised from the dead, how can some of you say that there is no resurrection of the dead? If there is no resurrection of the dead, then not even Christ has been raised. And if Christ has not been raised, our preaching is useless and so is your faith. More than that, we are then found to be false witnesses about God, for we have testified about God that he raised Christ from the dead. But he did not raise him if in fact the dead are not raised. For if the dead are not raised, then Christ has not been raised either. And if Christ has not been raised, your faith is futile; you are still in your sins. If only for this life we have hope in Christ, we are to be pitied more than all men.

But Christ has indeed been raised from the dead, the firstfruits of those who have fallen asleep. For since death came through a man, the resurrection of the dead comes also through a man. For as in Adam all die, so in Christ all will be made alive. But each in his own turn: Christ, the firstfruits; then, when he comes, those who belong to him. Then the end will come, when he hands over the kingdom to God the Father after he has destroyed all dominion, authority and power. For he must reign until he has put all his enemies under his feet. The last enemy to be destroyed is death.

1 Corinthians 15:12–26

> Jesus lives! thy terrors now
>   Can, O death, no more appal us;
> Jesus lives! by this we know
>   Thou, O grave, canst not enthral us.
> *Hallelujah!*

Christian Fürchtegott Gellert, 1715–69
tr. Frances Elizabeth Cox, 1812–97

I know that my redeemer lives

'I know that my Redeemer lives, and that in the end he
will stand upon the earth. And after my skin has been
destroyed, yet in my flesh I will see God; I myself will
see him with my own eyes – I, and not another. How
my heart yearns within me!'

Job 19:25–27

'This is what the Lord says – Israel's King and
Redeemer, the Lord Almighty: I am the first and I am
the last; apart from me there is no God. Who then is
like me? Let him proclaim it. Let him declare and lay
out before me what has happened since I established my
ancient people, and what is yet to come – yes, let him
foretell what will come. Do not tremble, do not be afraid.
Did I not proclaim this and foretell it long ago? You are
my witnesses. Is there any God besides me? No, there
is no other Rock; I know not one.'

Isaiah 44:6–8

> I know that my Redeemer lives:
> What joy the blest assurance gives!
> He lives, He lives, who once was dead;
> He lives, my everlasting Head.

Samuel Medley, 1738–99

Jesus, the bread of life

Jesus declared, 'I am the bread of life. He who comes to me will never go hungry, and he who believes in me will never be thirsty. But as I told you, you have seen me and still you do not believe. All that the Father gives me will come to me, and whoever comes to me I will never drive away. For I have come down from heaven not to do my will but to do the will of him who sent me. And this is the will of him who sent me, that I shall lose none of all that he has given me, but raise them up at the last day. For my Father's will is that everyone who looks to the Son and believes in him shall have eternal life, and I will raise him up at the last day.'

John 6:35—40

Jesus, Thou joy of loving hearts,
  Thou fount of life, Thou light of men,
From the best bliss that earth imparts,
  We turn unfilled to Thee again.

Thy truth unchanged hath ever stood;
  Thou savest those that on Thee call;
To them that seek Thee Thou art good,
  To them that find Thee, all in all.

We taste Thee, O Thou living Bread,
  And long to feast upon Thee still;
We drink of Thee, the fountain-head,
  And thirst our souls from Thee to fill.

Latin, c. 11th century,
tr. Ray Palmer, 1808—87

Why Jesus died

'Men of Israel, listen to this: Jesus of Nazareth was a man accredited by God to you by miracles, wonders and signs, which God did among you through him, as you yourselves know. This man was handed over to you by God's set purpose and foreknowledge; and you, with the help of wicked men, put him to death by nailing him to the cross. But God raised him from the dead, freeing him from the agony of death, because it was impossible for death to keep its hold on him. David said about him:

' "I saw the Lord always before me. Because he is at my right hand, I will not be shaken. Therefore my heart is glad and my tongue rejoices; my body also will live in hope, because you will not abandon me to the grave, nor will you let your Holy One see decay. You have made known to me the paths of life; you will fill me with joy in your presence." '

Acts 2:22–28

Was it the nails, O Saviour,
   That bound Thee to the tree?
Nay, 'twas Thine everlasting love,
   Thy love for me, for me.

O wonder of all wonders,
   That through Thy death for me
My open sins, my secret sins,
   Can all forgiven be!

Then melt my heart, O Saviour,
   Bend me, yes, break me down,
Until I own Thee Conqueror,
   And Lord and Sovereign crown.

Katharine Agnes May Kelly, 1869–1942

Salvation through Jesus

The next day the rulers, elders and teachers of the law met in Jerusalem. Annas the high priest was there, and so were Caiaphas, John, Alexander and the other men of the high priest's family. They had Peter and John brought before them and began to question them: 'By what power or what name did you do this?'

Then Peter, filled with the Holy Spirit, said to them: 'Rulers and elders of the people! If we are being called to account today for an act of kindness shown to a cripple and are asked how he was healed, then know this, you and all the people of Israel: It is by the name of Jesus Christ of Nazareth, whom you crucified but whom God raised from the dead, that this man stands before you healed. He is "the stone you builders rejected, which has become the capstone." Salvation is found in no-one else, for there is no other name under heaven given to men by which we must be saved.'

Acts 4:5–12

Jesus, we look to Thee,
  Thy promised presence claim;
Thou in the midst of us shalt be,
  Assembled in Thy Name.

Thy Name salvation is,
  Which here we come to prove;
Thy Name is life, and health, and peace,
  And everlasting love.

Present we know Thou art,
  But O Thyself reveal!
Now, Lord, let every bounding heart
  The mighty comfort feel.

Charles Wesley, 1707–88

The foundation of the church

[Paul's farewell to the Ephesian elders] 'And now, compelled by the Spirit, I am going to Jerusalem, not knowing what will happen to me there. I only know that in every city the Holy Spirit warns me that prison and hardships are facing me. However, I consider my life worth nothing to me, if only I may finish the race and complete the task the Lord Jesus has given me – the task of testifying to the gospel of God's grace.

'Now I know that none of you among whom I have gone about preaching the kingdom will ever see me again. Therefore, I declare to you today that I am innocent of the blood of all men. For I have not hesitated to proclaim to you the whole will of God. Keep watch over yourselves and all the flock of which the Holy Spirit has made you overseers. Be shepherds of the church of God, which he bought with his own blood. I know that after I leave, savage wolves will come in among you and will not spare the flock. Even from your own number men will arise and distort the truth in order to draw away disciples after them. So be on your guard!'

Acts 20:22–31

The church's one foundation
  Is Jesus Christ her Lord;
She is His new creation
  By water and the Word;
From heaven He came and sought her
  To be His holy bride;
With His own blood He bought her,
  And for her life He died.

Samuel John Stone, 1839–1900

Jesus Christ our Lord

Paul, a servant of Christ Jesus, called to be an apostle and set apart for the gospel of God – the gospel he promised beforehand through his prophets in the Holy Scriptures regarding his Son, who as to his human nature was a descendant of David, and who through the Spirit of holiness was declared with power to be the Son of God, by his resurrection from the dead: Jesus Christ our Lord. Through him and for his name's sake, we received grace and apostleship to call people from among all the Gentiles to the obedience that comes from faith. And you also are among those who are called to belong to Jesus. To all in Rome who are loved by God and called to be saints: Grace and peace to you from God our Father and from the Lord Jesus Christ.

Romans 1:1–7

Crown Him the Son of God,
 Before the worlds began:
And ye, who tread where He hath trod,
 Crown Him the Son of man:
Who every grief hath known
 That wrings the human breast,
And takes and bears them for His own,
 That all in Him may rest.

Crown Him the Lord of life,
 Who triumphed o'er the grace,
And rose victorious in the strife
 For those He came to save:
His glories now we sing
 Who died, and rose on high;
Who died eternal life to bring,
 And lives that death may die.

Matthew Bridges, 1800–94
and Godfrey Thring, 1823–1903

Not ashamed of the gospel

I long to see you so that I may impart to you some spiritual gift to make you strong – that is, that you and I may be mutually encouraged by each other's faith. I do not want you to be unaware, brothers, that I planned many times to come to you (but have been prevented from doing so until now) in order that I might have a harvest among you, just as I have had among the other Gentiles.

I am bound both to Greeks and non-Greeks, both to the wise and the foolish. That is why I am so eager to preach the gospel also to you who are at Rome.

I am not ashamed of the gospel, because it is the power of God for the salvation of everyone who believes: first for the Jew, then for the Gentile. For in the gospel a righteousness from God is revealed, a righteousness that is by faith from first to last, just as it is written: 'The righteous will live by faith.'

Romans 1:11–17

I'm not ashamed to own my Lord,
  Or to defend His cause;
Maintain the honour of His Word,
  The glory of His cross.

Isaac Watts, 1674–1748

Commitment to God

Now if we died with Christ, we believe that we will also live with him. For we know that since Christ was raised from the dead, he cannot die again; death no longer has mastery over him. The death he died, he died to sin once for all; but the life he lives, he lives to God.

In the same way, count yourselves dead to sin but alive to God in Christ Jesus. Therefore do not let sin reign in your mortal body so that you obey its evil desires. Do not offer the parts of your body to sin, as instruments of wickedness, but rather offer yourselves to God, as those who have been brought from death to life; and offer the parts of your body to him as instruments of righteousness. For sin shall not be your master, because you are not under law, but under grace.

Romans 6:8–14

In full and glad surrender
I give myself to Thee,
Thine utterly and only
And evermore to be.

O come and reign, Lord Jesus;
Rule over everything!
And keep me always loyal
And true to Thee, my King.

Frances Ridley Havergal, 1836–79

God's remedy for sin

So from now on we regard no-one from a worldly point of view. Though we once regarded Christ in this way, we do so no longer. Therefore, if anyone is in Christ, he is a new creation; the old has gone, the new has come! All this is from God, who reconciled us to himself through Christ and gave us the ministry of reconciliation: that God was reconciling the world to himself in Christ, not counting men's sins against them. And he has committed to us the message of reconciliation. We are therefore Christ's ambassadors, as though God were making his appeal through us. We implore you on Christ's behalf: Be reconciled to God. God made him who had no sin to be sin for us, so that in him we might become the righteousness of God. God's fellow-workers we urge you not to receive God's grace in vain. For he says, 'In the time of my favour I heard you, and in the day of salvation I helped you.' I tell you, now is the time of God's favour, now is the day of salvation.

2 Corinthians 5:16–6:2

Tell me the story slowly,
  That I may take it in –
That wonderful redemption,
  God's remedy for sin.
Tell me the story often,
  For I forget so soon;
The early dew of morning
  Has passed away at noon.

Tell me the old, old story,
Tell me the old, old story,
Tell me the old, old story,
  Of Jesus and His love.

Arabella Catherine Hankey, 1834–1911

The Lamb on the throne

Then I saw a Lamb, looking as if it had been slain,
standing in the centre of the throne, encircled by the
four living creatures and the elders. He had seven horns
and seven eyes, which are the seven spirits of God sent
out into all the earth. He came and took the scroll from
the right hand of him who sat on the throne. And when
he had taken it, the four living creatures and the
twenty-four elders fell down before the Lamb. Each one
had a harp and they were holding golden bowls full of
incense, which are the prayers of the saints. And they
sang a new song:

'You are worthy to take the scroll and to open its
seals, because you were slain, and with your blood you
purchased men for God from every tribe and language
and people and nation. You have made them to be a
kingdown and priests to serve our God, and they will
reign on the earth.'

Revelation 5:6–10

Crown Him with many crowns,
  The Lamb upon His throne;
Hark! how the heavenly anthem drowns
  All music but its own.
Awake, my soul, and sing
  Of Him who died for thee,
And hail Him as thy chosen King
  Through all eternity.

Matthew Bridges, 1800–94
and Godfrey Thring, 1823–1903

Worthy is the Lamb

Then I looked and heard the voice of many angels, numbering thousands upon thousands, and ten thousand times ten thousand. They encircled the throne and the living creatures and the elders. In a loud voice they sang: 'Worthy is the Lamb, who was slain, to receive power and wealth and wisdom and strength and honour and glory and praise!'

Then I heard every creature in heaven and on earth and under the earth and on the sea, and all that is in them, singing: 'To him who sits on the throne and to the Lamb be praise and honour and glory and power, for ever and ever!' The four living creatures said, 'Amen', and the elders fell down and worshipped.

Revelation 5:11–14

Come, let us join our cheerful songs
　　With angels round the throne;
Ten thousand thousand are their tongues,
　　But all their joys are one.

'Worthy the Lamb that died', they cry,
　　'To be exalted thus!'
'Worthy the Lamb', our lips reply,
　　'For He was slain for us!'

The whole creation join in one,
　　To bless the sacred Name
Of Him that sits upon the throne,
　　And to adore the Lamb.

Isaac Watts, 1674–1748

God is love

Dear friends, let us love one another, for love comes from God. Everyone who loves has been born of God and knows God. Whoever does not love does not know God, because God is love. This is how God showed his love among us: He sent his only begotten Son into the world that we might live through him. This is love: not that we loved God, but that he loved us and sent his Son as an atoning sacrifice for our sins. Dear friends, since God so loved us, we also ought to love one another. No-one has ever seen God; but if we love one another, God lives in us and his love is made complete in us.

We know that we live in him and he in us, because he has given us of his Spirit. And we have seen and testify that the Father has sent his Son to be the Saviour of the world. If anyone acknowledges that Jesus is the Son of God, God lives in him and he in God. And so we know and rely on the love God has for us.

1 John 4:7–16

I am so glad that our Father in heaven
Tells of His love in the book He has given:
Wonderful things in the Bible I see;
This is the dearest, that Jesus loves me.

I am so glad that Jesus loves me,
Jesus loves even me.

Though I forget Him, and wander away,
Still He doth love me wherever I stray;
Back to His dear loving arms do I flee,
When I remember that Jesus loves me.

Philipp Paul Bliss, 1838–76

The suffering servant

Just as there were many who were appalled at him –
his appearance was so disfigured beyond that of any
man and his form marred beyond human likeness – so
will he sprinkle many nations, and kings will shut their
mouths because of him. . . .

Who has believed our message and to whom has the
arm of the Lord been revealed? He grew up before him
like a tender shoot, and like a root out of dry ground. He
had no beauty or majesty to attract us to him, nothing
in his appearance that we should desire him. He was
despised and rejected by men, a man of sorrows, and
familiar with suffering. Like one from whom men hide
their faces he was despised, and we esteemed him not.

Isaiah 52:14–53:3

> O sacred head! sore wounded,
>   With grief and shame bowed down,
> How scornfully surrounded
>   With thorns, Thine only crown!
> How pale art Thou with anguish,
>   With sore abuse and scorn!
> How does that visage languish
>   Which once was bright as morn!
>
> Thy brief and bitter passion
>   Were all for sinners' gain
> Mine, mine was the transgression,
>   But Thine the deadly pain:
> Lo! here I fall, my Saviour;
>   'Tis I deserve Thy place;
> Look on me with Thy favour,
>   Vouchsafe to me Thy grace.

Paul Gerhardt, 1607–76
attributed to Bernard of Clairvaux, 1091–1153
tr. James Waddell Alexander, 1804–59

Man of sorrows

Surely he took up our infirmities and carried our sorrows, yet we considered him stricken by God, smitten by him, and afflicted. But he was pierced for our transgressions, he was crushed for our iniquities; the punishment that brought us peace was upon him, and by his wounds we are healed. We all, like sheep, have gone astray, each of us has turned to his own way; and the Lord has laid on him the iniquity of us all.

He was oppressed and afflicted, yet he did not open his mouth; he was led like a lamb to the slaughter, and as a sheep before her shearers is silent, so he did not open his mouth. By oppression and judgment he was taken away. And who can speak of his descendants? For he was cut off from the land of the living; for the transgression of my people he was stricken. He was assigned a grave with the wicked, and with the rich in his death, though he had done no violence, nor was any deceit in his mouth.

Isaiah 53:4–9

Man of Sorrows! what a name
For the Son of God, who came
Ruined sinners to reclaim!
    Hallelujah! what a Saviour!

Bearing shame and scoffing rude,
In my place condemned He stood;
Sealed my pardon with His blood:
    Hallelujah! what a Saviour!

Philipp Paul Bliss, 1838–76

Crowned with glory

Yet it was the Lord's will to crush him and cause him to suffer, and though the Lord makes his life a guilt offering, he will see his offspring and prolong his days, and the will of the Lord will prosper in his hand. After the suffering of his soul, he will see the light of life and be satisfied; by his knowledge my righteous servant will justify many, and he will bear their iniquities. Therefore I will give him a portion among the great, and he will divide the spoils with the strong, because he poured out his life unto death, and was numbered with the transgressors. For he bore the sin of many, and made intercession for the transgressors.

Isaiah 53:10–12

Look, ye saints! the sight is glorious;
　See the Man of Sorrows now,
From the fight returned victorious,
　Every knee to Him shall bow:
Crown Him! Crown Him!
　Crowns become the Victor's brow.

Crown the Saviour! angels, crown Him!
　Rich the trophies Jesus brings;
In the seat of power enthrone Him,
　While the vault of heaven rings:
Crown Him! Crown Him!
　Crown the Saviour King of kings!

Thomas Kelly, 1769–1855

Jesus, our Saviour

In the past God spoke to our forefathers through the prophets at many times in various ways, but in these last days he has spoken to us by his Son, whom he appointed heir of all things, and through whom he made the universe. The Son is the radiance of God's glory and the exact representation of his being, sustaining all things by his powerful word. After he had provided purification for sins, he sat down at the right hand of the Majesty in heaven.

Hebrews 1:1–3

For Christ did not enter a man-made sanctuary that was only a copy of the true one; he entered heaven itself, now to appear for us in God's presence. Nor did he enter heaven to offer himself again and again, the way the high priest enters the Most Holy Place every year with blood that is not his own. Then Christ would have had to suffer many times since the creation of the world. But now he has appeared once for all at the end of the ages to do away with sin by the sacrifice of himself. Just as man is destined to die once, and after that to face judgment, so Christ was sacrificed once to take away the sins of many people; and he will appear a second time, not to bear sin, but to bring salvation to those who are waiting for him.

Hebrews 9:24–28

Jesus the Saviour reigns,
  The God of truth and love:
When He had purged our stains,
  He took His seat above:

Lift up your heart, lift up your voice;
Rejoice, again I say, Rejoice.

Rejoice in glorious hope;
  Jesus the Judge shall come,
And take His servants up
  To their eternal home:

We soon shall hear the archangel's voice;
The trump of God shall sound, Rejoice!

Charles Wesley, 1707–88

The praise of God's glory

O Lord, our Lord, how majestic is your name in all the earth! You have set your glory above the heavens. From the lips of children and infants you have ordained praise because of your enemies, to silence the foe and the avenger.

When I consider your heavens, the work of your fingers, the moon and the stars, which you have set in place, what is man that you are mindful of him, the son of man that you care for him? You made him a little lower than the heavenly beings and crowned him with glory and honour. You made him ruler over the works of your hands; you put everything under his feet: all flocks and herds, and the beasts of the field, the birds of the air, and the fish of the sea, all that swim the paths of the seas.

O Lord, our Lord, how majestic is your name in all the earth!

Psalm 8:1–9

All creatures of our God and King,
Lift up your voice and with us sing:
   Hallelujah, Hallelujah!
Thou burning sun with golden beam,
Thou silver moon with softer gleam:

O praise Him, O praise Him,
Hallelujah, Hallelujah, Hallelujah!

Let all things their Creator bless,
And worship Him in humbleness,
   O praise Him, Hallelujah!
Praise, praise the Father, praise the Son,
And praise the Spirit, Three in One.

St Francis of Assisi, 1182–1226
tr. William Henry Draper, 1855–1933

Crucified ... and risen!

Against all hope, Abraham in hope believed and so became the father of many nations, just as it had been said to him, 'So shall your offspring be.' Without weakening in his faith, he faced the fact that his body was as good as dead – since he was about a hundred years old – and that Sarah's womb was also dead. Yet he did not waver through unbelief regarding the promise of God, but was strengthened in his faith and gave glory to God, being fully persuaded that God had power to do what he had promised. This is why 'it was credited to him as righteousness.' The words 'it was credited to him' were written not for him alone, but also for us, to whom God will credit righteousness – for us who believe in him who raised Jesus our Lord from the dead. He was delivered over to death for our sins and was raised to life for our justification.

Romans 4:18–25

For through the law I died to the law so that I might live for God. I have been crucified with Christ and I no longer live, but Christ lives in me. The life I live in the body, I live by faith in the Son of God, who loved me and gave himself for me.

Galatians 2:19–20

One day when heaven was filled with His praises,
   One day when sin was as black as could be,
Jesus came forth to be born of a virgin
   Dwelt amongst men, my example is He!

Living, He loved me; dying, He saved me;
Buried, He carried my sins far away!
Rising, He justified freely for ever;
One day He's coming – O glorious day!

J. Wilbur Chapman, 1859–1918

In all things God works for good

And we know that in all things God works for the good of those who love him, who have been called according to his purpose. For those God foreknew he also predestined to be conformed to the likeness of his Son, that he might be the firstborn among many brothers. And those he predestined, he also called; those he called, he also justified; those he justified, he also glorified.

Romans 8:28–30

Now I want you to know, brothers, that what has happened to me has really served to advance the gospel. As a result, it has become clear throughout the whole palace guard and to everyone else that I am in chains for Christ. Because of my chains, most of the brothers in the Lord have been encouraged to speak the word of God more courageously and fearlessly.

Philippians 1:12–14

Through the love of God our Saviour
　　All will be well;
Free and changeless is His favour,
　　All, all is well:
Precious is the blood that healed us;
Perfect is the grace that sealed us;
Strong the hand stretched forth to shield us;
　　All must be well.

Though we pass through tribulation,
　　All will be well;
Christ hath purchased full salvation,
　　All, all is well:
Happy still in God confiding,
Fruitful, if in Christ abiding,
Holy, through the Spirit's guiding;
　　All must be well.

Mary Peter, 1813–56

God leads his people on

By day the Lord went ahead of them in a pillar of cloud to guide them on their way and by night in a pillar of fire to give them light, so that they could travel by day or night. Neither the pillar of cloud by day nor the pillar of fire by night left its place in front of the people.

Exodus 13:21–22

Trust in the Lord and do good; dwell in the land and enjoy safe pasture. Delight yourself in the Lord and he will give you the desires of your heart.

Commit your way to the Lord; trust in him and he will do this: He will make your righteousness shine like the dawn, the justice of your cause like the noonday sun.

Be still before the Lord and wait patiently for him; do not fret when men succeed in their ways, when they carry out their wicked schemes.

Psalm 37:3–7

Guide me, O Thou great Jehovah,
    Pilgrim through this barren land;
I am weak, but Thou art mighty,
    Hold me with Thy powerful hand;
        Bread of heaven,
Feed me now and evermore.

William Williams, 1717–91
tr. Peter Williams, 1721–96

Becoming like Jesus

You were taught, with regard to your former way of life, to put off your old self, which is being corrupted by its deceitful desires; to be made new in the attitude of your minds; and to put on the new self, created to be like God in true righteousness and holiness.

Therefore each of you must put off falsehood and speak truthfully to his neighbour, for we are all members of one body. 'In your anger do not sin': Do not let the sun go down while you are still angry, and do not give the devil a foothold. He who has been stealing must steal no longer, but must work, doing something useful with his own hands, that he may have something to share with those in need.

Ephesians 4:22–28

O Jesus Christ, grow Thou in me,
　And all things else recede;
My heart be daily nearer Thee,
　From sin be daily freed.

Johann Caspar Lavater, 1741–1801
tr. Elizabeth Lee Smith, 1817–98

Seeking the lost

Jesus entered Jericho and was passing through. A man was there by name of Zacchaeus; he was a chief tax collector and was wealthy. He wanted to see who Jesus was, but being a short man he could not, because of the crowd. So he ran ahead and climbed a sycamore-fig tree to see him, since Jesus was coming that way.

When Jesus reached the spot, he looked up and said to him, 'Zacchaeus, come down immediately. I must stay at your house today.' So he came down at once and welcomed him gladly. All the people saw this and began to mutter, 'He has gone to be the guest of a "sinner".'

But Zacchaeus stood up and said to the Lord, 'Look, Lord! Here and now I give half of my possessions to the poor, and if I have cheated anybody out of anything, I will pay back four times the amount.' Jesus said to him, 'Today salvation has come to this house, because this man, too, is a son of Abraham. For the Son of Man came to seek and to save what was lost.'

Luke 19:1–9

Come, let us sing of a wonderful love,
    Tender and true;
Out of the heart of the Father above,
    Streaming to me and to you:
        Wonderful love
Dwells in the heart of the Father above.

Jesus, the Saviour, this gospel to tell
    Joyfully came;
Came with the helpless and hopeless to dwell,
    Sharing their sorrow and shame;
        Seeking the lost,
Saving, redeeming at measureless cost.

Robert Walmsley, 1831–1905

Boasting in Jesus

This is what the Lord says: 'Let not the wise man boast of his wisdom or the strong man boast of his strength or the rich man boast of his riches, but let him who boasts boast about this: that he understands and knows me, that I am the Lord, who exercises kindness, justice and righteousness on earth, for in these I delight,' declares the Lord.

Jeremiah 9:23–24

He chose the lowly things of this world and the despised things – and the things that are not – to nullify the things that are, so that no-one may boast before him. It is because of him that you are in Christ Jesus, who has become for us wisdom from God – that is, our righteousness, holiness and redemption. Therefore, as it is written: 'Let him who boasts boast in the Lord.'

1 Corinthians 1:28–31

May I never boast except in the cross of our Lord Jesus Christ, through which the world has been crucified to me, and I to the world. Neither circumcision nor uncircumcision means anything; what counts is a new creation.

Galatians 6:14–15

> Forbid it, Lord, that I should boast
>   Save in the death of Christ my God:
> All the vain things that charm me most,
>   I sacrifice them to His blood.

Isaac Watts, 1674–1748

Seek this first

Since, then, you have been raised with Christ, set your hearts on things above, where Christ is seated at the right hand of God. Set your minds on things above, not on earthly things. For you died, and your life is now hidden with Christ in God. When Christ, who is your life, appears, then you also will appear with him in glory.

Put to death, therefore, whatever belongs to your earthly nature: sexual immorality, impurity, lust, evil desires and greed, which is idolatry. Because of these, the wrath of God is coming. You used to walk in these ways, in the life you once lived. But now you must rid yourselves of all such things as these: anger, rage, malice, slander and filthy language from your lips. Do not lie to each other, since you have taken off your old self with its practices and have put on the new self, which is being renewed in knowledge in the image of its Creator. Here there is no Greek or Jew, circumcised or uncircumcised, barbarian, Scythian, slave or free, but Christ is all, and is in all.

Therefore, as God's chosen people, holy and dearly loved, clothe yourselves with compassion, kindness, humility, gentleness and patience. Bear with each other and forgive whatever grievances you may have against one another. Forgive as the Lord forgave you. And over all these virtues put on love, which binds them all together in perfect unity.

Colossians 3:1–14

Seek Him first; then, when forgiven,
Pardoned, made an heir of heaven,
Let your life to Him be given:
    Seek this first.

Georgianna Mary Taylor, 1848–1915

Jesus is on our side

My dear children, I write this to you so that you will not sin. But if anybody does sin, we have one who speaks to the Father in our defence – Jesus Christ, the Righteous One. He is the atoning sacrifice for our sins, and not only for ours but also for the sins of the whole world.

1 John 2:1–2

Because Jesus lives for ever, he has a permanent priesthood. Therefore he is able to save completely those who come to God through him, because he always lives to intercede for them. Such a high priest meets our need – one who is holy, blameless, pure, set apart from sinners, exalted above the heavens.

Hebrews 7:24–26

Before the throne of God above
    I have a strong, a perfect plea,
A great High Priest, whose Name is Love,
    Who ever lives and pleads for me.

My name is graven in His hands,
    My name is written on His heart;
I know that, while in heaven He stands,
    No tongue can bid me thence depart.

Charitie Lees De Chenez, 1841–1923

Be filled with the Spirit

Be very careful, then, how you live – not as unwise but as wise, making the most of every opportunity, because the days are evil. Therefore do not be foolish, but understand what the Lord's will is. Do not get drunk on wine, which leads to debauchery. Instead, be filled with the Spirit. Speak to one another with psalms, hymns and spiritual songs. Sing and make music in your heart to the Lord, always giving thanks to God the Father for everything, in the name of our Lord Jesus Christ.

Submit to one another out of reverence for Christ.

Ephesians 5:15–21

'I desire to do your will, O my God; your law is within my heart.'

Psalm 40:8

'But may all who seek you rejoice and be glad in you; may those who love your salvation always say, "The Lord be exalted!"'

Psalm 40:16

> O fill me with Thy fulness, Lord;
>   Until my very heart o'erflow
> In kindling thought and glowing word,
>   Thy love to tell, Thy praise to show.
>
> O use me, Lord, use even me,
>   Just as Thou wilt, and when, and where,
> Until Thy blessed face I see,
>   Thy rest, Thy joy, Thy glory share.

Frances Ridley Havergal, 1836–79

King of kings, Lord of lords

I saw heaven standing open and there before me was a white horse, whose rider is called Faithful and True. With justice he judges and makes war. His eyes are like blazing fire, and on his head are many crowns. He has a name written on him that no-one knows but he himself. He is dressed in a robe dipped in blood, and his name is the Word of God. The armies of heaven were following him, riding on white horses and dressed in fine linen, white and clean. Out of his mouth comes a sharp sword with which to strike down the nations. 'He will rule them with an iron sceptre.' He treads the winepress of the fury of the wrath of God Almighty. On his robe and on his thigh he has this name written: KING OF KINGS AND LORD OF LORDS.

Revelation 19:11–16

Hark, those bursts of acclamation!
Hark, those loud triumphant chords!
Jesus takes the highest station:
O what joy the sight affords!
Crown Him! Crown Him:
King of kings, and Lord of lords!

Thomas Kelly, 1769–1855

God's holiness and love

In the year that King Uzziah died, I saw the Lord seated on a throne, high and exalted, and the train of his robe filled the temple. Above him were seraphs, each with six wings: With two wings they covered their faces, with two they covered their feet, and with two they were flying. And they were calling to one another: 'Holy, holy, holy is the Lord Almighty; the whole earth is full of his glory.' At the sound of their voices the doorposts and thresholds shook and the temple was filled with smoke.

'Woe to me!' I cried. 'I am ruined! For I am a man of unclean lips, and I live among a people of unclean lips, and my eyes have seen the King, the Lord Almighty.'

Then one of the seraphs flew to me with a live coal in his hand, which he had taken with tongs from the altar. With it he touched my mouth and said, 'See, this has touched your lips; your guilt is taken away and your sin atoned for.'

Isaiah 6:1–7

> Eternal Light! Eternal Light!
>   How pure the soul must be,
> When, placed within Thy searching sight,
> It shrinks not, but with calm delight
>   Can live and look on Thee.
>
> There is a way for man to rise
>   To that sublime abode:
> An offering and a sacrifice,
> A Holy Spirit's energies,
>   An Advocate with God.

Thomas Binney, 1798–1874

The preciousness of Christ

'The kingdom of heaven is like treasure hidden in a field. When a man found it, he hid it again, and then in his joy went and sold all he had and bought that field.

Again, the kingdom of heaven is like a merchant looking for fine pearls. When he found one of great value, he went away and sold everything he had and bought it.'

Matthew 13:44–46

When Christ came as high priest of the good things that are already here, he went through the greater and more perfect tabernacle that is not man-made, that is to say, not a part of this creation. He did not enter by means of the blood of goats and calves; but he entered the Most Holy Place once for all by his own blood, having obtained eternal redemption. The blood of goats and bulls and the ashes of a heifer sprinkled on those who are ceremonially unclean sanctify them so that they are outwardly clean. How much more, then, will the blood of Christ, who through the eternal Spirit offered himself unblemished to God, cleanse our consciences from acts that lead to death, so that we may serve the living God!

Hebrews 9:11–14

> I've found the pearl of greatest price,
>   My heart doth sing for joy;
> And sing I must, for Christ is mine,
>   Christ shall my song employ.
>
> Christ is my Prophet, Priest, and King:
>   My Prophet full of light,
> My great High Priest before the throne,
>   My King of heavenly might.

John Mason, c. 1646–94

The power of sin

The Lord said, 'My Spirit will not contend with man for ever, for he is mortal; his days will be a hundred and twenty years.' The Lord saw how great man's wickedness on the earth had become, and that every inclination of the thoughts of his heart was only evil all the time. The Lord was grieved that he had made man on the earth, and his heart was filled with pain.

Genesis 6:3, 5–6

The heart is deceitful above all things and beyond cure. Who can understand it?

'I the Lord search the heart and examine the mind, to reward a man according to his conduct, according to what his deeds deserve.'

Jeremiah 17:9–10

> Plenteous grace with Thee is found,
>   Grace to cover all my sin;
> Let the healing streams abound,
>   Make and keep me pure within:
>
> Thou of life the fountain art,
>   Freely let me take of Thee;
> Spring Thou up within my heart,
>   Rise to all eternity.

Charles Wesley, 1707–88

Praise God!

I will extol the Lord at all times; his praise will always be on my lips. My soul will boast in the Lord; let the afflicted hear and rejoice. Glorify the Lord with me: let us exalt his name together.

I sought the Lord, and he answered me; he delivered me from all my fears. Those who look to him are radiant; their faces are never covered with shame. This poor man called, and the Lord heard him; he saved him out of all his troubles. The angel of the Lord encamps around those who fear him, and he delivers them.

Taste and see that the Lord is good; blessed is the man who takes refuge in him. Fear the Lord, you his saints, for those who fear him lack nothing. A righteous man may have many troubles, but the Lord delivers him from them all.

Psalm 34:1–9, 19

Through all the changing scenes of life,
 In trouble and in joy,
The praises of my God shall still
 My heart and tongue employ.

Fear Him, ye saints, and you will then
 Have nothing else to fear;
Make you His service your delight,
 Your wants shall be His care.

Nahum Tate, 1652–1715
and Nicholas Brady, 1659–1726

'I am with you'

But now, this is what the Lord says – he who created you, O Jacob, he who formed you, O Israel: 'Fear not, for I have redeemed you; I have summoned you by name; you are mine. When you pass through the waters, I will be with you; and when you pass through the rivers, they will not sweep over you. When you walk through the fire, you will not be burned; the flames will not set you ablaze. For I am the Lord, the Holy One of Israel, your Saviour; I give Egypt for your ransom, Cush and Seba in your stead. Since you are precious and honoured in my sight, and because I love you, I will give men in exchange for you, and people in exchange for your life. Do not be afraid, for I am with you; I will bring your children from the east and gather you from the west. I will say to the north, 'Give them up!' and to the south, 'Do not hold them back.' Bring my sons from afar and my daughters from the ends of the earth – everyone who is called by my name, whom I created for my glory, whom I formed and made.'

Isaiah 43:1–7

Fear not, He is with thee, O be not dismayed;
For He is thy God, and will still give thee aid:
He'll strengthen thee, help thee, and cause thee to stand,
Upheld by His righteous, omnipotent hand.

When through the deep waters He calls thee to go,
The rivers of grief shall not thee overflow;
For He will be with thee in trouble to bless,
And sanctify to thee thy deepest distress.

'K' in Rippon's *Selection*, 1787

The greatness of God

O Lord, you have searched me and you know me. You know when I sit and when I rise; you perceive my thoughts from afar. You discern my going out and my lying down; you are familiar with all my ways. Before a word is on my tongue you know it completely, O Lord.

You hem me in – behind and before; you have laid your hand upon me. Such knowledge is too wonderful for me, too lofty for me to attain.

Where can I go from your Spirit? Where can I flee from your presence? If I go up to the heavens, you are there; if I make my bed in the depths, you are there. If I rise on the wings of the dawn, if I settle on the far side of the sea, even there your hand will guide me, your right hand will hold me fast.

Psalm 139:1–10

Holy and Infinite! Viewless, Eternal!
　Veiled in the glory none can sustain,
None comprehendeth Thy Being supernal,
　Nor can the heaven of heavens contain.

Glorious in holiness, fearful in praises,
　Who shall not fear Thee and who shall not laud?
Anthems of glory Thy universe raises,
　Holy and infinite! Father and God!

Frances Ridley Havergal, 1836–79

Spiritual praise

You have not come to a mountain that can be touched and that is burning with fire; to darkness, gloom and storm; to a trumpet blast or to such a voice speaking words that those who heard it begged that no further word be spoken to them, because they could not bear what was commanded: 'If even an animal touches the mountain, it must be stoned.'

The sight was so terrifying that Moses said, 'I am trembling with fear.'

But you have come to Mount Zion, to the heavenly Jerusalem, the city of the living God. You have come to thousands upon thousands of angels in joyful assembly, to the church of the firstborn, whose names are written in heaven. You have come to God, the judge of all men, to the spirits of righteous men made perfect, to Jesus the mediator of a new covenant, and to the sprinkled blood that speaks a better word than the blood of Abel.

Hebrews 12:18–24

Praise Him, praise Him! Jesus, our blessed Redeemer;
  For our sins He suffered and bled and died.
He, our Rock, our hope of eternal salvation,
  Hail Him, hail Him! Jesus the crucified.
Loving Saviour, meekly enduring sorrow,
  Crowned with thorns that cruelly pierced His brow;
Once for us rejected, despised, and forsaken,
  Prince of glory, ever triumphant now.

Frances Jane Van Alstyne, 1820–1915

Worshipping God alone

And God spoke all these words: 'I am the Lord your God, who brought you out of Egypt, out of the land of slavery. You shall have no other gods before me. You shall not make for yourself an idol in the form of anything in heaven above or on the earth beneath or in the waters below. You shall not bow down to them or worship them; for I, the Lord your God, am a jealous God, punishing the children for the sin of the fathers to the third and fourth generation of those who hate me, but showing love to a thousand generations of those who love me and keep my commandments.'

Exodus 20:1–6

We know that anyone born of God does not continue to sin; the one who was born of God keeps him safe, and the evil one cannot harm him. We know that we are children of God, and that the whole world is under the control of the evil one. We know also that the Son of God has come and has given us understanding, so that we may know him who is true. And we are in him who is true – even in his Son Jesus Christ. He is the true God and eternal life.

Dear children, keep yourselves from idols.

1 John 5:18–21

> Jesus calls us from the worship
> Of the vain world's golden store,
> From each idol that would keep us,
> Saying, 'Christian, love me more!'
>
> In our joys and in our sorrow,
> Days of toil and hours of ease,
> Still He calls, in cares and pleasures,
> That we love Him more than these.

Cecil Frances Alexander, 1818–95

Serving Christ

Finally, all of you, live in harmony with one another; be sympathetic, love as brothers, be compassionate and humble. Do not repay evil with evil or insult with insult, but with blessing, because to this you were called so that you may inherit a blessing. For, 'Whoever would love life and see good days must keep his tongue from evil and his lips from deceitful speech. He must turn from evil and do good; he must seek peace and pursue it. For the eyes of the Lord are on the righteous and his ears are attentive to their prayer, but the face of the Lord is against those who do evil.'

Who is going to harm you if you are eager to do good? But even if you should suffer for what is right, you are blessed. 'Do not fear what they fear; do not be frightened.' But in your hearts set apart Christ as Lord. Always be prepared to give an answer to everyone who asks you to give the reason for the hope that you have. But do this with gentleness and respect, keeping a clear conscience, so that those who speak maliciously against your good behaviour in Christ may be ashamed of their slander. It is better, if it is God's will, to suffer for doing good than for doing evil. For Christ died for sins once for all, the righteous for the unrighteous, to bring you to God.

1 Peter 3:8–18

> I want a true regard,
>   A single, steady aim,
> Unmoved by threatening or reward,
>   To Thee and Thy great Name;
> A jealous, just concern
>   For Thine immortal praise;
> A pure desire that all may learn
>   And glorify Thy grace.

Charles Wesley, 1707–88

A faith for life

Now faith is being sure of what we hope for and certain of what we do not see. This is what the ancients were commended for.

By faith we understand that the universe was formed at God's command, so that what is seen was not made out of what was visible.

By faith Abel offered God a better sacrifice than Cain did. By faith he was commended as a righteous man, when God spoke well of his offerings. And by faith he still speaks, even though he is dead.

By faith Enoch was taken from this life, so that he did not experience death; he could not be found, because God had taken him away. For before he was taken, he was commended as one who pleased God. And without faith it is impossible to please God, because anyone who comes to him must believe that he exists and that he rewards those who earnestly seek him.

Hebrews 11:1–6

When we walk with the Lord,
In the light of His word,
   What a glory He shed on our way!
While we do His good will,
He abides with us still,
   And with all who will trust and obey!

Trust and obey!
For there's no other way
  To be happy in Jesus
But to trust and obey.

John Henry Sammis, 1846–1919

Practical Christian unity

All the believers were one in heart and mind. No-one claimed that any of his possessions was his own, but they shared everything they had. With great power the apostles continued to testify to the resurrection of the Lord Jesus, and much grace was upon them all. There were no needy persons among them. For from time to time those who owned lands or houses sold them, brought the money from the sales and put it at the apostles' feet, and it was distributed to anyone as he had need.

Joseph, a Levite from Cyprus, whom the apostles called Barnabas (which means Son of Encouragement), sold a field he owned and brought the money and put it at the apostles' feet.

Acts 4:32–37

    Blest be the tie that binds
      Our hearts in Christian love;
    The fellowship of kindred minds
      Is like to that above.

    Before our Father's throne
      We pour our ardent prayers;
    Our fears, our hopes, our aims are one,
      Our comforts and our cares.

John Fawcett, 1739–1817

Reverence for God's name

You shall not misuse the name of the Lord your God,
for the Lord will not hold anyone guiltless who misuses
his name.

Exodus 20:7

'Again, you have heard that it was said to the people
long ago, "Do not break your oath, but keep the oaths
you have made to the Lord." But I tell you, Do not swear
at all: either by heaven, for it is God's throne; or by the
earth, for it is his footstool; or by Jerusalem, for it is the
city of the Great King. And do not swear by your head,
for you cannot make even one hair white or black.
Simply let your "Yes" be "Yes", and your "No", "No";
anything beyond this comes from the evil one.'

Matthew 5:33–37

Shun evil companions; bad language disdain;
God's Name hold in reverence, nor take it in vain;
Be thoughtful and earnest, kind-hearted and true;
Look ever to Jesus, He will carry you through.

Horatio Richmond Palmer, 1834–1907

Resting in God

This is what the Sovereign Lord, the Holy One of Israel, says: 'In repentance and rest is your salvation, in quietness and trust is your strength, but you would have none of it. You said, 'No, we will flee on horses.' Therefore you will flee! You said, 'We will ride off on swift horses.' Therefore your pursuers will be swift! A thousand will flee at the threat of one; at the threat of five you will all flee away, till you are left like a flagstaff on a mountaintop, like a banner on a hill.'

Yet the Lord longs to be gracious to you; he rises to show you compassion. For the Lord is a God of justice. Blessed are all who wait for him!

Isaiah 30:15–18

Drop Thy still dews of quietness
    Till all our strivings cease:
Take from our souls the strain and stress,
And let our ordered lives confess
    The beauty of Thy peace.

John Greenleaf Whittier, 1807–92

Generous giving

As he looked up, Jesus saw the rich putting their gifts into the temple treasury. He also saw a poor widow put in two very small copper coins.

'I tell you the truth,' he said, 'this poor widow has put in more than all the others. All these people gave their gifts out of their wealth; but she out of her poverty put in all she had to live on.'

Luke 21:1–4

Remember this: Whoever sows sparingly will also reap sparingly, and whoever sows generously will also reap generously. Each man should give what he has decided in his heart to give, not reluctantly or under compulsion, for God loves a cheerful giver. And God is able to make all grace abound to you, so that in all things at all times, having all that you need, you will abound in every good work. As it is written: 'He has scattered abroad his gifts to the poor; his righteousness endures for ever.' Now he who supplies seed to the sower and bread for food will also supply and increase your store of seed and will enlarge the harvest of your righteousness. You will be made rich in every way so that you can be generous on every occasion, and through us your generosity will result in thanksgiving to God.

2 Corinthians 9:6–11

Take my silver and my gold,
Not a mite would I withhold;
Take my intellect, and use
Every power as Thou shalt choose.

Frances Ridley Havergal, 1836–79

God's special day

'Remember the Sabbath day by keeping it holy. Six days you shall labour and do all your work, but the seventh day is a Sabbath to the Lord your God. On it you shall not do any work, neither you, nor your son or daughter, nor your manservant or maidservant, nor your animals, nor the alien within your gates. For in six days the Lord made the heavens and the earth, the sea, and all that is in them, but he rested on the seventh day. Therefore the Lord blessed the Sabbath day and made it holy.'

Exodus 20:8–11

'If you keep your feet from breaking the Sabbath and from doing as you please on my holy day, if you call the Sabbath a delight and the Lord's holy day honourable, and if you honour it by not going your own way and not doing as you please or speaking idle words, then you will find joy in the Lord, and I will cause you to ride on the heights of the land and to feast on the inheritance of your father Jacob.' The mouth of the Lord has spoken.

Isaiah 58:13–14

Then he [Jesus] said to them, 'The Sabbath was made for man, not man for the Sabbath. So the Son of Man is Lord even of the Sabbath.'

Mark 2:27–28

O Sabbath rest by Galilee!
O calm of hills above.
Where Jesus knelt to share with Thee
The silence of eternity,
Interpreted by love.

John Greenleaf Whittier, 1807–92

Living God's way

Come, my children, listen to me; I will teach you the fear of the Lord. Whoever of you loves life and desires to see many good days, keep your tongue from evil and your lips from speaking lies. Turn from evil and do good; seek peace and pursue it.

Psalm 34:11–14

Blessed is the man who finds wisdom, the man who gains understanding, for she is more profitable than silver and yields better returns than gold. She is more precious than rubies; nothing you desire can compare with her. Long life is in her right hand; in her left hand are riches and honour. Her ways are pleasant ways, and all her paths are peace. She is a tree of life to those who embrace her; those who lay hold of her will be blessed.

Proverbs 3:13–18

And there's another country, I've heard of long ago –
Most dear to them that love her, most great to them
   that know –
We may not count her armies: we may not see
   her King –
Her fortress is a faithful heart, her pride is
   suffering –
And soul by soul and silently her shining bounds
   increase,
And her ways are ways of gentleness and all her
   paths are peace.

Cecil Spring Rice, 1859–1918

Children and parents

'Honour your father and your mother, so that you may
live long in the land the Lord your God is giving you.'

Exodus 20:12

Then he [Jesus] went down to Nazareth with them [his
parents] and was obedient to them. But his mother trea-
sured all these things in her heart. And Jesus grew in
wisdom and stature, and in favour with God and men.

Luke 2:51–52

Children, obey your parents in the Lord, for this is right.
'Honour your father and mother' – which is the first
commandment with a promise – 'that it may go well
with you and that you may enjoy long life on the earth.'

Fathers, do not exasperate your children; instead,
bring them up in the training and instruction of the
Lord.

Ephesians 6:1–4

And through all His wondrous childhood
He would honour and obey,
Love, and watch the lowly maiden
In whose gentle arms He lay.
Christian children all must be
Mild, obedient, good as He.

Cecil Frances Alexander, 1818–95

Obeying Christ

'Why do you call me, "Lord, Lord," and do not do what I say? I will show you what he is like who comes to me and hears my words and puts them into practice. He is like a man building a house, who dug down deep and laid the foundation on rock. When the flood came, the torrent struck that house but could not shake it, because it was well built. But the one who hears my words and does not put them into practice is like a man who built a house on the ground without a foundation. The moment the torrent struck that house, it collapsed and its destruction was complete.'

Luke 6:46—49

By the grace God has given me, I laid a foundation as an expert builder, and someone else is building on it. But each one should be careful how he builds. For no-one can lay any foundation other than the one already laid, which is Jesus Christ.

1 Corinthians 3:10—11

When we walk with the Lord,
In the light of His Word,
    What a glory He sheds on our way!
While we do His good will,
He abides with us still,
    And with all who will trust and obey!

Trust and obey!
For there's no other way
    To be happy in Jesus
But to trust and obey.

John Henry Sammis, 1846–1919

Building on Christ

If any man builds on this foundation using gold, silver, costly stones, wood, hay or straw, his work will be shown for what it is, because the Day will bring it to light. It will be revealed with fire, and the fire will test the quality of each man's work. If what he has built survives, he will receive his reward. If it is burned up, he will suffer loss; he himself will be saved, but only as one escaping through the flames.

Don't you know that you yourselves are God's temple and that God's Spirit lives in you? If anyone destroys God's temple, God will destroy him; for God's temple is sacred, and you are that temple.

Do not deceive yourselves. If any one of you thinks he is wise by the standards of this age, he should become a 'fool' so that he may become wise. For the wisdom of this world is foolishness in God's sight. As it is written: 'He catches the wise in their craftiness'; and again, 'The Lord knows that the thoughts of the wise are futile.' So then, no more boasting about men! All things are yours, whether Paul or Apollos or Cephas or the world or life or death or the present or the future – all are yours, and you are of Christ, and Christ is of God.

1 Corinthians 3:12–23

> Christ is our Corner-stone,
>   On Him alone we build;
> With His true saints alone
>   The courts of heaven are filled;
> On His great love
>   Our hopes we place
>   Of present grace
> And joys above.

Latin, 6th or 7th century
tr. John Chandler, 1806–76

The depth of sin

'You shall not commit adultery.'

Exodus 20:14

'You have heard that it was said, "Do not commit adultery." But I tell you that anyone who looks at a woman lustfully has already committed adultery with her in his heart. If your right eye causes you to sin, gouge it out and throw it away. It is better for you to lose one part of your body than for your whole body to be thrown into hell. And if your right hand causes you to sin, cut it off and throw it away. It is better for you to lose one part of your body than for your whole body to go into hell.'

Matthew 5:27–30

> I want a godly fear,
>   A quick-discerning eye
> That looks to Thee when sin is near,
>   And sees the tempter fly;
> A spirit still prepared,
>   And armed with jealous care,
> For ever standing on its guard
>   And watching unto prayer.

Charles Wesley, 1707–88

The way to true wisdom

James, a servant of God and of the Lord Jesus Christ,
To the twelve tribes scattered among the nations:
Greetings.

Consider it pure joy, my brothers, whenever you face
trials of many kinds, because you know that the testing
of your faith develops perseverance. Perseverance must
finish its work so that you may be mature and complete,
not lacking anything. If any of you lacks wisdom, he
should ask God, who gives generously to all without
finding fault, and it will be given to him. But when he
asks, he must believe and not doubt, because he who
doubts is like a wave of the sea, blown and tossed by
the wind. That man should not think he will receive
anything from the Lord; he is a double-minded man,
unstable in all he does.

James 1:1–7

Lead us, O Father, in the paths of peace:
  Without Thy guiding hand we go astray,
And doubts appal, and sorrows still increase;
  Lead us through Christ, the true and living Way.

Lead us, O Father, in the paths of truth:
  Unhelped by Thee, in error's maze we grope,
While passion stains and folly dims our youth,
  And age comes on uncheered by faith or hope.

William Henry Burleigh, 1812–71

The Christian's new life

'You shall not steal.'

Exodus 20:15

You were taught, with regard to your former way of life,
to put off your old self, which is being corrupted by its
deceitful desires; to be made new in the attitude of your
minds; and to put on the new self, created to be like God
in true righteousness and holiness. Therefore each of
you must put off falsehood and speak truthfully to his
neighbour, for we are all members of one body. 'In your
anger do not sin': Do not let the sun go down while you
are still angry, and do not give the devil a foothold. He
who has been stealing must steal no longer, but must
work, doing something useful with his own hands, that
he may have something to share with those in need.

Ephesians 4:22–28

> O Jesus, I have promised
>   To serve Thee to the end;
> Be Thou for ever near me,
>   My Master and my Friend:
> I shall not fear the battle
>   If Thou art by my side,
> Nor wander from the pathway
>   If Thou wilt be my Guide.
>
> O let me feel Thee near me:
>   The world is ever near;
> I see the sights that dazzle,
>   The tempting sounds I hear;
> My foes are ever near me,
>   Around me and within;
> But, Jesus, draw Thou nearer,
>   And shield my soul from sin.

John Ernest Bode, 1816–74

Light upon our way

The Lord said to Moses, 'Tell Aaron and his sons, "This is how you are to bless the Israelites. Say to them: The Lord bless you and keep you; the Lord make his face shine upon you and be gracious to you; the Lord turn his face towards you and give you peace." '

Numbers 6:22–26

Your statutes are wonderful; therefore I obey them. The unfolding of your words gives light; it gives understanding to the simple. I open my mouth and pant, longing for your commands. Turn to me and have mercy on me, as you always do to those who love your name. Direct my footsteps according to your word; let no sin rule over me. Redeem me from the oppression of men, that I may obey your precepts. Make your face shine upon your servant and teach me your decrees.

Psalm 119:129–135

> Lord, upon our blindness
> Thy pure radiance pour;
> For Thy loving kindness
> Make us love Thee more;
> And, when clouds are drifting
> Dark across our sky,
> Then, the veil uplifting,
> Father, be Thou nigh.

William Walsham How, 1823–97

He will keep us from falling

Paul and Timothy, servants of Christ Jesus,

To all the saints in Christ Jesus at Philippi, together with the overseers and deacons: Grace and peace to you from God our Father and the Lord Jesus Christ.

I thank my God every time I remember you. In all my prayers for all of you, I always pray with joy because of your partnership in the gospel from the first day until now, being confident of this, that he who began a good work in you will carry it on to completion until the day of Christ Jesus.

Philippians 1:1–6

To him who is able to keep you from falling and to present you before his glorious presence without fault and with great joy – to the only God our Saviour be glory, majesty, power and authority, through Jesus Christ our Lord, before all ages, now and for evermore! Amen.

Jude 24–25

The work which His goodness began,
    The arm of His strength will complete;
His promise is Yea and Amen,
    And never was forfeited yet.
Things future, nor things that are now,
    Not all things below nor above,
Can make Him His purpose forgo,
    Or sever my soul from His love.

Augustus Montague Toplady, 1740–78

Jesus is baptised

Then Jesus came from Galilee to the Jordan to be baptised by John. But John tried to deter him, saying, 'I need to be baptised by you, and do you come to me?'

Jesus replied, 'Let it be so now; it is proper for us to do this to fulfil all righteousness.' Then John consented.

As soon as Jesus was baptised, he went up out of the water. At that moment heaven was opened, and he saw the Spirit of God descending like a dove and lighting on him. And a voice from heaven said, 'This is my Son, whom I love; with him I am well pleased.'

Matthew 3:13–17

Come, gracious Spirit, heavenly Dove,
With light and comfort from above,
Be Thou our guardian, Thou our guide,
O'er every thought and step preside.

Lead us to Christ, the living Way,
Nor let us from His pastures stray;
Lead us to holiness, the road
That we must take to dwell with God.

Simon Browne, 1680–1732

The Counsellor will come

'Now I am going to him who sent me, yet none of you asks me, "Where are you going?" Because I have said these things, you are filled with grief. But I tell you the truth: It is for your good that I am going away. Unless I go away, the Counsellor will not come to you; but if I go, I will send him to you. When he comes, he will convict the world of guilt in regard to sin and righteousness and judgment: in regard to sin, because men do not believe in me; in regard to righteousness, because I am going to the Father, where you can see me no longer; and in regard to judgment, because the prince of this world now stands condemned.

'I have much more to say to you, more than you can now bear. But when he, the Spirit of truth, comes, he will guide you into all truth. He will not speak on his own; he will speak only what he hears, and he will tell you what is yet to come. He will bring glory to me by taking from what is mine and making it known to you. All that belongs to the Father is mine. That is why I said the Spirit will take from what is mine and make it known to you.

'In a little while you will see me no more, and then after a little while you will see me.'

John 16:5–16

Come, Holy Spirit, come,
  Let Thy bright beams arise;
Dispel the sorrow from our minds,
  The darkness from our eyes.

Convince us of our sin,
  Then lead to Jesus' blood;
And to our wondering view reveal
  The secret love of God.

Joseph Hart, 1712–68

The day of Pentecost

When the day of Pentecost came, they were all together in one place. Suddenly a sound like the blowing of a violent wind came from heaven and filled the whole house where they were sitting. They saw what seemed to be tongues of fire that separated and came to rest on each of them. All of them were filled with the Holy Spirit and began to speak in other tongues as the Spirit enabled them. Now there were staying in Jerusalem God-fearing Jews from every nation under heaven. When they heard this sound, a crowd came together in bewilderment, because each one heard them speaking in his own language. Utterly amazed, they asked: 'Are not all these men who are speaking Galileans? Then how is it that each of us hears them in his own native language? Parthians, Medes and Elamites; residents of Mesopotamia, Judea and Cappadocia, Pontus and Asia, Phrygia and Pamphylia, Egypt and the parts of Libya near Cyrene; visitors from Rome (both Jews and converts to Judaism); Cretans and Arabs – we hear them declaring the wonders of God in our own tongues!' Amazed and perplexed, they asked one another, 'What does this mean?'

Some, however, made fun of them and said, 'They have had too much wine.'

Acts 2:1–13

O Breath of life, come sweeping through us,
Revive your church with life and power;
O Breath of life, come, cleanse, renew us
And fit your church to meet this hour.

O Wind of God, come bend us, break us
Till humbly we confess our need;
Then, in your tenderness remake us,
Revive, restore – for this we plead.

Elizabeth A. P. Head, 1850–1936

Sealed with the Spirit

In him [Christ] we were also chosen, having been pre-destined according to the plan of him who works out everything in conformity with the purpose of his will, in order that we, who were the first to hope in Christ, might be for the praise of his glory. And you also were included in Christ when you heard the word of truth, the gospel of your salvation. Having believed, you were marked in him with a seal, the promised Holy Spirit, who is a deposit guaranteeing our inheritance until the redemption of those who are God's possession – to the praise of his glory.

Ephesians 1:11–14

Now it is God who makes both us and you stand firm in Christ. He anointed us, set his seal of ownership on us, and put his Spirit in our hearts as a deposit, guarantee-ing what is to come.

2 Corinthians 1:21–22

> Why should the children of a King
>   Go mourning all their days?
> Great Comforter, descend, and bring
>   Some tokens of Thy grace.
>
> Dost Thou not dwell in all Thy saints,
>   And seal the heirs of heaven?
> When wilt Thou banish my complaints,
>   And show my sins forgiven?
>
> Thou art the earnest of His love,
>   The pledge of joys to come,
> And Thy soft wings, celestial Dove,
>   Will safe convey me home.

Isaac Watts, 1674–1748

Do not put out the Spirit's fire

Do not grieve the Holy Spirit of God, with whom you were sealed for the day of redemption. Get rid of all bitterness, rage and anger, brawling and slander, along with every form of malice. Be kind and compassionate to one another, forgiving each other, just as in Christ God forgave you.

Ephesians 4:30–32

Be joyful always; pray continually; give thanks in all circumstances, for this is God's will for you in Christ Jesus.

Do not put out the Spirit's fire; do not treat prophecies with contempt. Test everything. Hold on to the good. Avoid every kind of evil.

May God himself, the God of peace, sanctify you through and through. May your whole spirit, soul and body be kept blameless at the coming of our Lord Jesus Christ. The one who calls you is faithful and he will do it.

1 Thessalonians 5:16–24

Come down, O Love divine
Seek Thou this soul of mine,
    And visit it with Thine own ardour glowing;
O Comforter, draw near,
Within my heart appear,
    And kindle it, Thy holy flame bestowing.

O let it freely burn,
Till earthly passions turn
    To dust and ashes, in its heat consuming;
And let Thy glorious light
Shine ever on my sight,
    And clothe me round, the while my path
      illuming.

Bianco da Siena, c. 1350–1434
tr. Richard Frederick Littledale, 1833–90

The moving of the Spirit

We did not follow cleverly invented stories when we told you about the power and coming of our Lord Jesus Christ, but we were eye-witnesses of his majesty. For he received honour and glory from God the Father when the voice came to him from the Majestic Glory, saying, 'This is my Son, whom I love; with him I am well pleased.' We ourselves heard this voice that came from heaven when we were with him on the sacred mountain.

And we have the word of the prophets made more certain, and you will do well to pay attention to it, as to a light shining in a dark place, until the day dawns and the morning star rises in your hearts. Above all, you must understand that no prophecy of Scripture came about by the prophet's own interpretation. For prophecy never had its origin in the will of man, but men spoke from God as they were carried along by the Holy Spirit.
2 Peter 1:16–21

Come, Holy Ghost, our hearts inspire,
  Let us Thine influence prove,
Source of the old prophetic fire,
  Fountain of light and love.

Come, Holy Ghost, for moved by Thee
  The prophets wrote and spoke;
Unlock the truth, Thyself the key,
  Unseal the sacred Book.

God, through Himself, we then shall know,
  If Thou within us shine,
And sound, with all Thy saints below,
  The depths of love divine.

Charles Wesley, 1707–88

Longing for God

As the deer pants for streams of water, so my soul pants for you, O God. My soul thirsts for God, for the living God. When can I go and meet with God? My tears have been my food day and night, while men say to me all day long, 'Where is your God?' These things I remember as I pour out my soul: how I used to go with the multitude, leading the procession to the house of God, with shouts of joy and thanksgiving among the festive throng.

Why are you downcast, O my soul? Why so disturbed within me? Put your hope in God, for I will yet praise him, my Saviour and my God.

Psalm 42:1–6

O Love divine, how sweet Thou art!
When shall I find my willing heart
   All taken up by Thee?
I thirst, I faint, I die to prove
The greatness of redeeming love,
   The love of Christ to me.

Charles Wesley, 1707–88

Following Christ

From that time on Jesus began to explain to his disciples that he must go to Jerusalem and suffer many things at the hands of the elders, chief priests and teachers of the law, and that he must be killed and on the third day be raised to life.

Peter took him aside and began to rebuke him. 'Never, Lord!' he said. 'This shall never happen to you!'

Jesus turned and said to Peter, 'Get behind me, Satan! You are a stumbling-block to me; you do not have in mind the things of God, but the things of men.'

Then Jesus said to his disciples, 'If anyone would come after me, he must deny himself and take up his cross and follow me. For whoever wants to save his life will lose it, but whoever loses his life for me will find it. What good will it be for a man if he gains the whole world, yet forfeits his soul? Or what can a man give in exchange for his soul? For the Son of Man is going to come in his Father's glory with his angels, and then he will reward each person according to what he has done. I tell you the truth, some who are standing here will not taste death before they see the Son of Man coming in his kingdom.'

Matthew 16:21–28

> O Love, that wilt not let me go,
>   I rest my weary soul in Thee;
> I give Thee back the life I owe,
> That in Thine ocean depths its flow
>   May richer, fuller be.

George Matheson, 1842–1906

Worship the Lord in holiness

Ascribe to the Lord, O mighty ones, ascribe to the Lord glory and strength. Ascribe to the Lord the glory due to his name; worship the Lord in the splendour of his holiness.

The voice of the Lord is over the waters; the God of glory thunders, the Lord thunders over the mighty waters. The voice of the Lord is powerful; the voice of the Lord is majestic. The voice of the Lord breaks the cedars; the Lord breaks in pieces the cedars of Lebanon. He makes Lebanon skip like a calf, Sirion like a young wild ox. The voice of the Lord strikes with flashes of lightning.

The Lord sits enthroned over the flood; the Lord is enthroned as King for ever. The Lord gives strength to his people; the Lord blesses his people with peace.

Psalm 29:1–7, 10–11

O worship the Lord in the beauty of holiness;
　Bow down before Him, His glory proclaim;
With gold of obedience and incense of lowliness,
　Kneel and adore Him, the Lord is His Name.

John Samuel Bewley Monsell, 1811–75

Life in the Spirit

So I say, live by the Spirit, and you will not gratify the desires of the sinful nature. For the sinful nature desires what is contrary to the Spirit, and the Spirit what is contrary to the sinful nature. They are in conflict with each other, so that you do not do what you want. But if you are led by the Spirit, you are not under law.

The acts of the sinful nature are obvious: sexual immorality, impurity and debauchery; idolatry and witchcraft; hatred, discord, jealousy, fits of rage, selfish ambition, dissensions, factions and envy; drunkenness, orgies, and the like. I warn you, as I did before, that those who live like this will not inherit the kingdom of God.

But the fruit of the Spirit is love, joy, peace, patience, kindness, goodness, faithfulness, gentleness and self-control. Against such things there is no law. Those who belong to Christ Jesus have crucified the sinful nature with its passions and desires. Since we live by the Spirit, let us keep in step with the Spirit. Let us not become conceited, provoking and envying each other.

Galatians 5:16–26

Holy Spirit, love divine,
Glow within this heart of mine;
Kindle every high desire;
Perish self in Thy pure fire.

Holy Spirit, joy divine,
Gladden Thou this heart of mine;
In the desert ways I'll sing:
Spring, O Well, for ever spring!

Samuel Longfellow, 1819–92

The cleansing of God

Have mercy on me, O God, according to your unfailing love; according to your great compassion blot out my transgressions. Wash away all my iniquity and cleanse me from my sin.

For I know my transgressions, and my sin is always before me. Against you, you only, have I sinned and done what is evil in your sight, so that you are proved right when you speak and justified when you judge. Surely I was sinful at birth, sinful from the time my mother conceived me. Surely you desire truth in the inner parts; you teach me wisdom in the inmost place.

Cleanse me with hyssop, and I shall be clean; wash me, and I shall be whiter than snow. Let me hear joy and gladness; let the bones you have crushed rejoice. Hide your face from my sins and blot out all my iniquity.

Psalm 51:1–9

Have Thine own way, Lord, have Thine own way;
Search me and try me, Master, today.
Whiter than snow, Lord, wash me just now,
As in Thy presence humbly I bow.

Adelaide Addison Pollard, 1862–1934

Create in me a pure heart

Create in me a pure heart, O God, and renew a steadfast spirit within me. Do not cast me from your presence or take your Holy Spirit from me. Restore to me the joy of your salvation and grant me a willing spirit, to sustain me.

Then I will teach transgressors your ways, and sinners will turn back to you. Save me from bloodguilt, O God, the God who saves me, and my tongue will sing of your righteousness. O Lord, open my lips, and my mouth will declare your praise. You do not delight in sacrifice, or I would bring it; you do not take pleasure in burnt offerings. The sacrifices of God are a broken spirit; a broken and contrite heart, O God, you will not despise.

In your good pleasure make Zion prosper; build up the walls of Jerusalem. Then there will be righteous sacrifices, whole burnt offerings to delight you; then bulls will be offered on your altar.

Psalm 51:10–19

A humble, lowly, contrite heart,
　Believing, true, and clean,
Which neither life nor death can part
　From Him that dwells within;

Thy nature, gracious Lord, impart;
　Come quickly from above;
Write Thy new Name upon my heart,
　Thy new best Name of love.

Charles Wesley, 1707–88

Praise the Lord, O my soul

Praise the Lord, O my soul; all my inmost being, praise his holy name. Praise the Lord, O my soul, and forget not all his benefits – who forgives all your sins and heals all your diseases, who redeems your life from the pit and crowns you with love and compassion, who satisfies your desires with good things so that your youth is renewed like the eagle's.

The Lord works righteousness and justice for all the oppressed. He made known his ways to Moses, his deeds to the people of Israel: The Lord is compassionate and gracious, slow to anger, abounding in love.

Praise the Lord, you his angels, you mighty ones who do his bidding, who obey his word. Praise the Lord, all his heavenly hosts, you his servants who do his will. Praise the Lord, all his works everywhere in his dominion. Praise the Lord, O my soul.

Psalm 103:1–8, 20–22

Praise, my soul, the King of heaven,
  To His feet they tribute bring;
Ransomed, healed, restored, forgiven,
  Who like thee His praise should sing?
    Praise Him! Praise Him!
Praise the everlasting King.

Angels, help us to adore Him;
  Ye behold Him face to face;
Sun and moon, bow down before Him,
  Dwellers all in time and space.
    Praise Him! Praise Him!
Praise with us the God of grace.

Henry Francis Lyte, 1793–1847

God's glorious grace

Peter, an apostle of Jesus Christ, To God's elect, strangers in the world, scattered throughout Pontus, Galatia, Cappadocia, Asia and Bithynia, who have been chosen according to the foreknowledge of God the Father, through the sanctifying work of the Spirit, for obedience to Jesus Christ and sprinkling by his blood: Grace and peace be yours in abundance.

Praise be to the God and Father of our Lord Jesus Christ! In his great mercy he has given us new birth into a living hope through the resurrection of Jesus Christ from the dead, and into an inheritance that can never perish, spoil or fade – kept in heaven for you, who through faith are shielded by God's power until the coming of the salvation that is ready to be revealed in the last time. In this you greatly rejoice, though now for a little while you may have had to suffer grief in all kinds of trials. These have come so that your faith – of greater worth than gold; which perishes even though refined by fire – may be proved genuine and may result in praise, glory and honour when Jesus Christ is revealed. Though you have not seen him, you love him; and even though you do not see him now, you believe in him and are filled with an inexpressible and glorious joy, for you are receiving the goal of your faith, the salvation of your souls.

1 Peter 1:1–9

On such love, my soul, still ponder,
    Love so great, so rich and free;
Say, while lost in holy wonder,
    'Why, O Lord, such love to me?'
        Hallelujah!
    Grace shall reign eternally.

John Kent, 1766–1843

The body and blood of Christ

While they were eating, Jesus took bread, gave thanks and broke it, and gave it to his disciples, saying, 'Take and eat; this is my body.' Then he took the cup, gave thanks and offered it to them, saying, 'Drink from it, all of you. This is my blood of the covenant, which is poured out for many for the forgiveness of sins. I tell you, I will not drink of this fruit of the vine from now on until that day when I drink it anew with you in my Father's kingdom.'

Matthew 26:26–29

For I received from the Lord what I also passed on to you: The Lord Jesus, on the night he was betrayed, took bread, and when he had given thanks, he broke it and said, 'This is my body, which is for you; do this in remembrance of me.' In the same way, after supper he took the cup, saying, 'This cup is the new covenant in my blood; do this, whenever you drink it, in remembrance of me.' For whenever you eat this bread and drink this cup, you proclaim the Lord's death until he comes.

Therefore, whoever eats the bread or drinks the cup of the Lord in an unworthy manner will be guilty of sinning against the body and blood of the Lord. A man ought to examine himself before he eats of the bread and drinks of the cup. For anyone who eats and drinks without recognising the body of the Lord eats and drinks judgment on himself. That is why many among you are weak and sick, and a number of you have fallen asleep.

1 Corinthians 11:23–30

> Here would I feed upon the bread of God,
>   Here drink with Thee the royal wine of heaven;
> Here would I lay aside each earthly load,
>   Here take afresh the calm of sin forgiven.

Horatius Bonar, 1808–89

JUNE 4

The message of the cross

For the message of the cross is foolishness to those who
are perishing, but to us who are being saved it is the
power of God. For it is written: 'I will destroy the wisdom
of the wise; the intelligence of the intelligent I will frustrate.' Where is the wise man? Where is the scholar?
Where is the philosopher of this age? Has not God made
foolish the wisdom of the world? For since in the wisdom
of God the world through its wisdom did not know him,
God was pleased through the foolishness of what was
preached to save those who believe. Jews demand
miraculous signs and Greeks look for wisdom, but we
preach Christ crucified: a stumbling-block to Jews and
foolishness to Gentiles, but to those whom God has
called, both Jews and Greeks, Christ the power of God
and the wisdom of God. For the foolishness of God is
wiser than man's wisdom, and the weakness of God is
stronger than man's strength. Brothers, think of what
you were when you were called. Not many of you were
wise by human standards; not many were influential;
not many were of noble birth. But God chose the foolish
things of the world to shame the wise; God chose the
weak things of the world to shame the strong.

1 Corinthians 1:18–27

We sing the praise of Him who died,
  Of Him who died upon the cross;
The sinner's hope let men deride,
  For this we count the world but loss.

The cross! it takes our guilt away;
  It holds the fainting spirit up;
It cheers with hope the gloomy day,
  And sweetens every bitter cup.

Thomas Kelly, 1769–1855

Singing joyfully to God

Shout for joy to the Lord, all the earth. Worship the Lord with gladness; come before him with joyful songs. Know that the Lord is God. It is he who made us, and we are his; we are his people, the sheep of his pasture.

Enter his gates with thanksgiving and his courts with praise; give thanks to him and praise his name. For the Lord is good and his love endures for ever; his faithfulness continues through all generations.

Psalm 100:1–5

May the glory of the Lord endure for ever; may the Lord rejoice in his works – he who looks at the earth, and it trembles, who touches the mountains, and they smoke.

I will sing to the Lord all my life; I will sing praise to my God as long as I live. May my meditation be pleasing to him, as I rejoice in the Lord. But may sinners vanish from the earth and the wicked be no more.

Praise the Lord, O my soul.

Praise the Lord.

Psalm 104:31–35

> All people on earth do dwell,
>   Sing to the Lord with cheerful voice;
> Him serve with fear, His praise forth tell,
>   Come ye before Him and rejoice.

William Kethe, d. 1594

Looking forward to the day of the Lord

But do not forget this one thing, dear friends: With the Lord a day is like a thousand years, and a thousand years are like a day. The Lord is not slow in keeping his promise, as some understand slowness. He is patient with you, not wanting anyone to perish, but everyone to come to repentance.

But the day of the Lord will come like a thief. The heavens will disappear with a roar; the elements will be destroyed by fire, and the earth and everything in it will be laid bare.

Since everything will be destroyed in this way, what kind of people ought you to be? You ought to live holy and godly lives as you look forward to the day of God and speed its coming. That day will bring about the destruction of the heavens by fire, and the elements will melt in the heat. But in keeping with his promise we are looking forward to a new heaven and a new earth, the home of righteousness.

So then, dear friends, since you are looking forward to this, make every effort to be found spotless, blameless and at peace with him.

2 Peter 3:8–14

O may we thus be found,
  Obedient to His Word,
Attentive to the trumpet's sound,
  And looking for our Lord!
O may we thus ensure
  A lot among the blest;
And watch a moment to secure
  An everlasting rest!

Charles Wesley, 1707–88

The cost of discipleship

When Jesus saw the crowd around him, he gave orders to cross to the other side of the lake. Then a teacher of the law came to him and said, 'Teacher, I will follow you wherever you go.'

Jesus replied, 'Foxes have holes and birds of the air have nests, but the Son of Man has nowhere to lay his head.'

Another disciple said to him, 'Lord, first let me go and bury my father.'

But Jesus told him, 'Follow me, and let the dead bury their own dead.'

Then he got into the boat and his disciples followed him. Without warning, a furious storm came up on the lake, so that the waves swept over the boat. But Jesus was sleeping. The disciples went and woke him, saying, 'Lord, save us! We're going to drown!'

He replied, 'You of little faith, why are you so afraid?' Then he got up and rebuked the winds and the waves, and it was completely calm.

The men were amazed and asked, 'What kind of man is this? Even the winds and the waves obey him!'

Matthew 8:18–27

> The foxes found rest,
> And the birds their nest,
>   In the shade of the cedar tree;
> But Thy couch was the sod,
> O Thou Son of God,
>   In the deserts of Galilee:
> O come to my heart, Lord Jesus!
>   There is room in my heart for Thee.

Emily Elizabeth Steele Elliott, 1836–97

—————— **JUNE 8** ——————

The armour of God

Finally, be strong in the Lord and in his mighty power.
Put on the full armour of God so that you can take your
stand against the devil's schemes. For our struggle is
not against flesh and blood, but against the rulers,
against the authorities, against the powers of this dark
world and against the spiritual forces of evil in the
heavenly realms. Therefore put on the full armour of
God, so that when the day of evil comes, you may be
able to stand your ground, and after you have done
everything, to stand. Stand firm then, with the belt of
truth buckled round your waist, with the breastplate of
righteousness in place, and with your feet fitted with
the readiness that comes from the gospel of peace. In
addition to all this, take up the shield of faith, with
which you can extinguish all the flaming arrows of the
evil on. Take the helmet of salvation and the sword of
the Spirit, which is the word of God. And pray in the
Spirit on all occasions with all kinds of prayers and
requests. With this in mind, be alert and always keep
on praying for all the saints.

Ephesians 6:10–18

Soldiers of Christ, arise,
  And put your armour on;
Strong in the strength which God supplies,
  Through His eternal Son;
Strong in the Lord of hosts,
  And in His mighty power;
Who in the strength of Jesus trusts
  Is more than conqueror.

Charles Wesley, 1707–88

Fight the good fight

But godliness with contentment is great gain. For we brought nothing into the world, and we can take nothing out of it. But if we have food and clothing, we will be content with that. People who want to get rich fall into temptation and a trap and into many foolish and harmful desires that plunge men into ruin and destruction. For the love of money is a root of all kinds of evil. Some people, eager for money, have wandered from the faith and pierced themselves with many griefs.

But you, man of God, flee from all this, and pursue righteousness, godliness, faith, love, endurance and gentleness. Fight the good fight of the faith. Take hold of the eternal life to which you were called when you made your good confession in the presence of many witnesses.

1 Timothy 6:6–12

> Fight the good fight with all thy might;
> Christ is thy strength, and Christ thy right;
> Lay hold on life, and it shall be
> Thy joy and crown eternally.

John Samuel Bewley Monsell, 1811–75

The battle belongs to the Lord

Then the Spirit of the Lord came upon Jahaziel son of
Zechariah, the son of Benaiah, the son of Jeiel, the son
of Mattaniah, a Levite and descendant of Asaph, as he
stood in the assembly.

He said, 'Listen, King Jehoshaphat and all who live
in Judah and Jerusalem! This is what the Lord says to
you: "Do not be afraid or discouraged because of this
vast army. For the battle is not yours, but God's.
Tomorrow march down against them. They will be
climbing up by the Pass of Ziz, and you will find them
at the end of the gorge in the Desert of Jeruel. You will
not have to fight this battle. Take up your positions;
stand firm and see the deliverance the Lord will give
you, O Judah and Jerusalem. Do not be afraid; do not
be discouraged. Go out to face them tomorrow, and the
Lord will be with you."'

2 Chronicles 20:14–17

We go in faith, our own great weakness feeling,
    And needing more each day Thy grace to know;
Yet from our hearts a song of triumph pealing:
    'We rest on Thee, and in Thy Name we go.'

We rest on Thee, our Shield and our Defender!
    Thine is the battle; Thine shall be the praise
When passing through the gates of pearly splendour,
    Victors, we rest with Thee through endless days.

Edith Adeline Gilling Cherry, 1872–97

Depending on God's strength

Strengthen the feeble hands, steady the knees that give way; say to those with fearful hearts, 'Be strong, do not fear; your God will come, he will come with vengeance; with divine retribution he will come to save you.'

Then will the eyes of the blind be opened and the ears of the deaf unstopped. Then will the lame leap like a deer, and the mute tongue shout for joy. Water will gush forth in the wilderness and streams in the desert. The burning sand will become a pool, the thirsty ground bubbling springs. In the haunts where jackals once lay, grass and reeds and papyrus will grow.

Isaiah 35:3–7

'Simon, Simon, Satan has asked to sift you as wheat. But I have prayed for you, Simon, that your faith may not fail. And when you have turned back, strengthen your brothers.' But he replied, 'Lord, I am ready to go with you to prison and to death.' Jesus answered, 'I tell you, Peter, before the cock crows today, you will deny three times that you know me.'

Luke 22:31–34

Thou seest our weakness, Lord;
　　Our hearts are known to Thee:
O lift Thou up the sinking hand,
　　Confirm the feeble knee!

Let us in life, in death,
　　Thy steadfast truth declare,
And publish with our latest breath
　　Thy love and guardian care.

Paul Gerhardt, 1607–76
tr. John Wesley, 1703–91

Separation of the peoples

'Then the King will say to those on his right, "Come, you who are blessed by my Father; take your inheritance, the kingdom prepared for you since the creation of the world. For I was hungry and you gave me something to eat, I was thirsty and you gave me something to drink, I was a stranger and you invited me in, I needed clothes and you clothed me, I was sick and you looked after me, I was in prison and you came to visit me."

'Then the righteous will answer him, "Lord, when did we see you hungry and feed you, or thirsty and give you something to drink? When did we see you a stranger and invite you in, or needing clothes and clothe you? When did we see you sick or in prison and go to visit you?"

'The King will reply, "I tell you the truth, whatever you did for one of the least of these brothers of mine, you did for me."

'Then he will say to those on his left, "Depart from me, you who are cursed, into the eternal fire prepared for the devil and his angels. For I was hungry and you gave me nothing to eat, I was thirsty and you gave me nothing to drink, I was a stranger and you did not invite me in, I needed clothes and you did not clothe me, I was sick and in prison and you did not look after me."

'They also will answer, "Lord, when did we see you hungry or thirsty or a stranger or needing clothes or sick or in prison, and did not help you?"

'He will reply, "I tell you the truth, whatever you did not do for one of the least of these, you did not do for me."

'Then they will go away to eternal punishment, but the righteous to eternal life.'

Matthew 25:34–46

At His call the dead awaken,
  Rise to life from earth and sea;
All the powers of nature, shaken
  By His look, prepare to flee;
    Careless sinner,
  What will then become of thee?

But those who have confessed,
  Loved and served the Lord below,
He will say, 'Come near, ye blessed,
  See the kingdom I bestow;
    You for ever
  Shall my love and glory know.'

John Newton, 1725–1807

How unsearchable are his judgments

When I applied my mind to know wisdom and to observe man's labour on earth – his eyes not seeing sleep day or night – then I saw all that God has done. No-one can comprehend what goes on under the sun. Despite all his efforts to search it out, man cannot discover its meaning. Even if a wise man claims he knows, he cannot really comprehend it.

Ecclesiastes 8:16–17

Oh, the depth of the riches of the wisdom and knowledge of God! How unsearchable his judgments, and his paths beyond tracing out! 'Who has known the mind of the Lord? Or who has been his counsellor?' 'Who has ever given to God, that God should repay him?' For from him and through him and to him are all things. To him be the glory for ever! Amen.

Romans 11:33–36

Holy and Infinite! limitless, boundless
    All Thy perfections and power and praise!
Ocean of Mystery! awful and soundless
    All Thine unsearchable judgements and ways!

Frances Ridley Havergal, 1836–79

————— **JUNE 14** —————

Making the most of the time

Devote yourselves to prayer, being watchful and thankful. And pray for us, too, that God may open a door for our message, so that we may proclaim the mystery of Christ, for which I am in chains. Pray that I may proclaim it clearly, as I should. Be wise in the way you act towards outsiders; make the most of every opportunity. Let your conversation be always full of grace, seasoned with salt, so that you may know how to answer everyone.

Tychicus will tell you all the news about me. He is a dear brother, a faithful minister and fellow-servant in the Lord. I am sending him to you for the express purpose that you may know about our circumstances and that he may encourage your hearts. He is coming with Onesimus, our faithful and dear brother, who is one of you. They will tell you everything that is happening here.

Colossians 4:2–9

> I would the precious time redeem,
>   And longer live for this alone,
> To spend, and to be spent, for them
>   Who have not yet my Saviour known;
> Fully on these my mission prove,
> And only breathe, to breathe Thy love.

Charles Wesley, 1707–88

I am with you

'If your brother sins against you, go and show him his
fault, just between the two of you. If he listens to you,
you have won your brother over. But if he will not listen,
take one or two others along, so that "every matter may
be established by the testimony of two or three witnesses." If he refuses to listen to them, tell it to the
church; and if he refuses to listen even to the church,
treat him as you would a pagan or a tax collector.

I tell you the truth, whatever you bind on earth will
be bound in heaven, and whatever you loose on earth
will be loosed in heaven.

'Again, I tell you that if two of you on earth agree
about anything you ask for, it will be done for you by
my Father in heaven. For where two or three come
together in my name, there am I with them.'

Matthew 18:15–20

> Jesus, where'er Thy people meet,
> There they behold Thy mercy-seat;
> Where'er they seek Thee Thou art found,
> And every place is hallowed ground.
>
> Here may we prove the power of prayer,
> To strengthen faith and sweeten care,
> To teach our faint desires to rise,
> And bring all heaven before our eyes.

William Cowper, 1731–1800

Jesus loves to answer prayer

Then he said to them, 'Suppose one of you has a friend, and he goes to him at midnight and says, "Friend, lend me three loaves of bread, because a friend of mine on a journey has come to me, and I have nothing to set before him."

'Then the one inside answers, "Don't bother me. The door is already locked, and my children are with me in bed. I can't get up and give you anything." I tell you, though he will not get up and give him the bread because he is his friend, yet because of the man's boldness he will get up and give him as much as he needs.

'So I say to you: Ask and it will be given to you; seek and you will find; knock and the door will be opened to you. For everyone who asks receives; he who seeks finds; and to him who knocks, the door will be opened.

'Which of you fathers, if your son asks for a fish, will give him a snake instead? Or if he ask for an egg, will give him a scorpion? If you then, though you are evil, know how to give good gifts to your children, how much more will your Father in heaven give the Holy Spirit to those who ask him!'

Luke 11:5–13

> Come, my soul, thy suit prepare,
> Jesus loves to answer prayer;
> He Himself has bid thee pray,
> Therefore will not say thee nay.
>
> Thou art coming to a King,
> Large petitions with thee bring;
> For His grace and power are such,
> None can ever ask too much.

John Newton, 1725–1807

The heavenly worship

In the centre, around the throne, were four living creatures, and they were covered with eyes, in front and
behind. The first living creature was like a lion, the
second was like an ox, the third had a face like a man,
the fourth was like a flying eagle. Each of the four living
creatures had six wings and was covered with eyes all
around, even under his wings. Day and night they never
stop saying: 'Holy, holy, holy is the Lord God Almighty,
who was, and is, and is to come.' Whenever the living
creatures give glory, honour and thanks to him who
sits on the throne and who lives for ever and ever, the
twenty-four elders fall down before him who sits on the
throne, and worship him who lives for ever and ever.
They lay their crowns before the throne and say: 'You
are worthy, our Lord and God, to receive glory and
honour and power, for you created all things, and by
your will they were created and have their being.'

Revelation 4:6–11

Finish then Thy new creation,
  Pure and spotless may we be;
Let us see Thy great salvation,
  Perfectly restored in Thee;
Changed from glory into glory,
  Till in heaven we take our place,
Till we cast our crowns before Thee,
  Lost in wonder, love and praise.

Charles Wesley, 1707–88

Jesus prays for his disciples

'I have revealed you to those whom you gave me out of the world. They were yours; you gave them to me and they have obeyed your word. Now they know that everything you have given me comes from you. For I gave them the words you gave me and they accepted them. They knew with certainty that I came from you, and they believed that you sent me. I pray for them, I am not praying for the world, but for those you have given me, for they are yours. All I have is yours, and all you have is mine. And glory has come to me through them. I will remain in the world no longer, but they are still in the world, and I am coming to you. Holy Father protect them by the power of your name – the name you gave me – so that they may be one as we are one. While I was with them, I protected them and kept them safe by that name you gave me. None has been lost except the one doomed to destruction so that Scripture would be fulfilled.'

John 17:6–12

In the hour of trial,
   Jesus, pray for me,
Lest by base denial
   I depart from Thee;
When Thou seest me waver,
   With a look recall,
Nor, for fear or favour,
   Suffer me to fall.

James Montgomery, 1771–1854

Proclaim his salvation!

Sing to the Lord a new song: sing to the Lord, all the earth. Sing to the Lord, praise his name; proclaim his salvation day after day. Declare his glory among the nations, his marvellous deeds among all peoples.

For great is the Lord and most worthy of praise; he is to be feared above all gods. For all the gods of the nations are idols, but the Lord made the heavens. Splendour and majesty are before him; strength and glory are in his sanctuary.

Ascribe to the Lord, O families of nations, ascribe to the Lord glory and strength. Ascribe to the Lord the glory due to his name; bring an offering and come into his courts. Worship the Lord in the splendour of his holiness; tremble before him, all the earth.

Psalm 96:1–9

Ye blessed souls at rest,
  Who ran this earthly race,
And now, from sin released,
  Behold the Saviour's face,
God's praises sound,
  As in His sight
  With sweet delight
Ye do abound.

Ye saints, who toil below,
  Adore your heavenly King,
And, onward as ye go,
  Some joyful anthem sing;
That what He gives,
  And praise Him still
  Through good and ill,
Who ever lives.

Richard Baxter, 1615–91

Jesus, our friend

'As the Father has loved me, so have I loved you. Now
remain in my love. If you obey my commands, you will
remain in my love, just as I have obeyed my Father's
commands and remain in his love. I have told you this
so that my joy may be in you and that your joy may be
complete. My command is this: Love each other as I have
loved you. Greater love has no-one than this, that he
lay down his life for his friends. You are my friends if
you do what I command. I no longer call you servants,
because a servant does not know his master's business.
Instead, I have called you friends, for everything that I
learned from my Father I have made known to you. You
did not choose me, but I chose you and appointed you to
go and bear fruit – fruit that will last. Then the Father
will give you whatever you ask in my name. This is my
command: Love each other.'

John 15:9–17

I've found a Friend, O such a Friend!
    He loved me ere I knew Him;
He drew me with the cords of love,
    And thus He bound me to Him;
And round my heart still closely twine
    Those ties which nought can sever;
For I am His, and He is mine,
    For ever and for ever.

I've found a Friend, O such a Friend!
    He bled, He died to save me;
And not alone the gift of life,
    But His own self He gave me.
Nought that I have mine own I'll call,
    I'll hold it for the Giver;
My heart, my strength, my life, my all
    Are His, and His for ever.

James Grindlay Small, 1817–88

The guidance of God

Then the angel of God, who had been travelling in front of Israel's army, withdrew and went behind them. The pillar of cloud also moved from in front and stood behind them, coming between the armies of Egypt and Israel. Throughout the night the cloud brought darkness to the one side and light to the other; so neither went near the other all night long.

Exodus 14:19–20

He did miracles in the sight of their fathers in the land of Egypt, in the region of Zoan. He divided the sea and led them through; he made the water stand firm like a wall. He guided them with the cloud by day and with light from the fire all night. He split the rocks in the desert and gave them water as abundant as the seas; he brought streams out of a rocky crag and made water flow down like rivers.

Psalm 78:12–16

Open Thou the crystal fountain
  Whence the healing stream doth flow;
Let the fiery, cloudy pillar
  Lead me all my journey through;
    Strong Deliverer,
  Be Thou still my strength and shield.

William Williams, 1717–91
tr. Peter Williams, 1721–96

God, our help in ages past

Lord, you have been our dwelling-place throughout all generations. Before the mountains were born or you brought forth the earth and the world, from everlasting to everlasting you are God. Satisfy us in the morning with your unfailing love, that we may sing for joy and be glad all our days. Make us glad for as many days as you have afflicted us, for as many years as we have seen trouble. May your deeds be shown to your servants, your splendour to their children.

May the favour of the Lord our God rest upon us; establish the work of our hands for us – yes, establish the work of our hands.

Psalm 90:1–2, 14–17

O God, our help in ages past,
  Our hope for years to come,
Our shelter from the stormy blast,
  And our eternal home;

Beneath the shadow of Thy throne
  Thy saints have dwelt secure;
Sufficient is Thine arm alone,
  And our defence is sure.

Isaac Watts, 1674–1748

Real service

Love must be sincere. Hate what is evil; cling to what is good. Be devoted to one another in brotherly love. Honour one another above yourselves. Never be lacking in zeal, but keep your spiritual fervour, serving the Lord. Be joyful in hope, patient in affliction, faithful in prayer. Share with God's people who are in need. Practise hospitality.

Bless those who persecute you; bless and do not curse. Rejoice with those who rejoice; mourn with those who mourn. Live in harmony with one another. Do not be proud, but be willing to associate with people of low position. Do not be conceited.

Do not repay anyone evil for evil. Be careful to do what is right in the eyes of everybody. If it is possible, as far as it depends on you, live in peace with everyone. Do not take revenge, my friends, but leave room for God's wrath, for it is written: 'It is mine to avenge; I will repay,' says the Lord. On the contrary: 'If your enemy is hungry, feed him; if he is thirsty, give him something to drink. In doing this, you will heap burning coals on his head.' Do not be overcome by evil, but overcome evil with good.

Romans 12:9–21

> The Lord is King! I own His power,
> His right to rule each day and hour;
> I own His claim on heart and will,
> And His demands I would fulfil.

Darley Terry, 1848–1934

Following Christ's example

Slaves, submit yourselves to your masters with all respect, not only to those who are good and considerate, but also to those who are harsh. For it is commendable if a man bears up under the pain of unjust suffering because he is conscious of God. But how is it to your credit if you receive a beating for doing wrong and endure it? But if you suffer for doing good and you endure it, this is commendable before God. To this you were called, because Christ suffered for you, leaving you an example, that you should follow in his steps. 'He committed no sin, and no deceit was found in his mouth.' When they hurled their insults at him, he did not retaliate; when he suffered, he made no threats. Instead, he entrusted himself to him who judges justly. He himself bore our sins in his body on the tree, so that we might die to sins and live for righteousness; by his wounds you have been healed. For you were like sheep going astray, but now you have returned to the Shepherd and Overseer of your souls.

1 Peter 2:18–25

O let me see Thy footmarks,
  And in them plant mine own:
My hope to follow duly
  Is in Thy strength alone.
O guide me, call me, draw me,
  Uphold me to the end;
And then in heaven receive me,
  My Saviour and my Friend.

John Ernest Bode, 1816–74

Loving the Lord Jesus

When they had finished eating, Jesus said to Simon Peter, 'Simon son of John, do you truly love me more than these?'

'Yes, Lord,' he said, 'you know that I love you.'

Jesus said, 'Feed my lambs.'

Again Jesus said, 'Simon son of John, do you truly love me?'

He answered, 'Yes, Lord, you know that I love you.'

Jesus said, 'Take care of my sheep.'

The third time he said to him, 'Simon son of John, do you love me?'

Peter was hurt because Jesus asked him the third time, 'Do you love me?' He said, 'Lord, you know all things; you know that I love you.'

Jesus said, 'Feed my sheep. I tell you the truth, when you were younger you dressed yourself and went where you wanted; but when you are old you will stretch out your hands, and someone else will dress you and lead you where you do not want to go.' Jesus said this to indicate the kind of death by which Peter would glorify God. Then he said to him, 'Follow me!'

John 21:15–19

My Jesus, I love Thee, I know Thou art mine;
For Thee all the pleasures of sin I resign;
My gracious Redeemer, my Saviour art Thou,
If ever I loved Thee, my Jesus, 'tis now.

William Ralph Featherstone, 1842–70

Strength in unity

How good and pleasant it is when brothers live together
in unity! It is like precious oil poured on the head, running down on the beard, running down on Aaron's beard,
down upon the collar of his robes. It is as if the dew of
Hermon were falling on Mount Zion. For there the Lord
bestows his blessing, even life for evermore.

Psalm 133:1–3

Two are better than one, because they have a good
return for their work: If one falls down, his friend can
help him up. But pity the man who falls and has no-one
to help him up! Also, if two lie down together, they will
keep warm. But how can one keep warm alone? Though
one may be overpowered, two can defend themselves. A
cord of three strands is not quickly broken.

Ecclesiastes 4:9–12

How beautiful the sight
        Of brethren who agree
In friendship to unite,
        And bonds of charity!
'Tis like the precious ointment shed
O'er all his robes from Aaron's head.

James Montgomery, 1771–1854

———————— **JUNE 27** ————————

Salvation at the cross

The soldiers also came up and mocked him. They offered him wine vinegar and said, 'If you are the king of the Jews, save yourself.'

There was a written notice above him, which read: THIS IS THE KING OF THE JEWS.

One of the criminals who hung there hurled insults at him: 'Aren't you the Christ? Save yourself and us!'

But the other criminal rebuked him. 'Don't you fear God,' he said, 'since you are under the same sentence? We are punished justly, for we are getting what our deeds deserve. But this man has done nothing wrong.'

Then he said, 'Jesus, remember me when you come into your kingdom.'

Jesus answered him, 'I tell you the truth, today you will be with me in paradise.'

Luke 23:36–43

> There is a fountain filled with blood
>   Drawn from Immanuel's veins;
> And sinners, plunged beneath that flood,
>   Lose all their guilty stains.
>
> The dying thief rejoiced to see
>   That fountain in his day;
> And there have I, though vile as he,
>   Washed all my sins away.

William Cowper, 1731–1800

The Spirit of God

Then Peter stood up with the Eleven, raised his voice and addressed the crowd: 'Fellow Jews and all of you who live in Jerusalem, let me explain this to you; listen carefully to what I say. These men are not drunk, as you suppose. It's only nine in the morning! No, this is what was spoken by the prophet Joel:

'"In the last days, God says, I will pour out my Spirit on all people. Your sons and daughters will prophesy, your young men will see visions, your old men will dream dreams. Even on my servants, both men and women, I will pour out my Spirit in those days, and they will prophesy. I will show wonders in the heaven above and signs on the earth below, blood and fire and billows of smoke. The sun will be turned to darkness and the moon to blood before the coming of the great and glorious day of the Lord. And everyone who calls on the name of the Lord will be saved."'

Acts 2:14–21

O Spirit of the living God,
In all Thy plenitude of grace,
Where'er the foot of man hath trod,
Descend on our apostate race.

Give tongues of fire and hearts of love
To preach the reconciling word;
Give power and unction from above,
Whene'er the joyful sound is heard.

Baptize the nations; far and nigh
The triumphs of the cross record;
The Name of Jesus glorify
Till every kindred call Him Lord.

James Montgomery, 1771–1854

Pure Father of light

Now Moses was tending the flock of Jethro his father-in-law, the priest of Midian, and he led the flock to the far side of the desert and came to Horeb, the mountain of God. There the angel of the Lord appeared to him in flames of fire from within a bush. Moses saw that though the bush was on fire it did not burn up. So Moses thought, 'I will go over and see this strange sight – why the bush does not burn up.'

When the Lord saw that he had gone over to look, God called to him from within the bush, 'Moses, Moses!'

And Moses said, 'Here I am.'

'Do not come any closer,' God said. 'Take off your sandals, for the place where you are standing is holy ground.' Then he said, 'I am the God of your father, the God of Abraham, the God of Isaac and the God of Jacob.' At this, Moses hid his face, because he was afraid to look at God.

Exodus 3:1–6

Great Father of glory, pure Father of light,
Thine angels adore Thee, all veiling their sight;
All laud we would render; O help us to see
'Tis only the splendour of light hideth Thee.

Walter Chalmers Smith, 1824–1908

The sacred name

The Lord said, 'I have indeed seen the misery of my people in Egypt. I have heard them crying out because of their slave drivers, and I am concerned about their suffering. So I have come down to rescue them from the hand of the Egyptians and to bring them up out of that land into a good and spacious land, a land flowing with milk and honey ... So now, go. I am sending you to Pharaoh to bring my people the Israelites out of Egypt.' But Moses said to God, 'Who am I, that I should go to Pharaoh and bring the Israelites out of Egypt?' And God said, 'I will be with you. And this will be the sign to you that it is I who have sent you: When you have brought the people out of Egypt, you will worship God on this mountain.' Moses said to God, 'Suppose I go to the Israelites and say to them, "The God of your fathers has sent me to you," and they ask me, "What is his name?" Then what shall I tell them?' God said to Moses, 'I AM WHO I AM. This is what you are to say to the Israelites: "I AM has sent me to you." '

God also said to Moses, 'Say to the Israelites, "The Lord, the God of your fathers – the God of Abraham, the God of Isaac and the God of Jacob – has sent me to you." This is my name for ever, the name by which I am to be remembered from generation to generation.'

Exodus 3:7–15

> The God of Abraham praise,
>   Who reigns enthroned above,
> Ancient of everlasting days,
>   And God of love.
> Jehovah! Great I AM!
>   By earth and heaven confessed;
> I bow and bless the sacred Name
>   For ever blessed.

Thomas Olivers, 1725–99

Be still

Come and see the works of the Lord, the desolations he has brought on the earth. He makes wars cease to the ends of the earth; he breaks the bow and shatters the spear, he burns the shields with fire. 'Be still, and know that I am God; I will be exalted among the nations, I will be exalted in the earth.'

The Lord Almighty is with us; the God of Jacob is our fortress.

Psalm 46:8–11

My heart is steadfast, O God, my heart is steadfast; I will sing and make music. Awake, my soul! Awake, harp and lyre! I will awaken the dawn.

I will praise you, O Lord, among the nations; I will sing of you among the peoples. For great is your love, reaching to the heavens; your faithfulness reaches to the skies.

Be exalted, O God, above the heavens; let your glory be over all the earth.

Psalm 57:7–11

Be still, my soul: the Lord is on thy side;
    Bear patiently the cross of grief or pain;
Leave to thy God to order and provide;
    In every change He faithful will remain.
Be still, my soul: thy best, thy heavenly Friend
Through thorny ways leads to a joyful end.

Katharina von Schlegel, b. 1697
tr. Jane Laurie Borthwick, 1813–97

Do not love the world

Do not love the world or anything in the world. If anyone loves the world, the love of the Father is not in him. For everything in the world – the cravings of sinful man, the lust of his eyes and the boasting of what he has and does – comes not from the Father but from the world. The world and its desires pass away, but the man who does the will of God lives for ever.

Dear children, this is the last hour; and as you have heard that the antichrist is coming, even now many antichrists have come. This is how we know it is the last hour. They went out from us, but they did not really belong to us. For if they had belonged to us, they would have remained with us; but their going showed that none of them belonged to us.

But you have an anointing from the Holy One, and all of you know the truth. I do not write to you because you do not know the truth, but because you do know it and because no lie comes from the truth. Who is the liar? It is the man who denies that Jesus is the Christ. Such a man is the antichrist – he denies the Father and the Son. No-one who denies the Son has the Father; whoever acknowledges the Son has the Father also.

1 John 2:15–23

> Let earth no more my heart divide,
> With Christ may I be crucified,
> To Thee with my whole soul aspire;
> Dead to the world and all its toys,
> Its idle pomp, and fading joys,
> Be Thou alone my one desire!

Charles Wesley, 1707–88

Because he first loved us

We love because he first loved us. If anyone says, 'I love God,' yet hates his brother, he is a liar. For anyone who does not love his brother, whom he has seen, cannot love God, whom he has not seen. And he has given us this command: Whoever loves God must also love his brother.

Everyone who believes that Jesus is the Christ is born of God, and everyone who loves the father loves his child as well. This is how we know that we love the children of God: by loving God and carrying out his commands. This is love for God: to obey his commands. And his commands are not burdensome, for everyone born of God overcomes the world. This is the victory that has overcome the world, even our faith. Who is it that overcomes the world? Only he who believes that Jesus is the Son of God.

1 John 4:19–5:5

> I love thee because Thou hast first loved me,
> And purchased my pardon on Calvary's tree;
> I love Thee for wearing the thorns on Thy brow,
> If ever I loved Thee, my Jesus, 'tis now.

William Ralph Featherstone, 1842–70

Praying to the Lord

This is the one who came by water and blood – Jesus Christ. He did not come by water only, but by water and blood. And it is the Spirit who testifies, because the Spirit is the truth. For there are three that testify: the Spirit, the water and the blood; and the three are in agreement. We accept man's testimony, but God's testimony is greater because it is the testimony of God, which he has given about his Son. Anyone who believes in the Son of God has this testimony in his heart. Anyone who does not believe God has made him out to be a liar, because he has not believed the testimony God has given about his Son. And this is the testimony: God has given us eternal life, and this life is in his Son. He who has the Son has life; he who does not have the Son of God does not have life.

I write these things to you who believe in the name of the Son of God so that you may know that you have eternal life. This is the confidence we have in approaching God: that if we ask anything according to his will, he hears us. And if we know that he hears us – whatever we ask – we know that we have what we asked of him.

1 John 5:6–15

> What a Friend we have in Jesus,
> All our sins and griefs to bear!
> What a privilege to carry
> Everything to God in prayer!
> O what peace we often forfeit,
> O what needless pain we bear,
> All because we do not carry
> Everything to God in prayer!

Joseph Medlicott Scriven, 1819–86

New life in Christ

When the men came to Jesus, they said, 'John the Baptist sent us to you to ask, "Are you the one who was to come, or should we expect someone else?" '

At that very time Jesus cured many who had diseases, sicknesses and evil spirits, and gave sight to many who were blind. So he replied to the messengers, 'Go back and report to John what you have seen and heard: The blind receive sight, the lame walk, those who have leprosy are cured, the deaf hear, the dead are raised, and the good news is preached to the poor. Blessed is the man who does not fall away on account of me.'

Luke 7:20–23

But because of his great love for us, God, who is rich in mercy, made us alive with Christ even when we were dead in transgressions – it is by grace you have been saved.

Ephesians 2:4–5

O for a thousand tongues to sing
   My great Redeemer's praise,
The glories of my God and King,
   The triumphs of His grace!

Jesus! the Name that charms our fears,
   That bids our sorrows cease;
'Tis music in the sinner's ears,
   'Tis life, and health, and peace.

He speaks, and, listening to His voice,
   New life the dead receive,
The mournful, broken hearts rejoice,
   The humble poor believe.

Charles Wesley, 1707–88

A perfect sacrifice

' "If the offering is a burnt offering from the herd, he is to offer a male without defect. He must present it at the entrance to the Tent of Meeting so that it will be acceptable to the Lord. He is to lay his hand on the head of the burnt offering, and it will be accepted on his behalf to make atonement for him. He is to slaughter the young bull before the Lord, and then Aaron's sons the priests shall bring the blood and sprinkle it against the altar on all sides at the entrance to the Tent of Meeting. He is to skin the burnt offering and cut it into pieces. The sons of Aaron the priest are to put fire on the altar and arrange wood on the fire. Then Aaron's sons the priests shall arrange the pieces, including the head and the fat, on the burning wood that is on the altar. He is to wash the inner parts and the legs with water, and the priest is to burn all of it on the altar. It is a burnt offering, an offering made by fire, an aroma pleasing to the Lord." '

Leviticus 1:3–9

Day after day every priest stands and performs his religious duties; again and again he offers the same sacrifices, which can never take away sins. But when this priest had offered for all time one sacrifice for sins, he sat down at the right hand of God.

Hebrews 10:11–12

Not all the blood of beasts,
  On Jewish altars slain,
Could give the guilty conscience peace
  Or wash away the stain.

But Christ, the heavenly Lamb,
  Takes all our sin away;
A sacrifice of nobler name,
  And richer blood than they.

Isaac Watts, 1674–1748

'I was blind but now I see'

A second time they [the Pharisees] summoned the man who had been blind. 'Give glory to God,' they said. 'We know this man is a sinner.' He replied, 'Whether he is a sinner or not, I don't know. One thing I do know. I was blind but now I see!'

Then they asked him, 'What did he do to you? How did he open your eyes?' He answered, 'I have told you already and you did not listen. Why do you want to hear it again? Do you want to become his disciples, too?'

Then they hurled insults at him and said, 'You are this fellow's disciple! We are disciples of Moses! We know that God spoke to Moses, but as for this fellow, we don't even know where he comes from.' The man answered, 'Now that is remarkable! You don't know where he comes from, yet he opened my eyes. We know that God does not listen to sinners. He listens to the godly man who does his will. Nobody has ever heard of opening the eyes of a man born blind. If this man were not from God, he could do nothing.' To this they replied, 'You were steeped in sin at birth; how dare you lecture us!' And they threw him out.

John 9:24–34

> Lord, I was blind! I could not see
>   In Thy marred visage any grace;
> But now the beauty of Thy face
>   In radiant vision dawns on me.
>
> Lord, Thou hast made the blind to see;
>   The deaf to hear, the dumb to speak,
> The dead to live; and lo, I break
>   The chains of my captivity!

William Tidd Matson, 1833–99

Overflowing praise

Great is the Lord and most worthy of praise; his greatness no-one can fathom. One generation will commend your works to another; they will tell of your mighty acts. They will speak of the glorious splendour of your majesty, and I will meditate on your wonderful works. They will tell of the power of your awesome works, and I will proclaim your great deeds. They will celebrate your abundant goodness and joyfully sing of your righteousness.

The Lord is gracious and compassionate, slow to anger and rich in love. The Lord is good to all; he has compassion on all he has made. All you have made will praise you, O Lord; your saints will extol you. They tell of the glory of your kingdom and speak of your might, so that all men may know of your mighty acts and the glorious splendour of your kingdom. Your kingdom is an everlasting kingdom, and your dominion endures through all generations.

Psalm 145:3–13

Holy, holy, holy, Lord God Almighty!
   All Thy works shall praise Thy Name, in earth and
     sky and sea;
Holy, holy, holy! merciful and mighty,
   God in Three Persons, blessed Trinity!

Reginald Heber, 1783–1826

Jesus brings the good news

He [Jesus] went to Nazareth, where he had been brought up, and on the Sabbath day he went into the synagogue, as was his custom. And he stood up to read. The scroll of the prophet Isaiah was handed to him. Unrolling it, he found the place where it is written:

'The Spirit of the Lord is on me, because he has anointed me to preach good news to the poor. He has sent me to proclaim freedom for the prisoners and recovery of sight for the blind, to release the oppressed, to proclaim the year of the Lord's favour.'

Then he rolled up the scroll, gave it back to the attendant and sat down. The eyes of everyone in the synagogue were fastened on him, and he began by saying to them, 'Today this scripture is fulfilled in your hearing.'

All spoke well of him and were amazed at the gracious words that came from his lips. 'Isn't this Joseph's son?' they asked.

Luke 4:14–22

Hark, the glad sound! the Saviour comes,
　　The Saviour promised long;
Let every heart prepare a throne,
　　And every voice a song.

He comes the prisoners to release,
　　In Satan's bondage held;
The gates of brass before Him burst,
　　The iron fetters yield.

He comes the broken heart to bind,
　　The bleeding soul to cure,
And with the treasures of His grace
　　To enrich the humble poor.

Philip Doddridge, 1702–51

Responding to God's love

'To the angel of the church in Laodicea write: These are the words of the Amen, the faithful and true witness, the ruler of God's creation. I know your deeds, that you are neither cold nor hot. I wish you were either one or the other! So, because you are lukewarm – neither hot nor cold – I am about to spit you out of my mouth. You say, 'I am rich; I have acquired wealth and do not need a thing.' But you do not realise that you are wretched, pitiful, poor, blind and naked. I counsel you to buy from me gold refined in the fire, so that you can become rich; and white clothes to wear, so that you can cover your shameful nakedness; and salve to put on your eyes, so that you can see.

Those whom I love I rebuke and discipline. So be earnest, and repent. Here I am! I stand at the door and knock. If anyone hears my voice and opens the door, I will come in and eat with him, and he with me.

To him who overcomes, I will give the right to sit with me on my throne, just as I overcame and sat down with my Father on his throne. He who has an ear, let him hear what the Spirit says to the churches.'

Revelation 3:14–22

> Jesus is seeking the wanderers yet;
>   Why do they roam?
> Love only waits to forgive and forget;
>   Home! weary wanderer, home!
> Wonderful love
> Dwells in the heart of the Father above.

Robert Walmsley, 1831–1905

Saving others

But, dear friends, remember what the apostles of our Lord Jesus Christ foretold. They said to you, 'In the last times there will be scoffers who will follow their own ungodly desires.' These are the men who divide you, who follow mere natural instincts and do not have the Spirit.

But you, dear friends, build yourselves up in your most holy faith and pray in the Holy Spirit. Keep yourselves in God's love as you wait for the mercy of our Lord Jesus Christ to bring you to eternal life.

Be merciful to those who doubt; snatch others from the fire and save them; to others show mercy, mixed with fear – hating even the clothing stained by corrupted flesh.

Jude 17–23

> I want an even strong desire,
>   I want a calmly fervent zeal
> To save poor souls out of the fire
>   To snatch them from the verge of hell,
> And turn them to a pardoning God,
> And quench the brands in Jesu's blood.
>
> Enlarge, inflame, and fill my heart
>   With boundless charity divine!
> So shall I all my strength exert,
>   And love them with a zeal like Thine;
> And lead them to Thy open side,
> The sheep for whom their Shepherd died.

Charles Wesley, 1707–88

God is faithful

Let us hold unswervingly to the hope we profess, for he who promised is faithful. And let us consider how we may spur one another on towards love and good deeds. Let us not give up meeting together, as some are in the habit of doing, but let us encourage one another – and all the more as you see the Day approaching.

Hebrews 10:23–25

'To the angel of the church in Smyrna write: These are the words of him who is the First and the Last, who died and came to life again. I know your afflictions and your poverty – yet you are rich! I know the slander of those who say they are Jews and are not, but are a synagogue of Satan. Do not be afraid of what you are about to suffer. I tell you, the devil will put some of you in prison to test you, and you will suffer persecution for ten days. Be faithful, even to the point of death, and I will give you the crown of life.'

Revelation 2:8–10

How good is the God we adore,
   Our faithful, unchangeable Friend!
His love is as great as His power,
   And knows neither measure nor end!

'Tis Jesus, the First and the Last,
   Whose Spirit shall guide us safe home;
We'll praise Him for all that is past,
   And trust Him for all that's to come.

Joseph Hart, 1712–68

Wholehearted loyalty

My servant Caleb has a different spirit and follows me wholeheartedly.

Numbers 14:24

Now the men of Judah approached Joshua at Gilgal, and Caleb son of Jephunneh the Kenizzite said to him, 'You know what the Lord said to Moses the man of God at Kadesh Barnea about you and me. I was forty years old when Moses the servant of the Lord sent me to Kadesh Barnea to explore the land. And I brought him back a report according to my convictions, but my brothers who went up with me made the hearts of the people melt with fear. I, however, followed the Lord my God wholeheartedly. So on that day Moses swore to me, "The land on which your feet have walked will be your inheritance and that of your children for ever, because you have followed the Lord my God wholeheartedly."

'Now then, just as the Lord promised, he has kept me alive for forty-five years since the time he said this to Moses, while Israel moved in the desert. So here I am today, eighty-five years old! I am still as strong today as the day Moses sent me out; I'm just as vigorous to go out to battle now as I was then.

Joshua 14:6–11

True-hearted, whole-hearted, faithful and loyal,
　King of our lives, by Thy grace we will be:
Under Thy standard, exalted and royal,
　Strong in Thy strength, we will battle for Thee.

Peal out the watchword, and silence it never,
　Song of our spirits rejoicing and free:
'True-hearted, whole-hearted, now and for ever,
　King of our lives, by Thy grace we will be!'

Frances Ridley Havergal, 1836–79

Our security in God

But Zion said, 'The Lord has forsaken me, the Lord has forgotten me.'

'Can a mother forget the baby at her breast and have no compassion on the child she has borne? Though she may forget, I will not forget you! See, I have engraved you on the palms of my hands; your walls are ever before me.'

Isaiah 49:14–16

'Are not two sparrows sold for a penny? Yet not one of them will fall to the ground apart from the will of your Father. And even the very hairs of your head are all numbered. So don't be afraid; you are worth more than many sparrows.'

Matthew 10:29–31

My name from the palms of His hands
  Eternity will not erase;
Impressed on His heart it remains,
  In marks of indelible grace;

Yes, I to the end shall endure,
  As sure as the earnest is given;
More happy, but not more secure,
  The glorified spirits in heaven.

Augustus Montague Toplady, 1740–78

The Lord, our hope

For you have been my hope, O Sovereign Lord, my confidence since my youth. From my birth I have relied on you; you brought me forth from my mother's womb. I will ever praise you. I have become like a portent to many, but you are my strong refuge. My mouth is filled with your praise, declaring your splendour all day long. Do not cast me away when I am old; do not forsake me when my strength is gone.

Psalm 71:5–9

For a thousand years in your sight are like a day that has just gone by, or like a watch in the night. You sweep men away in the sleep of death; they are like the new grass of the morning – though in the morning it springs up new, by evening it is dry and withered. All our days pass away under your wrath; we finish our years with a moan. The length of our days is seventy years – or eighty, if we have the strength; yet their span is but trouble and sorrow, for they quickly pass, and we fly away.

Who knows the power of your anger? For your wrath is as great as the fear that is due to you. Teach us to number our days aright, that we may gain a heart of wisdom.

Psalm 90:4–12

A thousand ages in Thy sight
　Are like an evening gone,
Short as the watch that ends the night
　Before the rising sun.

Our God, our help in ages past,
　Our hope for years to come,
Be thou our guard while troubles last,
　And our eternal home.

Isaac Watts, 1674–1748

Strong in Christ

You then, my son, be strong in the grace that is in Christ
Jesus. And the things you have heard me say in the
presence of many witnesses entrust to reliable men who
will also be qualified to teach others. Endure hardship
with us like a good soldier of Christ Jesus. No-one serving as a soldier gets involved in civilian affairs – he
wants to please his commanding officer. Similarly, if
anyone competes as an athlete, he does not receive the
victor's crown unless he competes according to the rules.
The hardworking farmer should be the first to receive
a share of the crops. Reflect on what I am saying, for
the Lord will give you insight into all this.

2 Timothy 2:1–7

Stand up, stand up for Jesus!
　　Stand in His strength alone:
The arm of flesh will fail you;
　　Ye dare not trust your own.
Put on the gospel armour,
　　Each piece put on with prayer;
Where duty calls, or danger,
　　Be never wanting there.

Stand up, stand up for Jesus!
　　The strife will not be long;
This day the noise of battle,
　　The next the victor's song.
To him that overcometh
　　A crown of life shall be;
He with the King of glory
　　Shall reign eternally.

George Duffield, 1818–88

A lifetime of praise

Praise the Lord. Praise the Lord, O my soul. I will praise the Lord all my life; I will sing praise to my God as long as I live.

Do not put your trust in princes, in mortal men, who cannot save. When their spirit departs, they return to the ground; on that very day their plans come to nothing.

Blessed is he whose help is the God of Jacob, whose hope is in the Lord his God, the Maker of heaven and earth, the sea, and everything in them – the Lord, who remains faithful for ever. He upholds the cause of the oppressed and gives food to the hungry. The Lord sets prisoners free, the Lord gives sight to the blind, the Lord lifts up those who are bowed down, the Lord loves the righteous. The Lord watches over the alien and sustains the fatherless and the widow, but he frustrates the ways of the wicked.

The Lord reigns for ever, your God, O Zion, for all generations. Praise the Lord.

Psalm 146:1–10

I'll praise my Maker while I've breath,
And when my voice is lost in death,
Praise shall employ my nobler powers;
My days of praise shall ne'er be past,
While life, and thought, and being last,
Or immortality endures.

The Lord gives eyesight to the blind;
The Lord supports the fainting mind;
He sends the labouring conscience peace;
He helps the stranger in distress,
The widow and the fatherless,
And grants the prisoner sweet release.

Isaac Watts, 1674–1748

A purpose in suffering

Praise our God, O peoples, let the sound of his praise be heard; he has preserved our lives and kept our feet from slipping. For you, O God, tested us; you refined us like silver.

Psalm 66:8–10

'For my own name's sake I delay my wrath; for the sake of my praise I hold it back from you, so as not to cut you off. See, I have refined you, though not as silver; I have tested you in the furnace of affliction. For my own sake, for my own sake, I do this. How can I let myself be defamed? I will not yield my glory to another.'

Isaiah 48:9–11

Dear friends, do not be surprised at the painful trial you are suffering, as though something strange were happening to you. But rejoice that you participate in the sufferings of Christ, so that you may be overjoyed when his glory is revealed.

1 Peter 4:12–13

> When through fiery trials thy pathway shall lie,
> His grace all-sufficient shall be thy supply;
> The flame shall not hurt thee, His only design
> Thy dross to consume and thy gold to refine.

'K' in Rippon's *Selection*, 1787

Listening to God

The boy Samuel ministered before the Lord under Eli. In those days the word of the Lord was rare; there were not many visions. One night Eli, whose eyes were becoming so weak that he could barely see, was lying down in his usual place. The lamp of God had not yet gone out, and Samuel was lying down in the temple of the Lord, where the ark of God was. Then the Lord called Samuel. Samuel answered, 'Here I am.' And he ran to Eli and said, 'Here I am; you called me.' But Eli said, 'I did not call; go back and lie down.' So he went and lay down.

Again the Lord called, 'Samuel!' And Samuel got up and went to Eli and said, 'Here I am; you called me.' 'My son,' Eli said, 'I did not call; go back and lie down.' Now Samuel did not yet know the Lord: The word of the Lord had not yet been revealed to him. The Lord called Samuel a third time, and Samuel got up and went to Eli and said, 'Here I am; you called me.'

Then Eli realized that the Lord was calling the boy. So Eli told Samuel, 'Go and lie down, and if he calls you, say, "Speak, Lord, for your servant is listening."' So Samuel went and lay down in his place. The Lord came and stood there, calling as at the other times, 'Samuel! Samuel!' Then Samuel said, 'Speak, for your servant is listening.'

1 Samuel 3:1–10

Master, speak! Thy servant heareth,
 Waiting for Thy gracious word,
Longing for Thy voice that cheereth,
 Master, let it now be heard.
I am listening, Lord, for Thee;
What hast Thou to say to me?

Frances Ridley Havergal, 1836–79

The Lord is King!

Ascribe to the Lord, O families of nations, ascribe to the Lord glory and strength, ascribe to the Lord the glory due to his name. Bring an offering and come before him; worship the Lord in the splendour of his holiness. Tremble before him, all the earth! The world is firmly established; it cannot be moved. Let the heavens rejoice, let the earth be glad; let them say among the nations, 'The Lord reigns!'

1 Chronicles 16:28–31

The Lord reigns, he is robed in majesty; the Lord is robed in majesty and is armed with strength. The world is firmly established; it cannot be moved. Your throne was established long ago; you are from all eternity.

The seas have lifted up, O Lord, the seas have lifted up their voice; the seas have lifted up their pounding waves. Mightier than the thunder of the great waters, mightier than the breakers of the sea – the Lord on high is mighty.

Your statutes stand firm; holiness adorns your house for endless days, O Lord.

Psalm 93:1–5

The Lord is King; lift up thy voice,
O earth, and all ye heavens rejoice!
From world to world the joy shall ring:
'The Lord Omnipotent is King!'

The Lord is King! child of the dust,
The Judge of all the earth is just:
Holy and true are all His ways;
Let every creature speak His praise.

Josiah Conder, 1789–1855

The king of glory

The earth is the Lord's, and everything in it, the world, and all who live in it; for he founded it upon the seas and established it upon the waters.

Who may ascend the hill of the Lord? Who may stand in his holy place? He who has clean hands and a pure heart, who does not lift up his soul to an idol or swear by what is false. He will receive blessing from the Lord and vindication from God his Saviour. Such is the generation of those who seek him, who seek your face, O God of Jacob.

Lift up your heads, O you gates; be lifted up, you ancient doors, that the King of glory may come in. Who is this King of glory? The Lord strong and mighty, the Lord mighty in battle. Lift up your heads, O you gates; lift them up, you ancient doors, that the King of glory may come in. Who is he, this King of glory? The Lord Almighty – he is the King of glory.

Psalm 24:1–10

> King of glory! Soul of bliss!
> *Hallelujah!*
> Everlasting life is this,
> Thee to know, Thy power to prove,
> Thus to sing, and thus to love.

Charles Wesley, 1707–88

Mary's song of praise

And Mary said: 'My soul glorifies the Lord and my spirit rejoices in God my Saviour, for he has been mindful of the humble state of his servant. From now on all generations will call me blessed, for the Mighty One has done great things for me – holy is his name. His mercy extends to those who fear him, from generation to generation. He has performed mighty deeds with his arm; he has scattered those who are proud in their inmost thoughts. He has brought down rulers from their thrones but has lifted up the humble. He has filled the hungry with good things but has sent the rich away empty. He has helped his servant Israel, remembering to be merciful to Abraham and his descendants for ever, even as he said to our fathers.' *Luke 1:46–55*

Tell out, my soul, the greatness of the Lord;
　Unnumbered blessings give my spirit voice;
Tender to me the promise of His Word;
　In God my Saviour shall my heart rejoice.

Tell out, my soul, the greatness of His Name!
　Make known His might, the deeds His arm has done;
His mercy sure, from age to age the same;
　His Holy Name – the Lord, the Mighty One.

Tell out, my soul, the greatness of His might!
　Powers and dominions lay their glory by.
Proud hearts and stubborn wills are put to flight,
　The hungry fed, the humble lifted high.

Tell out, my soul, the glories of His word!
　Firm in His promise, and His mercy sure,
Tell out, my soul, the greatness of the Lord
　To children's children and for evermore!

Timothy Dudley-Smith, b. 1926

In the strength of God

David said to the Philistine, 'You come against me with sword and spear and javelin, but I come against you in the name of the Lord Almighty, the God of the armies of Israel, whom you have defied. This day the Lord will hand you over to me, and I'll strike you down and cut off your head. Today I will give the carcasses of the Philistine army to the birds of the air and the beasts of the earth, and the whole world will know that there is a God in Israel. All those gathered here will know that it is not by sword or spear that the Lord saves; for the battle is the Lord's, and he will give all of you into our hands.'

As the Philistine moved closer to attack him, David ran quickly towards the battle line to meet him. Reaching into his bag and taking out a stone, he slung it and struck the Philistine on the forehead. The stone sank into his forehead, and he fell face down on the ground.

So David triumphed over the Philistine with a sling and a stone; without a sword in his hand he struck down the Philistine and killed him.

1 Samuel 17:45–50

'We rest on Thee', our Shield and our Defender!
    We go not forth alone against the foe;
Strong in Thy strength, safe in Thy keeping tender,
    'We rest on Thee, and in Thy Name we go.'

Edith Adeline Gilling Cherry, 1872–97

The eternal God is our refuge

'I will sing to the Lord, for he is highly exalted. The horse and its rider he has hurled into the sea. The Lord is my strength and my song; he has become my salvation. He is my God, and I will praise him, my father's God, and I will exalt him. The Lord is a warrior; the Lord is his name.'

Exodus 15:1–3

'There is no-one like the God of Jeshurun, who rides on the heavens to help you and on the clouds in his majesty. The eternal God is your refuge, and underneath are the everlasting arms. He will drive out your enemy before you, saying, 'Destroy him!' 'So Israel will live in safety alone; Jacob's spring is secure in a land of grain and new wine, where the heavens drop dew. Blessed are you, O Israel! Who is like you, a people saved by the Lord? He is your shield and helper and your glorious sword. Your enemies will cower before you, and you will trample down their high places.'

Deuteronomy 33:26–29

> We come unto our fathers' God;
>   Their Rock is our salvation;
> The eternal arms, their dear abode,
>   We make our habitation;
> We bring Thee, Lord, the praise they brought,
> We seek Thee as Thy saints have sought
>   In every generation.

Thomas Hornblower Gill, 1819–1906

Led by the Spirit

Those who live according to the sinful nature have their minds set on what that nature desires; but those who live in accordance with the Spirit have their minds set on what the Spirit desires. The mind of sinful man is death, but the mind controlled by the Spirit is life and peace; the sinful mind is hostile to God. It does not submit to God's law, nor can it do so. Those controlled by the sinful nature cannot please God.

You, however, are controlled not by the sinful nature but by the Spirit, if the Spirit of God lives in you. And if anyone does not have the Spirit of Christ, he does not belong to Christ. But if Christ is in you, your body is dead because of sin, yet your spirit is alive because of righteousness. And if the Spirit of him who raised Jesus from the dead is living in you, he who raised Christ from the dead will also give life to your mortal bodies through his Spirit, who lives in you.

Therefore, brothers, we have an obligation – but it is not to the sinful nature, to live according to it. For if you live according to the sinful nature, you will die; but if by the Spirit you put to death the misdeeds of the body, you will live, because those who are led by the Spirit of God are sons of God.

Romans 8:5–14

By Thine unerring Spirit led,
　We shall not in the desert stray;
We shall not full direction need,
　Nor miss our providential way;
As far from danger as from fear,
While love, almighty love, is near.

Charles Wesley, 1707–88

A life of faith

Is any one of you in trouble? He should pray. Is anyone happy? Let him sing songs of praise. Is any one of you sick? He should call the elders of the church to pray over him and anoint him with oil in the name of the Lord. And the prayer offered in faith will make the sick person well; the Lord will raise him up. If he has sinned, he will be forgiven. Therefore confess your sins to each other and pray for each other so that you may be healed. The prayer of a righteous man is powerful and effective.

Elijah was a man just like us. He prayed earnestly that it would not rain, and it did not rain on the land for three and a half years. Again he prayed, and the heavens gave rain, and the earth produced its crops.

My brothers, if one of you should wander from the truth and someone should bring him back, remember this: Whoever turns a sinner from the error of his way will save him from death and cover over a multitude of sins.

James 5:13–20

> While I am a pilgrim here,
> Let Thy love my spirit cheer;
> As my guide, my Guard, my Friend,
> Lead me to my journey's end.
>
> Show me what I have to do;
> Every hour my strength renew;
> Let me live a life of faith;
> Let me die Thy people's death.

John Newton, 1725–1807

'You are very great'

Praise the Lord, O my soul.

O Lord my God, you are very great; you are clothed
with splendour and majesty. He wraps himself in light
as with a garment; he stretches out the heavens like a
tent and lays the beams of his upper chambers on their
waters. He makes the clouds his chariot and rides on
the wings of the wind. He makes winds his messengers,
flames of fire his servants.

He set the earth on its foundations; it can never be
moved. You covered it with the deep as with a garment;
the waters stood above the mountains. But at your
rebuke the waters fled, at the sound of your thunder
they took to flight; they flowed over the mountains, they
went down into the valleys, to the place you assigned
for them. You set a boundary they cannot cross; never
again will they cover the earth.

Psalm 104:1–9

God, the blessed and only Ruler, the King of kings and
Lord of lords, who alone is immortal and who lives in
unapproachable fight, whom no-one has seen or can see.
To him be honour and might for ever. Amen.

1 Timothy 6:15–16

> Immortal, invisible, God only wise,
> In light inaccessible hid from our eyes,
> Most blessed, most glorious, the Ancient of Days,
> Almighty, victorious, thy great Name we praise.

Walter Chalmers Smith, 1824–1908

The Lord, my strength

I love you, O Lord, my strength.

The Lord is my rock, my fortress and my deliverer;
my God is my rock, in whom I take refuge. He is my
shield and the horn of my salvation, my stronghold. I
call to the Lord, who is worthy of praise, and I am saved
from my enemies.

The cords of death entangled me; the torrents of
destruction overwhelmed me. The cords of the grave
coiled around me; the snares of death confronted me. In
my distress I called to the Lord; I cried to my God for
help. From his temple he heard my voice; my cry came
before him, into his ears.

The earth trembled and quaked, and the foundations
of the mountains shook; they trembled because he was
angry.

Psalm 18:1–7

Be Thou my vision, O Lord of my heart;
Nought be all else to me, save that Thou art;
Thou my best thought, by day or by night,
Waking or sleeping, Thy presence my light.

Be thou my battle-shield, sword for the fight;
Be thou my armour, be Thou my might;
Thou my soul's shelter, Thou my high tower;
Raise thou me heavenward, O Power of my power.

Irish, c. 8th century
tr. Mary Elizabeth Byrne, 1880–1931
versified by Eleanor Henrietta Hull, 1860–1935

To live is Christ

Yes, and I will continue to rejoice, for I know that through your prayers and the help given by the Spirit of Jesus Christ, what has happened to me will turn out for my deliverance. I eagerly expect and hope that I will in no way be ashamed, but will have sufficient courage so that now as always Christ will be exalted in my body, whether by life or by death. For to me, to live is Christ and to die is gain. If I am to go on living in the body, this will mean fruitful labour for me. Yet what shall I choose? I do not know! I am torn between the two: I desire to depart and be with Christ, which is better by far; but it is more necessary for you that I remain in the body. Convinced of this, I know that I will remain, and I will continue with all of you for your progress and joy in the faith, so that through my being with you again your joy in Christ Jesus will overflow on account of me.

Whatever happens, conduct yourselves in a manner worthy of the gospel of Christ. Then, whether I come and see you or only hear about you in my absence, I will know that you stand firm in one spirit, contending as one man for the faith of the gospel without being frightened in any way by those who oppose you.

Philippians 1:18–28

When peace, like a river, attendeth my way,
　　When sorrows, like sea-billows, roll,
Whatever my lot, Thou hast taught me to say,
　　It is well, it is well with my soul.

For me be it Christ, be it Christ hence to live!
　　If Jordan above me shall roll,
No pang shall be mine, for in death as in life
　　Thou wilt whisper Thy peace to my soul.

Horatio Gates Spafford, 1828–88

Christ's word in our hearts

As God's chosen people, holy and dearly loved, clothe yourselves with compassion, kindness, humility, gentleness and patience. Bear with each other and forgive whatever grievances you may have against one another. Forgive as the Lord forgave you. And over all these virtues put on love, which binds them all together in perfect unity.

Let the peace of Christ rule in your hearts, since as members of one body you were called to peace. And be thankful. Let the word of Christ dwell in you richly as you teach and admonish one another with all wisdom, and as you sing psalms, hymns and spiritual songs with gratitude in your hearts to God. And whatever you do, whether in word or deed, do it all in the name of the Lord Jesus, giving thanks to God the Father through him.

Colossians 3:12–17

May the Word of God dwell richly
In my heart from hour to hour.
So that all may see I triumph
Only through His power.

Katie Barclay Wilkinson, 1859–1928

The call of wisdom

Does not wisdom call out? Does not understanding raise her voice? On the heights along the way, where the paths meet, she takes her stand; beside the gates leading into the city, at the entrances, she cries aloud: 'To you, O men, I call out; I raise my voice to all mankind. You who are simple, gain prudence; you who are foolish, gain understanding. Listen, for I have worthy things to say; I open my lips to speak what is right. My mouth speaks what is true, for my lips detest wickedness. All the words of my mouth are just; none of them is crooked or perverse. To the discerning all of them are right; they are faultless to those who have knowledge. Choose my instruction instead of silver, knowledge rather than choice gold, for wisdom is more precious than rubies, and nothing you desire can compare with her.

Proverbs 8:1–11

> Wisdom divine! who tells the price
> Of wisdom's costly merchandise?
> Wisdom to silver we prefer,
> And gold is dross compared to her.

Charles Wesley, 1707–88

Jesus' entry into Jerusalem

As they approached Jerusalem and came to Bethphage and Bethany at the Mount of Olives, Jesus sent two of his disciples, saying to them, 'Go to the village ahead of you, and just as you enter it, you will find a colt tied there, which no-one has ever ridden. Untie it and bring it here. If anyone asks you, "Why are you doing this?" tell him, "The Lord needs it and will send it back here shortly."'

They went and found a colt outside in the street, tied at a doorway. As they untied it, some people standing there asked, 'What are you doing, untying that colt?' They answered as Jesus had told them to, and the people let them go. When they brought the colt to Jesus and threw their cloaks over it, he sat on it. Many people spread their cloaks on the road, while others spread branches they had cut in the fields. Those who went ahead and those who followed shouted, 'Hosanna!' 'Blessed is he who comes in the name of the Lord!' 'Blessed is the coming kingdom of our father David!' 'Hosanna in the highest!'

Jesus entered Jerusalem and went to the temple. He looked around at everything, but since it was already late, he went out to Bethany with the Twelve.

Mark 11:1–11

> All glory, laud, and honour
> To Thee, Redeemer, King,
> To whom the lips of children
> Made sweet hosannas ring!
> Thou art the King of Israel,
> Thou David's royal Son,
> Who in the Lord's Name comest,
> The King and blessed One.

Theodulph of Orleans, c. 750–821
tr. John Mason Neale, 1818–66

The peace of Christ

Jesus replied, 'If anyone loves me, he will obey my teaching. My Father will love him, and we will come to him and make our home with him. He who does not love me will not obey my teaching. These words you hear are not my own; they belong to the Father who sent me.

'All this I have spoken while still with you. But the Counsellor, the Holy Spirit, whom the Father will send in my name, will teach you all things and will remind you of everything I have said to you. Peace I leave with you; my peace I give you. I do not give to you as the world gives. Do not let your hearts be troubled and do not be afraid.

'You heard me say, "I am going away and I am coming back to you." If you loved me, you would be glad that I am going to the Father, for the Father is greater than I. I have told you now before it happens, so that when it does happen you will believe. I will not speak with you much longer, for the prince of this world is coming. He has no hold on me, but the world must learn that I love the Father and that I do exactly what my Father has commanded me.

'Come now; let us leave.'

John 14:23–31

His for ever, only His;
　　Who the Lord and me shall part?
Ah, with what a rest of bliss
　　Christ can fill the loving heart!
Heaven and earth may fade and flee,
　　First-born light in gloom decline,
But while God and I shall be,
　　I am His and He is mine.

George Wade Robinson, 1828–77

The power of Jesus' name

While the beggar held on to Peter and John, all the people were astonished and came running to them in the place called Solomon's Colonnade. When Peter saw this, he said to them: 'Men of Israel, why does this surprise you? Why do you stare at us as if by our own power or godliness we have made this man walk? The God of Abraham, Isaac and Jacob, the God of our fathers, has glorified his servant Jesus. You handed him over to be killed, and you disowned him before Pilate, though he had decided to let him go. You disowned the Holy and Righteous One and asked that a murderer be released to you. You killed the author of life, but God raised him from the dead. We are witnesses of this. By faith in the name of Jesus, this man whom you see and know was made strong. It is Jesus' name and the faith that comes through him that has given this complete healing to him, as you can all see.'

Acts 3:11–16

> All hail the power of Jesus' Name!
> Let angels prostrate fall;
> Bring forth the royal diadem
> To crown Him Lord of all.
>
> O that with yonder sacred throng
> We at His feet may fall,
> Join in the everlasting song,
> And crown Him Lord of all!

Edward Perronet, 1726–92
and John Rippon, 1751–1836

God's perfect way

'To the faithful you show yourself faithful, to the blameless you show yourself blameless, to the pure you show yourself pure, but to the crooked you show yourself shrewd. You save the humble, but your eyes are on the haughty to bring them low. You are my lamp, O Lord; the Lord turns my darkness into light. With your help I can advance against a troop; with my God I can scale a wall.

'As for God, his way is perfect; the word of the Lord is flawless. He is a shield for all who take refuge in him. For who is God besides the Lord? And who is the Rock except our God? It is God who arms me with strength and makes my way perfect. He makes my feet like the feet of a deer; he enables me to stand on the heights. He trains my hands for battle; my arms can bend a bow of bronze. You give me your shield of victory; you stoop down to make me great. You broaden the path beneath me, so that my ankles do not turn over.'

2 Samuel 22:26–37

Thou God of truth and love,
  We seek Thy perfect way,
Ready Thy choice to approve,
  Thy providence to obey:
Enter into Thy wise design,
And sweetly lose our will in Thine.

Charles Wesley, 1707–88

Asking for wisdom

At Gibeon the Lord appeared to Solomon during the night in a dream, and God said, 'Ask for whatever you want me to give you.'

Solomon answered, 'You have shown great kindness to your servant, my father David, because he was faithful to you and righteous and upright in heart. You have continued this great kindness to him and have given him a son to sit on his throne this very day.

'Now, O Lord my God, you have made your servant king in place of my father David. But I am only a little child and do not know how to carry out my duties. Your servant is here among the people you have chosen, a great people, too numerous to count or number. So give your servant a discerning heart to govern your people and to distinguish between right and wrong. For who is able to govern this great people of yours?'

The Lord was pleased that Solomon had asked for this. So God said to him, 'Since you have asked for this and not for long life or wealth for yourself, nor have asked for the death of your enemies but for discernment in administering justice, I will do what you have asked. I will give you a wise and discerning heart, so that there will never have been anyone like you, nor will there ever be. Moreover, I will give you what you have not asked for – both riches and honour – so that in your lifetime you will have no equal among kings. And if you walk in my ways and obey my statutes and commands as David your father did, I will give you a long life.' Then Solomon awoke – and he realised it had been a dream.

1 Kings 3:5–15

Be Thou my wisdom, Thou my true word;
I ever with Thee, Thou with me, Lord;
Thou my great Father, I Thy true son;
Thou in me dwelling, and I with Thee one.

Irish, c. 8th century
tr. Mary Elizabeth Byrne, 1830–1931
versified by Eleanor Henrietta Hull, 1860–1935

The quietness of God

And the word of the Lord came to him: 'What are you doing here, Elijah?' He replied, 'I have been very zealous for the Lord God Almighty. The Israelites have rejected your covenant, broken down your altars, and put your prophets to death with the sword. I am the only one left, and now they are trying to kill me too.'

The Lord said, 'Go out and stand on the mountain in the presence of the Lord, for the Lord is about to pass by.' Then a great and powerful wind tore the mountains apart and shattered the rocks before the Lord, but the Lord was not in the wind. After the wind there was an earthquake, but the Lord was not in the earthquake. After the earthquake came a fire, but the Lord was not in the fire. And after the fire came a gentle whisper. When Elijah heard it, he pulled his cloak over his face and went out and stood at the mouth of the cave.

Then a voice said to him, 'What are you doing here, Elijah?' He replied, 'I have been very zealous for the Lord God Almighty. The Israelites have rejected your covenant, broken down your altars, and put your prophets to death with the sword. I am the only one left, and now they are trying to kill me too.' The Lord said to him, 'Go back the way you came, and go to the Desert of Damascus. When you get there, anoint Hazael king over Aram.'

1 Kings 19:9–15

Breathe through the heats of our desire
   Thy coolness and Thy balm;
Let sense be dumb – let flesh retire;
Speak through the earthquake, wind, and fire,
   O still small voice of calm!

John Greenleaf Whittier, 1807–92

My times are in your hand

But I trust in you, O Lord; I say, 'You are my God.' My times are in your hands; deliver me from my enemies and from those who pursue me. Let your face shine on your servant; save me in your unfailing love. Let me not be put to shame, O Lord, for I have cried out to you; but let the wicked be put to shame and lie silent in the grave. Let their lying lips be silenced, for with pride and contempt they speak arrogantly against the righteous.

How great is your goodness, which you have stored up for those who fear you, which you bestow in the sight of men on those who take refuge in you. In the shelter of your presence you hide them from the intrigues of men; in your dwelling you keep them safe from accusing tongues.

Praise to the Lord, for he showed his wonderful love to me when I was in a besieged city. In my alarm I said, 'I am cut off from your sight!' Yet you heard my cry for mercy when I called to you for help.

Love the Lord, all his saints! The Lord preserves the faithful, but the proud he pays back in full. Be strong and take heart, all you who hope in the Lord.

Psalm 31:14–24

My times are in Thy hand,
    Whatever they may be,
Pleasing or painful, dark or bright,
    As best may seem to Thee.

My times are in Thy hand:
    Why should I doubt or fear?
A Father's hand will never cause
    His child a needless tear.

William Freeman Lloyd, 1791–1853

The Ancient of Days

'As I looked, thrones were set in place, and the Ancient of Days took his seat. His clothing was as white as snow; the hair on his head was white like wool. His throne was flaming with fire, and its wheels were all ablaze. A river of fire was flowing, coming out from before him. Thousands upon thousands attended him; ten thousand times ten thousand stood before him. The court was seated, and the books were opened.

'Then I continued to watch because of the boastful words the horn was speaking. I kept looking until the beast was slain and its body destroyed and thrown into the blazing fire. (The other beasts had been stripped of their authority, but were allowed to live for a period of time.)

'In my vision at night I looked, and there before me was one like a son of man, coming with the clouds of heaven. He approached the Ancient of Days and was led into his presence. He was given authority, glory and sovereign power; all peoples, nations and men of every language worshipped him. His dominion is an everlasting dominion that will not pass away, and his kingdom is one that will never be destroyed.'

Daniel 7:9–14

O worship the King,
　All-glorious above,
O gratefully sing
　His power and His love:
Our Shield and Defender,
　The Ancient of Days,
Pavilioned in splendour
　And girded with praise.

Robert Grant, 1779–1838

Before the throne of God

Then one of the elders asked me, 'These in white robes – who are they, and where did they come from?' I answered, 'Sir, you know.'

And he said, 'These are they who have come out of the great tribulation; they have washed their robes and made them white in the blood of the Lamb. Therefore, they are before the throne of God and serve him day and night in his temple; and he who sits on the throne will spread his tent over them. Never again will they hunger; never again will they thirst. The sun will not beat upon them, nor any scorching heat. For the Lamb at the centre of the throne will be their shepherd; he will lead them to springs of living water. And God will wipe away every tear from their eyes.'

Revelation 7:13–17

Glorious things of thee are spoken,
    Zion, city of our God!
He, whose word cannot be broken,
    Formed thee for His own abode.
On the Rock of Ages founded,
    What can shake thy sure repose?
With salvation's walls surrounded,
    Thou may'st smile at all thy foes.

Round each habitation hovering,
    See! the cloud and fire appear,
For a glory and a covering,
    Showing that the Lord is near:
Blest inhabitants of Zion,
    Washed in the Redeemer's blood –
Jesus, whom their souls rely on,
    Makes them kings and priests to God.

John Newton, 1725–1807

The unending reign

The seventh angel sounded his trumpet, and there were loud voices in heaven, which said: 'The kingdom of the world has become the kingdom of our Lord and of his Christ, and he will reign for ever and ever.'

And the twenty-four elders, who were seated on their thrones before God, fell on their faces and worshipped God, saying: 'We give thanks to you, Lord God Almighty, the One who is and who was, because you have taken your great power and have begun to reign. The nations were angry; and your wrath has come. The time has come for judging the dead, and for rewarding your servants the prophets and your saints and those who reverence your name, both small and great – and for destroying those who destroy the earth.'

Then God's temple in heaven was opened, and within his temple was seen the ark of his covenant. And there came flashes of lightning, rumblings, peals of thunder, an earthquake and a great hailstorm.

Revelation 11:15–19

Praise Him, praise Him! Jesus, our blessed Redeemer;
  Sing, O earth, His wonderful love proclaim!
Hail Him, hail Him! highest archangels in glory,
  Strength and honour give to His holy Name.
Like a shepherd, Jesus will guard His children,
  In His arms He carries them all day long;
O ye saints that dwell in the mountains of Zion,
  Praise Him, praise Him! ever in joyful song.

Frances Jane Van Alstyne, 1820–1915

'They overcame him'

And there was war in heaven. Michael and his angels
fought against the dragon, and the dragon and his
angels fought back. But he was not strong enough, and
they lost their place in heaven. The great dragon was
hurled down – that ancient serpent called the devil or
Satan, who leads the whole world astray. He was hurled
to the earth, and his angels with him.

Then I heard a loud voice in heaven say: 'Now have
come the salvation and the power and the kingdom of
our God, and the authority of his Christ. For the accuser
of our brothers, who accuses them before our God day
and night, has been hurled down. They overcame him
by the blood of the Lamb and by the word of their testimony; they did not love their lives so much as to shrink
from death. Therefore rejoice, you heavens and you who
dwell in them! But woe to the earth and the sea, because
the devil has gone down to you! He is filled with fury,
because he knows that his time is short.'

Revelation 12:7–12

Give me the wings of faith to rise
    Within the veil, and see
The saints above, how great their joys,
    How bright their glories be.

Once they were mourning here below,
    With sighing and with tears;
They wrestled hard, as we do now,
    With sins and doubts and fears.

I ask them whence their victory came;
    They, with united breath,
Ascribe their conquest to the Lamb,
    Their triumph to His death.

Isaac Watts, 1674–1748

Rest for the saints

Then I saw another angel flying in mid-air, and he had the eternal gospel to proclaim to those who live on the earth – to every nation, tribe, language and people. He said in a loud voice, 'Fear God and give him glory, because the hour of his judgment has come. Worship him who made the heavens, the earth, the sea and the springs of water.'

A second angel followed and said, 'Fallen! Fallen is Babylon the Great, which made all the nations drink the maddening wine of her adulteries.'

A third angel followed them and said in a loud voice: 'If anyone worships the beast and his image and receives his mark on the forehead or on the hand, he, too, will drink of the wine of God's fury, which has been poured full strength into the cup of his wrath. He will be tormented with burning sulphur in the presence of the holy angels and of the Lamb. And the smoke of their torment rises for ever and ever. There is no rest day or night for those who worship the beast and his image, or for anyone who receives the mark of his name.' This calls for patient endurance on the part of the saints who obey God's commandments and remain faithful to Jesus.

Then I heard a voice from heaven say, 'Write: Blessed are the dead who die in the Lord from now on.' 'Yes,' says the Spirit, 'they will rest from their labour, for their deeds will follow them.'

Revelation 14:6–13

For all the saints who from their labours rest,
Who Thee by faith before the world confessed,
Thy name, O Jesu, be for ever blest.
    Alleluia!

Thou wast their Rock, their Fortress, and their
    Might;
Thou, Lord, their Captain in the well fought fight;
Thou in the darkness drear their one true Light.
    Alleluia!

O may Thy soldiers, faithful, true, and bold,
Fight as the saints who nobly fought of old,
And win, with them, the victor's crown of gold!
    Alleluia!

William Walsham How, 1823–97

True freedom

To the Jews who had believed him, Jesus said, 'If you hold to my teaching, you are really my disciples. Then you will know the truth, and the truth will set you free.' They answered him, 'We are Abraham's descendants and have never been slaves of anyone. How can you say that we shall be set free?'

Jesus replied, 'I tell you the truth, everyone who sins is a slave to sin. Now a slave has no permanent place in the family, but a son belongs to it for ever. So if the Son sets you free, you will be free indeed. I know you are Abraham's descendants. Yet you are ready to kill me, because you have no room for my word. I am telling you what I have seen in the Father's presence, and you do what you have heard from your father.'

'Abraham is our father,' they answered. 'If you were Abraham's children,' said Jesus, 'then you would do the things Abraham did. As it is, you are determined to kill me, a man who has told you the truth that I heard from God. Abraham did not do such things. You are doing the things your own father does.' 'We are not illegitimate children,' they protested. 'The only Father we have is God himself.'

John 8:31–41

Long my imprisoned spirit lay
   Fast bound in sin and nature's night;
Thine eye diffused a quickening ray,
   I woke, the dungeon flamed with light;
My chains fell off, my heart was free,
I rose, went forth, and followed Thee.

Charles Wesley, 1707–88

Freedom in Christ

It is for freedom that Christ has set us free. Stand firm, then, and do not let yourselves be burdened again by a yoke of slavery.

Mark my words! I, Paul, tell you that if you let yourselves be circumcised, Christ will be of no value to you at all. Again I declare to every man who lets himself be circumcised that he is required to obey the whole law. You who are trying to be justified by law have been alienated from Christ; you have fallen away from grace. But by faith we eagerly await through the Spirit the righteousness for which we hope. For in Christ Jesus neither circumcision nor uncircumcision has any value. The only thing that counts is faith expressing itself through love.

You were running a good race. Who cut in on you and kept you from obeying the truth? That kind of persuasion does not come from the one who calls you. 'A little yeast works through the whole batch of dough.' I am confident in the Lord that you will take no other view. The one who is throwing you into confusion will pay the penalty, whoever he may be. Brothers, if I am still preaching circumcision, why am I still being persecuted? In that case the offence of the cross has been abolished. As for those agitators, I wish they would go the whole way and emasculate themselves.

Galatians 5:1–12

Give us holy freedom,
  Fill our hearts with love,
Draw us, holy Jesus,
  To the realms above.

George Rundle Prynne, 1818–1903

God, our friend

Now Moses used to take a tent and pitch it outside the
camp some distance away, calling it the 'tent of meeting'. Anyone enquiring of the Lord would go to the tent
of meeting outside the camp. And whenever Moses went
out to the tent, all the people rose and stood at the
entrances to their tents, watching Moses until he
entered the tent. As Moses went into the tent, the pillar
of cloud would come down and stay at the entrance,
while the Lord spoke with Moses. Whenever the people
saw the pillar of cloud standing at the entrance to the
tent, they all stood and worshipped, each at the entrance
to his tent. The Lord would speak to Moses face to face,
as a man speaks with his friend. Then Moses would
return to the camp, but his young assistant Joshua son
of Nun did not leave the tent.

Exodus 33:7–11

A man of many companions may come to ruin, but there
is a friend who sticks closer than a brother.

Proverbs 18:24

> I've found a Friend, O such a Friend,
>   So kind, and true, and tender!
> So wise a Counsellor and Guide,
>   So mighty a Defender!
> From Him who loves me now so well
>   What power my soul can sever?
> Shall life or death, or earth or hell?
>   No! I am His for ever.

James Grindlay Small, 1817–88

The final harvest

Jesus told them another parable, 'The kingdom of heaven is like a man who sowed good seed in his field. But while everyone was sleeping, his enemy came and sowed weeds among the wheat, and went away. When the wheat sprouted and formed heads, then the weeds also appeared. The owner's servants came to him and said, "Sir, didn't you sow good seed in your field? Where then did the weeds come from?" "An enemy did this," he replied. The servants asked him, "Do you want us to go and pull them up?" "No," he answered, "because while you are pulling the weeds, you may root up the wheat with them. Let both grow together until the harvest. At that time I will tell the harvesters: First collect the weeds and tie them in bundles to be burned; then gather the wheat and bring it into my barn."'

Matthew 13:24–30

All the world is God's own field,
Fruit unto His praise to yield;
Wheat and tares together sown,
Unto joy or sorrow grown;
First the blade, and then the ear,
Then the full corn shall appear:
Lord of harvest, grant that we
Wholesome grain and pure may be.

Even so, Lord, quickly come
To Thy final harvest-home:
Gather Thou Thy people in,
Free from sorrow, free from sin;
There, for ever purified,
In Thy presence to abide:
Come, with all Thine angels come,
Raise the glorious harvest-home.

Henry Alford, 1810–71

The light of God's word

Your word is a lamp to my feet and a light for my path.
I have taken an oath and confirmed it, that I will follow
your righteous laws. I have suffered much; preserve my
life, O Lord, according to your word. Accept, O Lord, the
willing praise of my mouth, and teach me your laws.
Though I constantly take my life in my hands, I will not
forget your law. The wicked have set a snare for me,
but I have not strayed from your precepts. Your statutes
are my heritage for ever; they are the joy of my heart.
My heart is set on keeping your decrees to the very end.

Psalm 119:105–112

'As the rain and the snow come down from heaven, and
do not return to it without watering the earth and
making it bud and flourish, so that it yields seed for the
sower and bread for the eater, so is my word that goes
out from my mouth: It will not return to me empty, but
will accomplish what I desire and achieve the purpose
for which I sent it.'

Isaiah 55:10–11

> O Word of God incarnate,
> O Wisdom from on high,
> O Truth unchanged, unchanging,
> O Light of our dark sky,
> We praise Thee for the radiance
> That from the hallowed page,
> A lantern to our footsteps,
> Shines on from age to age.

William Walsham How, 1823–97

Melt my heart, O God

Jesus said to the man with the shrivelled hand, 'Stand up in front of everyone.' Then Jesus asked them, 'Which is lawful on the Sabbath: to do good or to do evil, to save life or to kill?' But they remained silent.

He looked round at them in anger and, deeply distressed at their stubborn hearts, said to the man, 'Stretch out your hand.' He stretched it out, and his hand was completely restored. Then the Pharisees went out and began to plot with the Herodians how they might kill Jesus.

Mark 3:3–6

So, as the Holy Spirit says: 'Today, if you hear his voice, do not harden your hearts as you did in the rebellion, during the time of testing in the desert, where your fathers tested and tried me and for forty years saw what I did. That is why I was angry with that generation, and I said, 'Their hearts are always going astray, and they have not known my ways.' So I declared on oath in my anger, "They shall never enter my rest." '

See to it, brothers, that none of you has a sinful, unbelieving heart that turns away from the living God. But encourage one another daily, as long as it is called Today, so that none of you may be hardened by sin's deceitfulness.

Hebrews 3:7–13

> The stone to flesh again convert,
>   The veil of sin again remove;
> Sprinkle thy blood upon my heart,
>   And melt it by Thy dying love;
> This rebel heart by love subdue,
> And make it soft, and make it new.

Charles Wesley, 1707–88

To whom shall we go?

On hearing it, many of his disciples said, 'This is a hard teaching. Who can accept it?' Aware that his disciples were grumbling about this, Jesus said to them, 'Does this offend you? What if you see the Son of Man ascend to where he was before! The Spirit gives life; the flesh counts for nothing. The words I have spoken to you are spirit and they are life. Yet there are some of you who do not believe.' For Jesus had known from the beginning which of them did not believe and who would betray him. He went on to say, 'This is why I told you that no-one can come to me unless the Father has enabled him.'

From this time many of his disciples turned back and no longer followed him. 'You do not want to leave too, do you?' Jesus asked the Twelve.

Simon Peter answered him, 'Lord, to whom shall we go? You have the words of eternal life. We believe and know that you are the Holy One of God.' Then Jesus replied, 'Have I not chosen you, the Twelve? Yet one of you is a devil!' (He meant Judas, the son of Simon Iscariot, who, though one of the Twelve, was later to betray him.)

John 6:60–71

I need thee every hour, most gracious Lord;
No tender voice like Thine can peace afford.

*I need Thee, O I need Thee! every hour I need Thee;
O bless me now, my Saviour! I come to Thee.*

Annie Sherwood Hawks, 1835–1918

The fellowship of the church

But to each one of us grace has been given as Christ apportioned it. This is why it says: 'When he ascended on high, he led captives in his train and gave gifts to men.' (What does 'he ascended' mean except that he also descended to the lower, earthly regions? He who descended is the very one who ascended higher than all the heavens, in order to fill the whole universe.) It was he who gave some to be apostles, some to be prophets, some to be evangelists, and some to be pastors and teachers, to prepare God's people for works of service, so that the body of Christ may be built up until we all reach unity in the faith and in the knowledge of the Son of God and become mature, attaining to the whole measure of the fulness of Christ.

Then we will no longer be infants, tossed back and forth by the waves, and blown here and there by every wind of teaching and by the cunning and craftiness of men in their deceitful scheming. Instead, speaking the truth in love, we will in all things grow up into him who is the Head, that is, Christ. From him the whole body, joined and held together by every supporting ligament, grows and builds itself up in love, as each part does its work.

Ephesians 4:7–16

> Move and actuate and guide;
> Divers gifts to each divide;
> Placed according to Thy will,
> Let us all our work fulfil;
> Never from our office move;
> Needful to each other prove;
> Use the grace on each bestowed,
> Tempered by the art of God.

Charles Wesley, 1707–88

Joy in Jerusalem

I rejoiced with those who said to me, 'Let us go to the
house of the Lord.' Our feet are standing in your gates,
O Jerusalem.

Jerusalem is built like a city that is closely compacted
together. That is where the tribes go up, the tribes of
the Lord, to praise the name of the Lord according to the
statute given to Israel. There the thrones for judgment
stand, the thrones of the house of David.

Pray for the peace of Jerusalem: 'May those who love
you be secure. May there be peace within your walls
and security within your citadels.' For the sake of my
brothers and friends, I will say, 'Peace be within you.'
For the sake of the house of the Lord our God, I will
seek your prosperity.

Psalm 122:1–9

How pleased and blest was I
To hear the people cry,
   'Come, let us seek our God today!'
Yes, with a cheerful zeal
We haste to Zion's hill,
   And there our vows and honours pay.

My tongue repeats her vows,
Peace to this sacred house!
   For there my friends and kindred dwell;
And, since my glorious God
Makes thee His blest abode,
   My soul shall ever love thee well!

Isaac Watts, 1674–1748

The city of our God

Great is the Lord, and most worthy of praise, in the city of our God, his holy mountain. It is beautiful in its loftiness, the joy of the whole earth. Like the utmost heights of Zaphon is Mount Zion, the city of the Great King. God is in her citadels; he has shown himself to be her fortress.

As we have heard, so have we seen in the city of the Lord Almighty, in the city of our God: God makes her secure for ever.

Within your temple, O God, we meditate on your unfailing love. Like your name, O God, your praise reaches to the ends of the earth; your right hand is filled with righteousness. Mount Zion rejoices, the villages of Judah are glad because of your judgments.

Walk about Zion, go round her, count her towers, consider well her ramparts, view her citadels, that you may tell of them to the next generation. For this God is our God for ever and ever; he will be our guide even to the end.

Psalm 48:1–3, 8–14

> The hill of Zion yields
>   A thousand sacred sweets,
> Before we reach the heavenly fields,
>   Or walk the golden streets.
>
> Then let our songs abound,
>   And every tear be dry;
> We're marching through Immanuel's ground
>   To fairer worlds on high.

Isaac Watts, 1674–1748

The love of Jesus

The revelation of Jesus Christ, which God gave him to show his servants what must soon take place. He made it known by sending his angel to his servant John, who testifies to everything he saw – that is, the word of God and the testimony of Jesus Christ. Blessed is the one who reads the words of this prophecy, and blessed are those who hear it and take to heart what is written in it, because the time is near.

John, to the seven churches in the province of Asia: Grace and peace to you from him who is, and who was, and who is to come, and from the seven spirits before his throne, and from Jesus Christ, who is the faithful witness, the firstborn from the dead, and the ruler of the kings of the earth.

To him who loves us and has freed us from our sins by his blood, and has made us to be a kingdom and priests to serve his God and Father – to him be glory and power for ever and ever! Amen.

Revelation 1:1–6

Jesus loves me, this I know,
For the Bible tells me so;
Little ones to Him belong,
They are weak, but He is strong.

Yes, Jesus loves me,
Yes, Jesus loves me,
Yes, Jesus loves me,
    The Bible tells me so.

Anna Bartlett Warner, 1827–1915

Fulfilling our calling

'Blessed are you when people insult you, persecute you and falsely say all kinds of evil against you because of me. Rejoice and be glad, because great is your reward in heaven, for in the same way they persecuted the prophets who were before you.

'You are the salt of the earth. But if the salt loses its saltiness, how can it be made salty again? It is no longer good for anything, except to be thrown out and trampled by men.

'You are the light of the world. A city on a hill cannot be hidden. Neither do people light a lamp and put it under a bowl. Instead they put it on its stand, and it gives light to everyone in the house. In the same way, let your light shine before men, that they may see your good deeds and praise your Father in heaven.'

Matthew 5:11–16

A charge to keep I have,
  A God to glorify,
A never-dying soul to save,
  And fit it for the sky:

To serve the present age,
  My calling to fulfil:
O may it all my powers engage
  To do my Master's will!

Charles Wesley, 1707–88

Christ, our cornerstone

Therefore, rid yourselves of all malice and all deceit, hypocrisy, envy, and slander of every kind. Like new-born babies, crave pure spiritual milk, so that by it you may grow up in your salvation, now that you have tasted that the Lord is good.

As you come to him, the living Stone – rejected by men but chosen by God and precious to him – you also, like living stones, are being built into a spiritual house to be a holy priesthood, offering spiritual sacrifices acceptable to God through Jesus Christ. For in Scripture it says: 'See, I lay a stone in Zion, a chosen and precious cornerstone, and the one who trusts in him will never put to shame.'

Now to you who believe, this stone is precious. But to those who do not believe, 'The stone the builders rejected has become the capstone,' and, 'A stone that causes men to stumble and a rock that makes them fall.'

They stumble because they disobey the message – which is also what they were destined for.

1 Peter 2:1–8

Christ is our Corner-stone,
  On him alone we build;
With His true saints alone
  The courts of heaven are filled;
On His great love
  Our hopes we place
  Of present grace
And joys above.

Latin, 6th or 7th century
tr. John Chandler, 1806–76

Seeing the king

He who walks righteously and speaks what is right, who rejects gain from extortion and keeps his hand from accepting bribes, who stops his ears against plots of murder and shuts his eyes against contemplating evil – that is the man who will dwell on the heights, whose refuge will be the mountain fortress. His bread will be supplied, and water will not fail him.

Your eyes will see the king in his beauty and view a land that stretches afar. In your thoughts you will ponder the former terror: 'Where is that chief officer? Where is the one who took the revenue? Where is the officer in charge of the towers?' You will see those arrogant people no more, those people of an obscure speech, with their strange, incomprehensible tongue.

Look upon Zion, the city of our festivals; your eyes will see Jerusalem, a peaceful abode, a tent that will not be moved; its stakes will never be pulled up, nor any of its ropes broken. There the Lord will be our Mighty One. It will be like a place of broad rivers and streams.

Isaiah 33:15–21

The King there, in His beauty,
  Without a veil is seen;
It were a well-spent journey,
  Though seven deaths lay between;
The Lamb with His fair army
  Doth on Mount Zion stand,
And glory, glory dwelleth
  In Immanuel's land.

The bride eyes not her garment,
  But her dear bridegroom's face;
I will not gaze at glory,
  But on my King of grace;
Not at the crown He giveth,
  But on His pierced hand:
The Lamb is all the glory
  Of Immanuel's land.

Anne Ross Cousin, 1824–1906

Delighting in the Lord

Lord, you have assigned me my portion and my cup; you have made my lot secure. The boundary lines have fallen for me in pleasant places; surely I have a delightful inheritance.

I will praise the Lord, who counsels me; even at night my heart instructs me. I have set the Lord always before me. Because he is at my right hand, I shall not be shaken.

Therefore my heart is glad and my tongue rejoices; my body also will rest secure, because you will not abandon me to the grave, nor will you let your Holy One see decay. You have made known to me the path of life; you will fill me with joy in your presence, with eternal pleasures at your right hand.

Psalm 16:5–11

> Jesus, the very thought of Thee
>   With sweetness fills my breast;
> But sweeter far Thy face to see,
>   And in Thy presence rest.
>
> Jesus, our only joy be Thou,
>   As Thou our prize wilt be;
> Jesus, be thou our glory now,
>   And through eternity.

Bernard of Clairvaux, 1091–1153
tr. Edward Caswall, 1814–78

Finishing the course

In the presence of God and of Christ Jesus, who will judge the living and the dead, and in view of his appearing and his kingdom, I give you this charge: Preach the Word; be prepared in season and out of season; correct, rebuke and encourage – with great patience and careful instruction. For the time will come when men will not put up with sound doctrine. Instead, to suit their own desires, they will gather around them a great number of teachers to say what their itching ears want to hear. They will turn their ears away from the truth and turn aside to myths. But you, keep your head in all situations, endure hardship, do the work of an evangelist, discharge all the duties of your ministry.

For I am already being poured out like a drink offering, and the time has come for my departure. I have fought the good fight, I have finished the race, I have kept the faith. Now there is in store for me the crown of righteousness, which the Lord, the righteous Judge, will award to me on that day – and not only to me, but also to all who have longed for his appearing.

2 Timothy 4:1–8

Run the straight race through God's good grace,
Lift up thine eyes and seek His face;
Life with its path before thee lies,
Christ is the way, and Christ the prize.

Faint not nor fear, His arms are near;
He changeth not, and thou art dear;
Only believe, and thou shalt see
That Christ is all in all to thee.

John Samuel Bewley Monsell, 1811–75

The giver of all things

'Praise be to you, O Lord, God of our father Israel, from everlasting to everlasting. Yours, O Lord, is the greatness and the power and the glory and the majesty and the splendour, for everything in heaven and earth is yours. Yours, O Lord, is the kingdom; you are exalted as head over all. Wealth and honour come from you; you are the ruler of all things. In your hands are strength and power to exalt and give strength to all. Now, our God, we give you thanks, and praise your glorious name.

'But who am I, and who are my people, that we should be able to give as generously as this? Everything comes from you, and we have given you only what comes from your hand. We are aliens and strangers in your sight, as were all our forefathers. Our days on earth are like a shadow, without hope. O Lord our God, as for all this abundance that we have provided for building you a temple for your Holy Name, it comes from your hand, and all of it belongs to you. I know, my God, that you test the heart, and are pleased with integrity.

1 Chronicles 29:10–16

O Lord of heaven, and earth, and sea,
To Thee all praise and glory be;
How shall we show our love to Thee,
    Who givest all?

To Thee, from whom we all derive
Our life, our gifts, our power to give!
O may we ever with Thee live,
    Who givest all!

Christopher Wordsworth, 1807–85

Loving the Saviour

Let him kiss me with the kisses of his mouth – for your love is more delightful than wine. Pleasing is the fragrance of your perfumes; your name is like perfume poured out. No wonder the maidens love you! Take me away with you – let us hurry! Let the king bring me into his chambers.

We rejoice and delight in you; we will praise your love more than wine.

How right they are to adore you!

Song of Songs 1:2–4

Now one of the Pharisees invited Jesus to have dinner with him, so he went to the Pharisee's house and reclined at the table. When a woman who had lived a sinful life in that town learned that Jesus was eating at the Pharisee's house, she brought an alabaster jar of perfume, and as she stood behind him at his feet weeping, she began to wet his feet with her tears. Then she wiped them with her hair, kissed them and poured perfume on them.

Luke 7:36–38

There is a Name I love to hear;
    I love to sing its worth;
It sounds like music in mine ear,
    The sweetest Name on earth.

*O how I love the Saviour's name,
    The sweetest name on earth.*

Jesus, the Name I love so well,
    The Name I love to hear:
No saint on earth its worth can tell,
    No heart conceive how dear.

Frederick Whitfield, 1829–1904

The great shepherd

You who bring good tidings to Zion, go up on a high mountain. You who bring good tidings to Jerusalem, lift up your voice with a shout, lift it up, do not be afraid; say to the towns of Judah, 'Here is your God!' See, the Sovereign Lord comes with power, and his arm rules for him. See, his reward is with him, and his recompense accompanies him. He tends his flocks like a shepherd: He gathers the lambs in his arms and carries them close to his heart; he gently leads those that have young.

Isaiah 40:9–11

' "For this is what the Sovereign Lord says: I myself will search for my sheep and look after them. As a shepherd looks after his scattered flock when he is with them, so will I look after my sheep. I will rescue them from all the places where they were scattered on a day of clouds and darkness. I will bring them out from the nations and gather them from the countries, and I will bring them into their own land. I will pasture them on the mountains of Israel, in the ravines and in all the settlements in the land. I will tend them in a good pasture, and the mountain heights of Israel will be their grazing land. There they will lie down in good grazing land, and there they will feed in a rich pasture on the mountains of Israel. I myself will tend my sheep and make them lie down, declares the Sovereign Lord. I will search for the lost and bring back the strays. I will bind up the injured and strengthen the weak, but the sleek and the strong I will destroy. I will shepherd the flock with justice." '

Ezekiel 34:11–16

Saviour, like a shepherd lead us,
  Much we need Thy tender care;
In Thy pleasant pastures feed us;
  For our use Thy folds prepare:
    Blessed Jesus!
  Thou hast bought us, Thine we are.

Anonymous

As white as snow

Hear the word of the Lord, you rulers of Sodom; listen to the law of our God, you people of Gomorrah! 'The multitude of your sacrifices – what are they to me?' says the Lord. 'I have more than enough of burnt offerings, of rams and the fat of fattened animals; I have no pleasure in the blood of bulls and lambs and goats. . . . Stop bringing meaningless offerings! Your incense is detestable to me. New Moons, Sabbaths and convocations – I cannot bear your evil assemblies. Your New Moon festivals and your appointed feasts my soul hates. They have become a burden to me; I am weary of bearing them. When you spread out your hands in prayer, I will hide my eyes from you; even if you offer many prayers, I will not listen. Your hands are full of blood; wash and make yourselves clean. Take your evil deeds out of my sight! Stop doing wrong, learn to do right! Seek justice, encourage the oppressed. Defend the cause of the fatherless, plead the case of the widow.

'Come now, let us reason together,' says the Lord. 'Though your sins are like scarlet, they shall be as white as snow, though they are red as crimson, they shall be like wool.

Isaiah 1:10–18

What a wonderful redemption!
  Never can a mortal know
How my sin, tho' red like crimson,
  Can be whiter than the snow.

All that thrills my soul is Jesus;
  He is more than life to me;
And the fairest of ten thousand,
  In my blessed Lord I see.

Thoro Harris

The Lord's servant

'Here is my servant, whom I uphold, my chosen one in whom I delight; I will put my Spirit on him and he will bring justice to the nations. He will not shout or cry out, or raise his voice in the streets. A bruised reed he will not break, and a smouldering wick he will not snuff out. In faithfulness he will bring forth justice; he will not falter or be discouraged till he establishes justice on earth. In his law the islands will put their hope.'

This is what God the Lord says – he who created the heavens and stretched them out, who spread out the earth and all that comes out of it, who gives breath to its people, and life to those who walk on it: 'I, the Lord, have called you in righteousness; I will take hold of your hand. I will keep you and will make you to be a covenant for the people and a light for the Gentiles, to open eyes that are blind, to free captives from prison and to release from the dungeon those who sit in darkness.'

Isaiah 42:1–7

> With joy we meditate the grace
> Of our High Priest above;
> His heart is made of tenderness,
> And overflows with love.
>
> He'll never quench the smoking flax,
> But raise it to a flame;
> The bruised reed He never breaks,
> Nor scorns the meanest name.
>
> Then let our humble faith address
> His mercy and His power:
> We shall obtain delivering grace
> In the distressing hour.

Isaac Watts, 1674–1784

Clothed in God's righteousness

'For I, the Lord, love justice; I hate robbery and iniquity.
In my faithfulness I will reward them and make an
everlasting covenant with them. Their descendants will
be known among the nations and their offspring among
the peoples. All who see them will acknowledge that
they are a people the Lord has blessed.'

I delight greatly in the Lord; my soul rejoices in my
God. For he has clothed me with garments of salvation
and arrayed me in a robe of righteousness, as a
bridegroom adorns his head like a priest, and as a bride
adorns herself with her jewels. For as the soil makes
the young plant come up and a garden causes seeds to
grow, so the Sovereign Lord will make righteousness
and praise spring up before all nations.

Isaiah 61:8–11

A debtor to mercy alone,
  Of covenant mercy I sing;
Nor fear, with Thy righteousness on,
  My person and offering to bring;
The terrors of law and of God
  With me can have nothing to do;
My Saviour's obedience and blood
  Hide all my transgressions from view.

Augustus Montague Toplady, 1740–78

Resting in God

Therefore, since the promise of entering his rest still
stands, let us be careful that none of you be found to
have fallen short of it. For we also have had the gospel
preached to us, just as they did; but the message they
heard was of no value to them, because those who heard
did not combine it with faith. Now we who have believed
enter that rest, just as God has said, "So I declared on
oath in my anger, "They shall never enter my rest.'"
And yet his work has been finished since the creation
of the world. For somewhere he has spoken about the
seventh day in these words: 'And on the seventh day
God rested from all his work.' And again in the passage
above he says, 'They shall never enter my rest.'

Hebrews 4:1–5

O give Thine own sweet rest to me,
That I may speak with soothing power
A word in season, as from thee,
To weary ones in needful hour.

Frances Ridley Havergal, 1836–79

Commitment from the heart

So whether you eat or drink or whatever you do, do it all for the glory of God. Do not cause anyone to stumble, whether Jews, Greeks or the church of God – even as I try to please everybody in every way. For I am not seeking my own good but the good of many, so that they may be saved. Follow my example, as I follow the example of Christ.

1 Corinthians 10:31–11:1

The end of all things is near. Therefore be clear minded and self-controlled so that you can pray. Above all, love each other deeply, because love covers over a multitude of sins. Offer hospitality to one another without grumbling. Each one should use whatever gift he has received to serve others, faithfully administering God's grace in its various forms. If anyone speaks, he should do it as one speaking the very words of God. If anyone serves, he should do it with the strength God provides, so that in all things God may be praised through Jesus Christ. To him be the glory and the power for ever and ever. Amen.

1 Peter 4:7–11

Fill every part of me with praise;
Let all my being speak
Of thee and of Thy love, O Lord,
Poor though I be and weak.

So shall no part of day or night
From sacredness be free;
But all my life, in every step,
Be fellowship with Thee.

Horatius Bonar, 1808–89

Loved with everlasting love

'At that time,' declares the Lord, 'I will be the God of all the clans of Israel, and they will be my people.'

This is what the Lord says: 'The people who survive the sword will find favour in the desert; I will come to give rest to Israel.'

The Lord appeared to us in the past, saying: 'I have loved you with an everlasting love; I have drawn you with loving-kindness. I will build you up again and you will be rebuilt, O Virgin Israel. Again you will take up your tambourines and go out to dance with the joyful. Again you will plant vineyards on the hills of Samaria; the farmers will plant them and enjoy their fruit. There will be a day when watchmen cry out on the hills of Ephraim, "Come, let us go to Zion, to the Lord our God." '

Jeremiah 31:1–6

Loved with everlasting love,
    Led by grace that love to know,
Spirit, breathing from above,
    Thou hast taught me it is so.
O this full and perfect peace!
    O this transport all divine!
In a love which cannot cease,
    I am His and He is mine.

George Wade Robinson, 1838–77

Coming to life

'Son of man, can these bones live?' I said, 'O Sovereign Lord, you alone know.' Then he said to me, 'Prophesy to these bones and say to them, "Dry bones, hear the word of the Lord! This is what the Sovereign Lord says to these bones: I will make breath enter you, and you will come to life. I will attach tendons to you and make flesh come upon you and cover you with skin; I will put breath in you, and you will come to life. Then you will know that I am the Lord."'

So I prophesied as I was commanded. And as I was prophesying, there was a noise, a rattling sound, and the bones came together, bone to bone. I looked, and tendons and flesh appeared on them and skin covered them, but there was no breath in them.

Then he said to me, 'Prophesy to the breath; prophesy, son of man, and say to it, "This is what the Sovereign Lord says: Come from the four winds, O breath, and breathe into these slain, that they may live."' So I prophesied as he commanded me, and breath entered them; they came to life and stood up on their feet – a vast army.

Ezekiel 37:3–10

God, who is rich in mercy, made us alive with Christ even when we were dead in transgressions – it is by grace you have been saved.

Ephesians 2:4–5

Lord, I was dead! I could not stir
　My lifeless soul to come to Thee;
But now, since Thou hast quickened me,
　I rise from sin's dark sepulchre.

William Tidd Matson, 1833–99

Into Christ's fold

'I tell you the truth, the man who does not enter the sheep pen by the gate, but climbs in by some other way, is a thief and a robber. The man who enters by the gate is the shepherd of his sheep. The watchman opens the gate for him, and the sheep listen to his voice. He calls his own sheep by name and leads them out. When he has brought out all his own, he goes on ahead of them, and his sheep follow him because they know his voice. But they will never follow a stranger; in fact, they will run away from him because they do not recognise a stranger's voice.' Jesus used this figure of speech, but they did not understand what he was telling them.

Therefore Jesus said again, 'I tell you the truth, I am the gate for the sheep. All who ever came before me were thieves and robbers, but the sheep did not listen to them. I am the gate; whoever enters through me will be saved. He will come in and go out, and find pasture. The thief comes only to steal and kill and destroy; I have come that they may have life, and have it to the full.'

John 10:1–10

> Out of the fear and dread of the tomb,
>   Jesus, I come; Jesus, I come;
> Into the joy and light of Thy home,
>   Jesus, I come to Thee.
> Out of the depths of ruin untold,
> Into the peace of Thy sheltering fold,
> Ever Thy glorious face to behold,
>   Jesus, I come to Thee.

William True Sleeper, 1840–1920

Returning to God

'Come, let us return to the Lord. He has torn us to pieces but he will heal us; he has injured us but he will bind up our wounds. After two days he will revive us; on the third day he will restore us, that we may live in his presence. Let us acknowledge the Lord; let us press on to acknowledge him. As surely as the sun rises, he will appear; he will come to us like the winter rains, like the spring rains that water the earth.'

'What can I do with you, Ephraim? What can I do with you, Judah? Your love is like the morning mist, like the early dew that disappears.'

Hosea 6:1–4

Come, let us to the Lord our God
    With contrite hearts return:
Our God is gracious, nor will leave
    The desolate to mourn.

Long hath the night of sorrow reigned;
    The dawn shall bring us light;
God shall appear, and we shall rise
    With gladness in His sight.

Our hearts, if God we seek to know,
    Shall know Him and rejoice;
His coming like the morn shall be,
    Like morning songs His voice.

Scottish Paraphrases, 1781

Preparing to meet God

'Therefore this is what I will do to you, Israel, and because I will do this to you, prepare to meet your God, O Israel.' He who forms the mountains, creates the wind, and reveals his thoughts to man, he who turns dawn to darkness, and treads the high places of the earth – the Lord God Almighty is his name.

Hear this word, O house of Israel, this lament I take up concerning you: 'Fallen is Virgin Israel, never to rise again, deserted in her own land, with no-one to lift her up.'

This is what the Sovereign Lord says: 'The city that marches out a thousand strong for Israel will have only a hundred left; the town that marches out a hundred strong will have only ten left.'

This is what the Lord says to the house of Israel: 'Seek me and live; do not seek Bethel, do not go to Gilgal, do not journey to Beersheba. For Gilgal will surely go into exile, and Bethel will be reduced to nothing.' Seek the Lord and live, or he will sweep through the house of Joseph like a fire; it will devour, and Bethel will have no-one to quench it.

Amos 4:12–5:6

Prepare me, gracious God,
　　To stand before Thy face!
Thy Spirit must the work perform,
　　For it is all of grace.

In Christ's obedience clothe,
　　And wash me in His blood:
So shall I lift my head with joy
　　Among the sons of God.

Robert Elliott, 1763

The triumph of God's kingdom

In the last days the mountain of the Lord's temple will be established as chief among the mountains; it will be raised above the hills, and peoples will stream to it.

Many nations will come and say, 'Come, let us go to the mountain of the Lord, to the house of the God of Jacob. He will teach us his ways, so that we may walk in his paths.' The law will go out from Zion, the word of the Lord from Jerusalem. He will judge between many peoples and will settle disputes for strong nations far and wide. They will beat their swords into ploughshares and their spears into pruning hooks. Nation will not take up sword against nation, nor will they train for war any more. Every man will sit under his own vine and under his own fig-tree, and no-one will make them afraid, for the Lord Almighty has spoken. All the nations may walk in the name of their gods; we will walk in the name of the Lord our God for ever and ever.
Micah 4 : 1 – 5

Jesus, immortal King, go on;
The glorious day will soon be won;
Thine enemies prepare to flee,
And leave the conquered world to Thee.

Then shall contending nations rest,
For love shall reign in every breast;
Weapons, for war designed, shall cease,
Or then be implements of peace.

Thomas Kelly, 1769 – 1855

The way to life

O Lord, are you not from everlasting? My God, my Holy
One, we will not die. O Lord, you have appointed them
to execute judgment; O Rock, you have ordained them
to punish. Your eyes are too pure to look on evil; you
cannot tolerate wrong. Why then do you tolerate the
treacherous? Why are you silent while the wicked swallow up those more righteous than themselves?

Habakkuk 1:12–13

With what shall I come before the Lord and bow down
before the exalted God? Shall I come before him with
burnt offerings, with calves a year old? Will the Lord
be pleased with thousands of rams, with ten thousand
rivers of oil? Shall I offer my firstborn for my transgression, the fruit of my body for the sin of my soul? He
has showed you, O man, what is good. And what does
the Lord require of you? To act justly and to love mercy
and to walk humbly with your God.

Micah 6:6–8

> Wherewith, O God, Shall I draw near,
>   And bow myself before Thy face?
> How in Thy purer eyes appear?
>   What shall I bring to gain Thy grace?
>
> Jesus, the Lamb of God, hath bled;
>   He bore our sins upon the tree;
> Beneath our curse He bowed His head;
>   'Tis finished! He hath died for me!
>
> Who'er to Thee themselves approve
>   Must take the path Thy Word hath showed,
> Justice pursue, and mercy love,
>   And humbly walk by faith with God.

Charles Wesley, 1707–88

When all is dark

Who among you fears the Lord and obeys the word of his servant? Let him who walks in the dark, who has no light, trust in the name of the Lord and rely on his God. But now, all you who light fires and provide yourselves with flaming torches, go, walk in the light of your fires and of the torches you have set ablaze. This is what you shall receive from my hand: You will lie down in torment.

'Listen to me, you who pursue righteousness and who seek the Lord: Look to the rock from which you were cut and to the quarry from which you were hewn; look to Abraham, your father, and to Sarah, who gave you birth. When I called him he was but one, and I blessed him and made him many. The Lord will surely comfort Zion and will look with compassion on all her ruins; he will make her deserts like Eden, her wastelands like the garden of the Lord. Joy and gladness will be found in her, thanksgiving and the sound of singing.'

Isaiah 50:10–51:3

Lead, kindly Light, amid the encircling gloom
   Lead Thou me on!
The night is dark, and I am far from home;
   Lead Thou me on!
Keep Thou my feet; I do not ask to see
The distant scene; one step enough for me.

John Henry Newman, 1801–90

Heirs of God, co-heirs with Christ

Now if we are children, then we are heirs – heirs of God and co-heirs with Christ, if indeed we share in his sufferings in order that we may also share in his glory.

I consider that our present sufferings are not worth comparing with the glory that will be revealed in us. The creation waits in eager expectation for the sons of God to be revealed. For the creation was subjected to frustration, not by its own choice, but by the will of the one who subjected it, in hope that the creation itself will be liberated from its bondage to decay and brought into the glorious freedom of the children of God.

Romans 8:17–21

What from Christ that soul shall sever,
    Bound by everlasting bands?
Once in Him, in Him for ever,
    Thus the eternal cov'nant stands:
      None shall pluck thee
From the Strength of Israel's hands.

Heirs of God, joint-heirs with Jesus,
    Long ere time its race begun;
To His Name eternal praises;
    O what wonders He hath done!
      One with Jesus,
By eternal union one.

John Kent, 1766–1843

The work of the Holy Spirit

We know that the whole creation has been groaning as in the pains of childbirth right up to the present time. Not only so, but we ourselves, who have the firstfruits of the Spirit, groan inwardly as we wait eagerly for our adoption as sons, the redemption of our bodies. For in this hope we were saved. But hope that is seen is no hope at all. Who hopes for what he already has? But if we hope for what we do not yet have, we wait for it patiently.

In the same way, the Spirit helps us in our weakness. We do not know what we ought to pray for, but the Spirit himself intercedes for us with groans that words cannot express.

Romans 8:22–26

His Holy Spirit dwelleth
　Within my willing heart,
Tames it, when it rebelleth,
　And soothes the keenest smart;
And when my soul is lying
　Weak, trembling and oppressed,
He pleads with groans and sighing
　That cannot be expressed.

To mine His Spirit speaketh
　Sweet words of soothing power,
How God, for him that seeketh
　For rest, hath rest in store:
There God Himself prepareth
　My heritage and lot,
And though my body weareth,
　My heaven shall fail me not.

Paul Gerhardt, 1607–76
tr. Richard Massie, 1800–87

More than conquerors

What, then, shall we say in response to this? If God is for us, who can be against us? He who did not spare his own Son, but gave him up for us all – how will he not also, along with him, graciously give us all things? Who will bring any charge against those whom God has chosen? It is God who justifies. Who is he that condemns? Christ Jesus, who died – more than that, who was raised to life – is at the right hand of God and is also interceding for us. Who shall separate us from the love of Christ? Shall trouble or hardship or persecution or famine or nakedness or danger or sword? As it is written: 'For your sake we face death all day long; we are considered as sheep to be slaughtered.' No, in all these things we are more than conquerors through him who loved us. For I am convinced that neither death nor life, neither angels nor demons, neither the present nor the future, nor any powers, neither height nor depth, nor anything else in all creation, will be able to separate us from the love of God that is in Christ Jesus our Lord.

Romans 8:31–39

No more we doubt Thee, glorious Prince of life;
Life is nought without Thee: aid us in our strife,
Make us more than conquerors, through Thy
   deathless love;
Bring us safe through Jordan to Thy home above.

Thine be the glory, risen, conquering Son,
Endless is the victory Thou o'er death hast won!

Edmond Louis Budry, 1854–1932
tr. Richard Birch Hoyle, 1875–1939

Do not worry

'And why do you worry about clothes? See how the lilies of the field grow. They do not labour or spin. Yet I tell you that not even Solomon in all his splendour was dressed like one of these. If that is how God clothes the grass of the field, which is here today and tomorrow is thrown into the fire, will he not much more clothe you, O you of little faith? So do not worry, saying, 'What shall we eat?' or 'What shall we drink?' or 'What shall we wear?' For the pagans run after all these things, and your heavenly Father knows that you need them. But seek first his kingdom and his righteousness, and all these things will be given to you as well. Therefore do not worry about tomorrow, for tomorrow will worry about itself. Each day has enough trouble of its own.'

Matthew 6:28–34

Seek ye his first God's peace and blessing –
Ye have all if this possessing;
Come, your need and sin confessing:
　　Seek him first.

Seek this first, His promise trying –
It is sure, all need supplying;
Heavenly things – on Him relying –
　　Seek ye first.

Georgianna Mary Taylor, 1848–1915

Built on rock

'Therefore everyone who hears these words of mine and puts them into practice is like a wise man who built his house on the rock. The rain came down, the streams rose, and the winds blew and beat against that house, yet it did not fall, because it had its foundation on the rock. But everyone who hears these words of mine and does not put them into practice is like a foolish man who built his house on sand. The rain came down, the streams rose, and the winds blew and beat against that house, and it fell with a great crash.'

When Jesus had finished saying these things, the crowds were amazed at his teaching, because he taught as one who had authority, and not as their teachers of the law.

Matthew 7:24–29

When darkness seems to veil His face,
I rest on His unchanging grace;
In every high and stormy gale
My anchor holds within the veil.

On Christ, the solid Rock, I stand;
All other ground is sinking sand.

His oath, His covenant, and blood
Support me in the 'whelming flood:
When all around my soul gives way,
He then is all my hope and stay.

Edward Mote, 1797–1874,
and others

The gentle Father

As a father has compassion on his children, so the Lord has compassion on those who fear him; for he knows how we are formed, he remembers that we are dust. As for man, his days are like grass, he flourishes like a flower of the field; the wind blows over it and it is gone, and its place remembers it no more. But from everlasting to everlasting the Lord's love is with those who fear him, and his righteousness with their children's children – with those who keep his covenant and remember to obey his precepts.

The Lord has established his throne in heaven, and his kingdom rules over all.

Psalm 103:13–19

Father-like, He tends and spares us,
    Well our feeble frame He knows;
In His hands He gently bears us,
    Rescues us from all our foes:
        Praise Him! Praise Him!
    Widely as His mercy flows.

Frail as summer's flower we flourish;
    Blows the wind, and it is gone;
But while mortals rise and perish
    God endures unchanging on.
        Praise Him! Praise Him!
    Praise the high eternal One.

Henry Francis Lyte, 1793–1847

Calming the storm

That day when evening came, he said to his disciples,
'Let us go over to the other side.' Leaving the crowd
behind, they took him along, just as he was, in the boat.
There were also other boats with him. A furious squall
came up, and the waves broke over the boat, so that it
was nearly swamped. Jesus was in the stern, sleeping
on a cushion. The disciples woke him and said to him,
'Teacher, don't you care if we drown?'

He got up, rebuked the wind and said to the waves,
'Quiet! Be still!' Then the wind died down and it was
completely calm.

He said to his disciples, 'Why are you so afraid? Do
you still have no faith?'

They were terrified and asked each other, 'Who is
this? Even the wind and the waves obey him!'

Mark 4:35–41

Praise to the Lord, Who, when tempests their
    warfare are waging,
Who, when the elements madly around Thee are
    raging,
  Biddeth them cease,
  Turneth their fury to peace,
Whirlwinds and waters assuaging.

Joachim Neander, 1650–80
tr. Catherine Winkworth, 1829–78, and others

The friend of sinners

'I tell you, among those born of women there is no-one greater than John; yet the one who is least in the kingdom of God is greater than he.' (All the people, even the tax collectors, when they heard Jesus' words, acknowledged that God's way was right, because they had been baptised by John. But the Pharisees and experts in the law rejected God's purpose for themselves, because they had not been baptised by John.)

'To what, then, can I compare the people of this generation? What are they like? They are like children sitting in the market-place and calling out to each other: "We played the flute for you, and you did not dance; we sang a dirge, and you did not cry." For John the Baptist came neither eating bread nor drinking wine, and you say, "He has a demon." The Son of Man came eating and drinking, and you say, "Here is a glutton and a drunkard, a friend of tax collectors and 'sinners'." But wisdom is proved right by all her children.'

Luke 7:28–35

One there is above all others,
  Well deserves the name of Friend;
His is love beyond a brother's,
  Costly, free, and knows no end:
They who once His kindness prove,
Find it everlasting love.

When He lived on earth abased
  'Friend of sinners' was His Name;
Now above all glory raised,
  He rejoices in the same;
Still He calls them brethren, friends,
And to all their wants attends.

John Newton, 1725–1807

Bearing fruit for God

'A farmer went out to sow his seed. As he was scattering the seed, some fell along the path; it was trampled on, and the birds of the air ate it up. Some fell on rock, and when it came up, the plants withered because they had no moisture. Other seed fell among thorns, which grew up with it and choked the plants. Still other seed fell on good soil. It came up and yielded a crop, a hundred times more than was sown.'

'This is the meaning of the parable: The seed is the word of God. Those along the path are the ones who hear, and then the devil comes and takes away the word from their hearts, so that they may not believe and be saved. Those on the rock are the ones who receive the word with joy when they hear it, but they have no root. They believe for a while, but in the time of testing they fall away. The seed that fell among thorns stands for those who hear, but as they go on their way they are choked by life's worries, riches and pleasures, and they do not mature. But the seed on good soil stands for those with a noble and good heart, who hear the word, retain it, and by persevering produce a crop.

Luke 8:5–8, 11–15

Let not the foe of Christ and man
    This holy seed remove,
But give it root in every heart
    To bring forth fruits of love.

Let not the world's deceitful cares
    The rising plant destroy,
But let it yield a hundredfold
    The fruits of peace and joy.

John Cawood, 1775–1852

Our king of glory

Then he [Jesus] said to them all: 'If anyone would come after me, he must deny himself and take up his cross daily and follow me. For whoever wants to save his life will lose it, but whoever loses his life for me will save it. What good is it for a man to gain the whole world, and yet lose or forfeit his very self? If anyone is ashamed of me and my words, the Son of Man will be ashamed of him when he comes in his glory and in the glory of the Father and of the holy angels.'   *Luke 9:23–26*

Therefore God exalted him [Christ Jesus] to the highest place and gave him the name that is above every name, that at the name of Jesus every knee should bow, in heaven and on earth and under the earth, and every tongue confess that Jesus Christ is Lord, to the glory of God the Father.   *Philippians 2:9–11*

> At the Name of Jesus
>   Every knee shall bow,
> Every tongue confess Him
>   King of glory now.
> 'Tis the Father's pleasure
>   We should call Him Lord,
> Who from the beginning
>   Was the mighty Word.
>
> Brothers, this Lord Jesus
>   Shall return again
> With His Father's glory,
>   With His angel train;
> For all wreaths of empire
>   Meet upon His brow,
> And our hearts confess Him
>   King of glory now.

Caroline Maria Noel, 1817–77

The harvest field

Jesus went through all the towns and villages, teaching in their synagogues, preaching the good news of the kingdom and healing every disease and sickness. When he saw the crowds, he had compassion on them, because they were harassed and helpless, like sheep without a shepherd. Then he said to his disciples, 'The harvest is plentiful but the workers are few. Ask the Lord of the harvest, therefore, to send out workers into his harvest field.'

Matthew 9:35–38

Revive us, Lord! Is zeal abating
   While harvest fields are vast and white?
Revive us, Lord, the world is waiting,
   Equip Thy church to spread the light.

Elizabeth A. P. Head, 1850–1936

Let earth receive the king

Sing to the Lord a new song, for he has done marvellous things; his right hand and his holy arm have worked salvation for him. The Lord has made his salvation known and revealed his righteousness to the nations. He has remembered his love and his faithfulness to the house of Israel; all the ends of the earth have seen the salvation of our God.

Shout for joy to the Lord, all the earth, burst into jubilant song with music; make music to the Lord with the harp, with the harp and the sound of singing, with trumpets and the blast of the ram's horn – shout for joy before the Lord, the King.

Let the sea resound, and everything in it, the world, and all who live in it. Let the rivers clap their hands, let the mountains sing together for joy; let them sing before the Lord, for he comes to judge the earth. He will judge the world in righteousness and the peoples with equity.

Psalm 98:1–9

Joy to the world! the Lord is come!
    Let earth receive her King;
Let every heart prepare Him room,
    And heaven and nature sing.

Joy to the earth! the Saviour reigns!
    Let men their songs employ;
While fields and floods, rocks, hills and plains,
    Repeat the sounding joy.

He rules the world with truth and grace,
    And makes the nations prove
The glories of His righteousness,
    The wonders of His love.

Isaac Watts, 1674–1748

Our Lord God Almighty reigns!

The twenty-four elders and the four living creatures fell down and worshipped God, who was seated on the throne. And they cried: 'Amen, Hallelujah!'

Then a voice came from the throne, saying: 'Praise our God, all you his servants, you who fear him, both small and great!'

Then I heard what sounded like a great multitude, like the roar of rushing waters and like loud peals of thunder, shouting: 'Hallelujah! For our Lord God Almighty reigns. Let us rejoice and be glad and give him glory! For the wedding of the Lamb has come, and his bride has made herself ready. Fine linen, bright and clean, was given her to wear.' (Fine linen stands for the righteous acts of the saints.)

Then the angel said to me, 'Write: "Blessed are those who are invited to the wedding supper of the Lamb!"' And he added, 'These are the true words of God.'

At this I fell at his feet to worship him. But he said to me, 'Do not do it! I am a fellow-servant with you and with your brothers who hold to the testimony of Jesus. Worship God! For the testimony of Jesus is the spirit of prophecy.'

Revelation 19:4–10

He reigns! ye saints, exalt your strains:
Your God is King, your Father reigns;
And He is at the Father's side,
The Man of love, the Crucified.

One Lord, one empire, all secures:
He reigns – and life and death are yours;
Through earth and heaven one song shall ring,
'The Lord Omnipotent is King!'

Josiah Conder, 1789–1855

Looking at Christ

'And I will pour out on the house of David and the inhabitants of Jerusalem a spirit of grace and supplication. They will look on me, the one they have pierced, and they will mourn for him as one mourns for an only child, and grieve bitterly for him as one grieves for a firstborn son.'

Zechariah 12:10

One of the soldiers pierced Jesus' side with a spear, bringing a sudden flow of blood and water. The man who saw it has given testimony, and his testimony is true. He knows that he tells the truth, and he testifies so that you also may believe. These things happened so that the scripture would be fulfilled: 'Not one of his bones will be broken,' and, as another scripture says, 'They will look on the one they have pierced.'

John 19:34–37

Since we have been justified through faith, we have peace with God through our Lord Jesus Christ.

Romans 5:1

I hear the words of love,
  I gaze upon the blood,
I see the mighty sacrifice,
  And I have peace with God.

'Tis everlasting peace,
  Sure as Jehovah's Name;
'Tis stable as His steadfast throne,
  For evermore the same.

Horatius Bonar, 1808–89

Loving God

Hear, O Israel: The Lord our God, the Lord is one. Love the Lord your God with all your heart and with all your soul and with all your strength. These commandments that I give you today are to be upon your hearts. Impress them on your children. Talk about them when you sit at home and when you walk along the road, when you lie down and when you get up. Tie them as symbols on your hands and bind them on your foreheads. Write them on the door-frames of your houses and on your gates.

Deuteronomy 6:4–9

'Teacher, which is the greatest commandment in the Law?'

Jesus replied: ' "Love the Lord your God with all your heart and with all your soul and with all your mind." This is the first and greatest commandment. And the second is like it: "Love your neighbour as yourself." All the Law and the Prophets hang on these two commandments.'

Matthew 22:36–40

Thee will I love, my strength, my tower,
Thee will I love, my joy, my crown,
Thee will I love with all my power,
In all Thy works, and Thee alone;
Thee will I love, till the pure fire
Fill my whole soul with chaste desire.

Johann Scheffler, 1624–77
tr. John Wesley, 1703–91

Watching for the Lord's coming

'Be dressed ready for service and keep your lamps burning, like men waiting for their master to return from a wedding banquet, so that when he comes and knocks they can immediately open the door for him. It will be good for those servants whose master finds them watching when he comes. I tell you the truth, he will dress himself to serve, will have them recline at the table and will come and wait on them. It will be good for those servants whose master finds them ready, even if he comes in the second or third watch of the night. But understand this: If the owner of the house had known at what hour the thief was coming, he would not have let his house be broken into. You also must be ready, because the Son of Man will come at an hour when you do not expect him.'

Luke 12:35–40

Let all your lamps be bright,
    And trim the golden flame;
Gird up your loins as in His sight,
    For holy is His Name.

Watch! 'tis your Lord's command,
    And while we speak He's near;
Mark the first signal of His hand,
    And ready all appear.

Christ shall the banquet spread
    With His own royal hand,
And raise that faithful servant's head
    Amid the angelic band.

Philip Doddridge, 1702–51

'Increase our faith!'

Jesus said to his disciples: 'Things that cause people to sin are bound to come, but woe to that person through whom they come. It would be better for him to be thrown into the sea with a millstone tied round his neck than for him to cause one of these little ones to sin. So watch yourselves.

'If your brother sins, rebuke him, and if he repents, forgive him. If he sins against you seven times a day, and seven times comes back to you and says, "I repent," forgive him.'

The apostles said to the Lord, 'Increase our faith!'

He replied, 'If you have faith as small as a mustard seed, you can say to this mulberry tree, "Be uprooted and planted in the sea," and it will obey you.'

Luke 17:1–6

O for a faith that will not shrink,
Though pressed by many a foe;
That will not tremble on the brink
Of poverty or woe;
Lord, give me such a faith as this,
And then, whate'er may come,
I taste e'en now the hallowed bliss
Of an eternal home.

William Hiley Bathurst, 1796–1877

Growing in Christ

For this reason, ever since I heard about your faith in the Lord Jesus and your love for all the saints, I have not stopped giving thanks for you, remembering you in my prayers. I keep asking that the God of our Lord Jesus Christ, the glorious Father, may give you the Spirit of wisdom and revelation, so that you may know him better. I pray also that the eyes of your heart may be enlightened in order that you may know the hope to which he has called you, the riches of his glorious inheritance in the saints, and his incomparably great power for us who believe. That power is like the working of his mighty strength, which he exerted in Christ when he raised him from the dead and seated him at his right hand in the heavenly realms, for above all rule and authority, power and dominion, and every title that can be given, not only in the present age but also in the one to come. And God placed all things under his feet and appointed him to be head over everything for the church, which is his body, the fulness of him who fills everything in every way.

Ephesians 1:15–23

Lo! Thy presence now is filling
    All Thy church in every place;
Fill my heart too; make me willing
    In this season of Thy grace;
Come, Thou King of glory, come,
Deign to make my heart Thy home,
There abide and rule alone,
As upon Thy heavenly throne!

Gerhard Tersteegen, 1697–1769
tr. Catherine Winkworth, 1827–78

The presence of God

Moses said to the Lord, 'You have been telling me, "Lead these people," but you have not let me know whom you will send with me. You have said, "I know you by name and you have found favour with me." If you are pleased with me, teach me your ways so I may know you and continue to find favour with you. Remember that this nation is your people.'

The Lord replied, 'My Presence will go with you, and I will give you rest.'

Then Moses said to him, 'If your Presence does not go with us, do not send us up from here. How will anyone know that you are pleased with me and with your people unless you go with us? What else will distinguish me and your people from all the other people on the face of the earth?'

And the Lord said to Moses, 'I will do the very thing you have asked, because I am pleased with you and I know you by name.'

Exodus 33:12–17

Lord, it is not life to live
    If Thy presence Thou deny;
Lord, if Thou Thy presence give,
    'Tis no longer death to die:
Source and giver of repose,
    Singly from Thy smile it flows;
Peace and happiness are Thine;
Mine they are, if Thou art mine.

Augustus Montague Toplady, 1740–78

'Show me your glory'

Then Moses said, 'Now show me your glory.'

And the Lord said, 'I will cause all my goodness to pass in front of you, and I will proclaim my name, the Lord, in your presence. I will have mercy on whom I will have mercy, and I will have compassion on whom I will have compassion. But,' he said, 'you cannot see my face, for no-one may see me and live.'

Then the Lord said, 'There is a place near me where you may stand on a rock. When my glory passes by, I will put you in a cleft in the rock and cover you with my hand until I have passed by. Then I will remove my hand and you will see my back; but my face must not be seen.'

Exodus 33:18–23

Show me Thy face! – one transient gleam
  Of loveliness divine,
And I shall never think or dream
  Of other love save Thine;
All lesser light will darken quite,
  All lower glories wane;
The beautiful of earth will scarce
  Seem beautiful again.

Show me Thy face! – my faith and love
  Shall henceforth fixed be,
And nothing here have power to move
  My soul's serenity;
My life shall seem a trance, a dream,
  And all I feel and see,
Illusive, visionary – Thou
  The one reality!

Anonymous

Trusting God for pardon

To some who were confident of their own righteousness
and looked down on everybody else, Jesus told this parable: 'Two men went up to the temple to pray, one a
Pharisee and the other a tax collector. The Pharisee
stood up and prayed about himself: 'God, I thank you
that I am not like other men – robbers, evildoers, adul-
terers – or even like this tax collector. I fast twice a
week and give a tenth of all I get.'

'But the tax collector stood at a distance. He would
not even look up to heaven, but beat his breast and said,
'God, have mercy on me, a sinner.'

I tell you that this man, rather than the other, went
home justified before God. For everyone who exalts himself will be humbled, and he who humbles himself will
be exalted.'

Luke 18:9–14

I am trusting Thee for pardon,
    At Thy feet I bow;
For Thy grace and tender mercy,
    Trusting now.

I am trusting Thee for cleansing
    In the crimson flood;
Trusting Thee to make me holy
    By Thy blood.

Frances Ridley Havergal, 1836–79

Doing good to all

Brothers, if someone is caught in a sin, you who are spiritual should restore him gently. But watch yourself, or you also may be tempted. Carry each other's burdens, and in this way you will fulfil the law of Christ. If anyone thinks he is something when he is nothing, he deceives himself. Each one should test his own actions. Then he can take pride in himself, without comparing himself to somebody else, for each one should carry his own load.

Anyone who receives instruction in the word must share all good things with his instructor.

Do not be deceived: God cannot be mocked. A man reaps what he sows. The one who sows to please his sinful nature, from that nature will reap destruction; the one who sows to please the Spirit, from the Spirit will reap eternal life. Let us not become weary in doing good, for at the proper time we will reap a harvest if we do not give up. Therefore, as we have opportunity, let us do good to all people, especially to those who belong to the family of believers.

Galatians 6:1–10

Lord, speak to me, that I may speak
  In living echoes of Thy tone;
As Thou hast sought, so let me seek
  Thy erring children lost and lone.

O lead me, Lord, that I may lead
  The wandering and the wavering feet,
O feed me, Lord, that I may feed
  Thy hungering ones with manna sweet,

O strengthen me, that, while I stand
  Firm on the rock, and strong in Thee,
I may stretch out a loving hand
  To wrestlers with the troubled sea.

Frances Ridley Havergal, 1836–79

His love endures for ever

Give thanks to the Lord, for he is good.
His love endures for ever.
Give thanks to the God of gods.
His love endures for ever.
Give thanks to the Lord of lords:
His love endures for ever.

to him who alone does great wonders.
His love endures for ever.
who by his understanding made the heavens,
His love endures for ever.
who spread out the earth upon the waters,
His love endures for ever.
who made the great lights –
His love endures for ever.
the sun to govern the day,
His love endures for ever.
the moon and stars to govern the night;
His love endures for ever.
to him who struck down the firstborn of Egypt
His love endures for ever.
and brought Israel out from among them
His love endures for ever.
with a mighty hand and outstretched arm;
His love endures for ever.

Psalm 136:1–12

Give to our God immortal praise;
Mercy and truth are all His ways;
Wonders of grace to God belong,
Repeat His mercies in your song.

Give to the Lord of lords renown,
The King of kings with glory crown:
His mercies ever shall endure,
When lords and kings are known no more.

He built the earth, He spread the sky,
And fixed the starry lights on high:
Wonders of grace to God belong,
Repeat His mercies in your song.

Isaac Watts, 1674–1748

God's great love

Then the Lord came down in the cloud and stood there with him and proclaimed his name, the Lord. And he passed in front of Moses, proclaiming, 'The Lord, the Lord, the compassionate and gracious God, slow to anger, abounding in love and faithfulness, maintaining love to thousands, and forgiving wickedness, rebellion and sin. Yet he does not leave the guilty unpunished; he punishes the children and their children for the sin of the fathers to the third and fourth generation.'

Moses bowed to the ground at once and worshipped. 'O Lord, if I have found favour in your eyes,' he said, 'then let the Lord go with us. Although this is a stiff-necked people, forgive our wickedness and our sin, and take us as your inheritance.'

Then the Lord said, 'I am making a covenant with you. Before all your people I will do wonders never before done in any nation in all the world. The people you live among will see how awesome is the work that I, the Lord, will do for you. Obey what I command you today.'

Exodus 34:5–11

There's a wideness in God's mercy,
    Like the wideness of the sea;
There's a kindness in His justice,
    Which is more than liberty.

For the love of God is broader
    Than the measures of man's mind;
And the heart of the Eternal
    Is most wonderfully kind.

Frederick William Faber, 1814–63

My glory all the cross

See, a king will reign in righteousness and rulers will rule with justice. Each man will be like a shelter from the wind and a refuge from the storm, like streams of water in the desert and the shadow of a great rock in a thirsty land.

Isaiah 32:1–2

For Christ did not send me to baptise, but to preach the gospel – not with words of human wisdom, lest the cross of Christ be emptied of its power.

For the message of the cross is foolishness to those who are perishing, but to us who are being saved it is the power of God. For it is written: 'I will destroy the wisdom of the wise; the intelligence of the intelligent I will frustrate.'

1 Corinthians 1:17–19

> Upon that cross of Jesus
>   Mine eye at times can see
> The very dying form of One
>   Who suffered there for me;
> And from my smitten heart, with tears,
>   Two wonders I confess –
> The wonders of His glorious love,
>   And my own worthlessness.
>
> I take, O cross, thy shadow,
>   For my abiding place;
> I ask no other sunshine than
>   The sunshine of His face;
> Content to let the world go by,
>   To know no gain nor loss –
> My sinful self my only shame,
>   My glory all the cross.

Elizabeth Cecilia Clephane, 1830–69

Working with all our heart

Wives, submit to your husbands, as is fitting in the Lord.

Husbands, love your wives and do not be harsh with them.

Children, obey your parents in everything, for this pleases the Lord.

Fathers, do not embitter your children, or they will become discouraged.

Slaves, obey your earthly masters in everything; and do it, not only when their eye is on you and to win their favour, but with sincerity of heart and reverence for the Lord. Whatever you do, work at it with all your heart, as working for the Lord, not for men, since you know that you will receive an inheritance from the Lord as a reward. It is the Lord Christ you are serving. Anyone who does wrong will be repaid for his wrong, and there is no favouritism.

Masters, provide your slaves with what is right and fair, because you know that you also have a Master in heaven.

Colossians 3:18–4:1

> Teach me, my God and King,
> In all things Thee to see,
> And what I do in anything
> To do it as for Thee.

George Herbert, 1593–1633

The pure in heart

'Blessed are the pure in heart, for they will see God.'
Matthew 5:8

And I – in righteousness I shall see your face; when I awake, I shall be satisfied with seeing your likeness.
Psalm 17:15

Surely God is good to Israel, to those who are pure in heart.

Psalm 73:1

Make every effort to live in peace with all men and to be holy; without holiness no-one will see the Lord.
Hebrews 12:14

> Blest are the pure in heart,
>   For they shall see their God;
> The secret of the Lord is theirs;
>   Their soul is Christ's abode.
>
> Still to the lowly soul
>   He doth Himself impart,
> And for His dwelling and His throne
>   Chooseth the pure in heart.
>
> Lord, we Thy presence seek:
>   May ours this blessing be;
> Give us a pure and lowly heart, –
>   A temple meet for Thee.

John Keble, 1792–1866,
and William John Hall, 1793–1861

Christ in us

John replied, 'A man can receive only what is given him from heaven. You yourselves can testify that I said, 'I am not the Christ but am sent ahead of him.' The bride belongs to the bridegroom. The friend who attends the bridegroom waits and listens for him, and is full of joy when he hears the bridegroom's voice. That joy is mine, and it is now complete. He must become greater; I must become less. The one who comes from above is above all; the one who is from the earth belongs to the earth, and speaks as one from the earth. The one who comes from heaven is above all. He testifies to what he has seen and heard, but no-one accepts his testimony. The man who has accepted it has certified that God is truthful. For the one whom God has sent speaks the words of God, for God gives the Spirit without limit. The Father loves the Son and has placed everything in his hands. Whoever believes in the Son has eternal life, but whoever rejects the Son will not see life, for God's wrath remains on him.'

John 3:27–36

My dear children, for whom I am again in the pains of childbirth until Christ is formed in you.

Galatians 4:19

> Each day let Thy supporting might
>   My weakness still embrace;
> My darkness vanish in Thy light,
>   Thy life my death efface.
>
> Make this poor self grow less and less,
>   Be Thou my life and aim;
> O make me daily, through Thy grace,
>   More meet to bear. Thy Name!

Johann Caspar Lavater, 1741–1801
tr. Elizabeth Lee Smith, 1817–98

Trusting in God

The Lord is my light and my salvation – whom shall I fear? The Lord is the stronghold of my life – of whom shall I be afraid? When evil men advance against me to devour my flesh, when my enemies and my foes attack me, they will stumble and fall. Though an army besiege me, my heart will not fear; though war break out against me, even then will I be confident.

Do not hide your face from me, do not turn your servant away in anger; you have been my helper. Do not reject me or forsake me, O God my Saviour. Though my father and mother forsake me, the Lord will receive me. Teach me your way, O Lord; lead me in a straight path because of my oppressors. Do not hand me over to the desire of my foes, for false witnesses rise up against me, breathing out violence.

I am still confident of this: I will see the goodness of the Lord in the land of the living. Wait for the Lord; be strong and take heart and wait for the Lord.

Psalm 27:1–3, 9–14

> God is my strong salvation;
>   What foe have I to fear?
> In darkness and temptation
>   My light, my help is near.
>
> Though hosts encamp around me,
>   Firm to the fight I stand;
> What terror can confound me,
>   With God at my right hand?

James Montgomery, 1771–1854

Real worship

Come, let us sing for joy to the Lord; let us shout aloud to the Rock of our salvation. Let us come before him with thanksgiving and extol him with music and song.

For the Lord is the great God, the great King above all gods. In his hand are the depths of the earth, and the mountain peaks belong to him. The sea is his, for he made it, and his hands formed the dry land.

Come, let us bow down in worship, let us kneel before the Lord our Maker; for he is our God and we are the people of his pasture, the flock under his care.

Today, if you hear his voice, do not harden your hearts as you did at Meribah, as you did that day at Massah in the desert.

Psalm 95:1–8

My God, how wonderful Thou art!
    Thy majesty how bright!
How beautiful Thy mercy-seat,
    In depths of burning light!

How wonderful, how beautiful,
    The sight of Thee must be,
Thine endless wisdom, boundless power,
    And aweful purity!

Frederick William Faber, 1814–63

The Lord has done great things

When the Lord brought back the captives to Zion, we
were like men who dreamed. Our mouths were filled
with laughter, our tongues with songs of joy. Then it
was said among the nations, 'The Lord has done great
things for them.' The Lord has done great things for us,
and we are filled with joy.

Restore our fortunes, O Lord, like streams in the
Negev. Those who sow in tears will reap with songs of
joy. He who goes out weeping, carrying seed to sow, will
return with songs of joy, carrying sheaves with him.

Psalm 126:1–6

> Now thank we all our God,
> With hearts, and hands, and voices;
> Who wondrous things hath done,
> In whom His world rejoices;
> Who, from our mothers' arms,
> Hath blessed us on our way
> With countless gifts of love,
> And still is ours today.

Martin Rinkart, 1586–1649
tr. Catherine Winkworth, 1827–78

What God has prepared for his own

When I came to you, brothers, I did not come with eloquence or superior wisdom as I proclaimed to you the testimony about God. For I resolved to know nothing while I was with you except Jesus Christ and him crucified. I came to you in weakness and fear, and with much trembling. My message and my preaching were not with wise and persuasive words, but with a demonstration of the Spirit's power, so that your faith might not rest on men's wisdom, but on God's power.

We do, however, speak a message of wisdom among the mature, but not the wisdom of this age or of the rulers of this age, who are coming to nothing. No, we speak of God's secret wisdom, a wisdom that has been hidden and that God destined for our glory before time began. None of the rulers of this age understood it, for if they had, they would not have crucified the Lord of glory. However, as it is written: 'No eye has seen, no ear has heard, no mind has conceived what God has prepared for those who love him' – but God has revealed it to us by his Spirit.

1 Corinthians 2:1–10

Glories upon glories
    Has our God prepared,
By the souls that love Him
    One day to be shared;
Eye has not beheld them,
    Ear has never heard,
Nor of these has uttered
    Thought or speech a word.
Forward, marching forward,
    Clad in armour bright,
Till the veil be lifted,
    Till our faith be sight.

Henry Alford, 1810–71

Wisdom from the Spirit

The Spirit searches all things, even the deep things of God. For who among men knows the thoughts of a man except the man's spirit within him? In the same way no-one knows the thoughts of God except the Spirit of God. We have not received the spirit of the world but the Spirit who is from God, that we may understand what God has freely given us. This is what we speak, not in words taught us by human wisdom but in words taught by the Spirit, expressing spiritual truths in spiritual words. The man without the Spirit does not accept the things that come from the Spirit of God, for they are foolishness to him, and he cannot understand them, because they are spiritually discerned. The spiritual man makes judgments about all things, but he himself is not subject to any man's judgment: 'For who has known the mind of the Lord that he may instruct him?' But we have the mind of Christ.

1 Corinthians 2:10–16

Send us the Spirit of Thy Son,
To make the depths of Godhead known,
To make us share the life divine;
　　Send Him the sprinkled blood to apply,
　　Send Him our souls to sanctify,
And show and seal us ever Thine.

So shall we pray, and never cease,
So shall we thankfully confess
Thy wisdom, truth, and power, and love;
　　With joy unspeakable adore,
　　And bless and praise Thee evermore,
And serve Thee as Thy hosts above.

Charles Wesley, 1707–88

The paradise to come

The Spirit of the Lord will rest on him – the Spirit of wisdom and of understanding, the Spirit of counsel and of power, the Spirit of knowledge and of the fear of the Lord – and he will delight in the fear of the Lord.

He will not judge by what he sees with his eyes, or decide by what he hears with his ears; but with righteousness he will judge the needy, with justice he will give decisions for the poor of the earth. He will strike the earth with the rod of his mouth; with the breath of his lips he will slay the wicked. Righteousness will be his belt and faithfulness the sash round his waist.

The wolf will live with the lamb, the leopard will lie down with the goat, the calf and the lion and the yearling together; and a little child will lead them. The cow will feed with the bear, their young will lie down together, and the lion will eat straw like the ox. The infant will play near the hole of the cobra, and the young child put his hand into the viper's nest. They will neither harm nor destroy on all my holy mountain, for the earth will be full of the knowledge of the Lord as the waters cover the sea.

Isaiah 11:2–9

God is working His purpose out as year succeeds to
    year.
God is working His purpose out, and the time is
    drawing near;
Nearer and nearer draws the time, the time that
    shall surely be,
When the earth shall be filled with the glory of God
    as the waters cover the sea.

Arthur Campell Ainger, 1841–1919

Teach me your way

Show me your ways, O Lord, teach me your paths; guide
me in your truth and teach me, for you are God my
Saviour, and my hope is in you all day long. Remember
O Lord, your great mercy and love, for they are from of
old. Remember not the sins of my youth and my rebellious ways; according to your love remember me, for you
are good, O Lord.

Good and upright is the Lord; therefore he instructs
sinners in his ways.

He guides the humble in what is right and teaches
them his way. All the ways of the Lord are loving and
faithful for those who keep the demands of his covenant.
For the sake of your name, O Lord, forgive my iniquity,
though it is great. Who, then, is the man that fears the
Lord? He will instruct him in the way chosen for him.
He will spend his days in prosperity, and his descendants will inherit the land. The Lord confides in those
who fear him; he makes his covenant known to them.

Psalm 25:4–14

> Long as my life shall last,
>   Teach me Thy way;
> Where'er my lot be cast,
>   Teach me Thy way;
> Until the race is run,
> Until the journey's done,
> Until the crown is won,
>   Teach me Thy way.

Benjamin Mansell Ramsey, 1849–1923

God's great mercy

Oh, the depth of the riches of the wisdom and knowledge of God! How unsearchable his judgments, and his paths beyond tracing out! 'Who has known the mind of the Lord?' Or who has been his counsellor?' 'Who has ever given to God, that God should repay him?' For from him and through him and to him are all things. To him be the glory for ever! Amen.

Therefore, I urge you, brothers, in view of God's mercy, to offer your bodies as living sacrifices, holy and pleasing to God – this is your spiritual act of worship. Do not conform any longer to the pattern of this world, but be transformed by the renewing of your mind. Then you will be able to test and approve what God's will is – his good, pleasing and perfect will.

Romans 11:33–12:2

When all Thy mercies, O my God,
    My rising soul surveys,
Transported with the view, I'm lost
    In wonder, love, and praise.

Through every period of my life
    Thy goodness I'll pursue,
And after death in distant worlds
    The glorious theme renew.

Through all eternity to Thee
    A joyful song I'll raise;
But O! eternity's too short
    To utter all Thy praise!

Joseph Addison, 1672–1719

Growing in grace

All over the world this gospel is bearing fruit and growing, just as it has been doing among you since the day you heard it and understood God's grace in all its truth. You learned it from Epaphras, our dear fellow-servant, who is a faithful minister of Christ on our behalf, and who also told us of your love in the Spirit. For this reason, since the day we heard about you, we have not stopped praying for you and asking God to fill you with the knowledge of his will through all spiritual wisdom and understanding. And we pray this in order that you may live a life worthy of the Lord and may please him in every way: bearing fruit in every good work, growing in the knowledge of God, being strengthened with all power according to his glorious might so that you may have great endurance and patience, and joyfully giving thanks to the Father, who has qualified you to share in the inheritance of the saints in the kingdom of light. For he has rescued us from the dominion of darkness and brought us into the kingdom of the Son he loves, in whom we have redemption, the forgiveness of sins

Colossians 1: 6–14

It passeth praises, that dear love of Thine,
My Saviour, Jesus, yet this heart of mine
Would sing that love, so full, so rich, so free,
Which brings a rebel sinner, such as me,
    Nigh unto God.

O fill me, Jesus, Saviour, with Thy love!
Lead, lead me to the living fount above;
Thither may I, in simple faith, draw nigh,
And never to another fountain fly,
    But unto Thee.

Mary Shekleton, 1827–83

The supremacy of Christ

He [Christ] is the image of the invisible God, the first-born over all creation. For by him all things were created: things in heaven and on earth, visible and invisible, whether thrones or powers or rulers or authorities; all things were created by him and for him. He is before all things, and in him all things hold together. And he is the head of the body, the church; he is the beginning and the firstborn from among the dead, so that in everything he might have the supremacy. For God was pleased to have all his fulness dwell in him, and through him to reconcile to himself all things, whether things on earth or things in heaven, by making peace through his blood, shed on the cross.

Colossians 1: 15–20

Thou art the Everlasting Word,
    The Father's only Son;
God manifestly seen and heard,
    And heaven's beloved One.

Worthy, O Lamb of God, art Thou,
That every knee to Thee should bow!

In Thee, most perfectly expressed,
    The Father's glories shine:
Of the full Deity possessed,
    Eternally divine:

True image of the Infinite,
    Whose essence is concealed;
Brightness of uncreated light;
    The heart of God revealed.

Josiah Conder, 1789–1855

Coming to Christ

Since, then, we know what it is to fear the Lord, we try to persuade men. What we are is plain to God, and I hope it is also plain to your conscience. We are not trying to commend ourselves to you again, but are giving you an opportunity to take pride in us, so that you can answer those who take pride in what is seen rather than in what is in the heart. If we are out of our mind, it is for the sake of God; if we are in our right mind, it is for you. For Christ's love compels us, because we are convinced that one died for all, and therefore all died. And he died for all, that those who live should no longer live for themselves but for him who died for them and was raised again.

So from now on we regard no-one from a worldly point of view. Though we once regarded Christ in this way, we do so no longer. Therefore, if anyone is in Christ, he is a new creation; the old has gone, the new has come!

2 Corinthians 5:11–17

Come, ye sinners, poor and wretched,
   Weak and wounded, sick and sore;
Jesus ready stands to save you,
   Full of pity joined with power;
     He is able,
   He is willing; doubt no more!

Lo, the incarnate God, ascended,
   Pleads the merit of His blood;
Venture on Him, venture wholly,
   Let no other trust intrude;
     None but Jesus
   Can do helpless sinners good.

Joseph Hart, 1712–68

Christ, the curse of the law

All who rely on observing the law are under a curse, for it is written: 'Cursed is everyone who does not continue to do everything written in the Book of the Law.' Clearly no-one is justified before God by the law, because, 'The righteous will live by faith.' The law is not based on faith; on the contrary, 'The man who does these things will live by them.' Christ redeemed us from the curse of the law by becoming a curse for us, for it is written: 'Cursed is everyone who is hung on a tree.' He redeemed us in order that the blessing given to Abraham might come to the Gentiles through Christ Jesus, so that by faith we might receive the promise of the Spirit.

Galatians 3:10–14

> Guilty, vile, and helpless, we;
> Spotless Lamb of God was He:
> Full atonement! – can it be?
> Hallelujah! what a Saviour!

Philipp Paul Bliss, 1833–76

For ever with the Lord

'Lord,' Martha said to Jesus, 'if you had been here, my brother would not have died. But I know that even now God will give you whatever you ask.'

Jesus said to her, 'Your brother will rise again.'

Martha answered, 'I know he will rise again in the resurrection at the last day.'

Jesus said to her, 'I am the resurrection and the life. He who believes in me will live, even though he dies; and whoever lives and believes in me will never die. Do you believe this?'

'Yes, Lord,' she told him, 'I believe that you are the Christ, the Son of God, who was to come into the world.'
John 11:21–27

For the Lord himself will come down from heaven, with a loud command, with the voice of the archangel and with the trumpet call of God, and the dead in Christ will rise first. After that, we who are still alive and are left will be caught up together with them in the clouds to meet the Lord in the air. And so we will be with the Lord for ever.
1 Thessalonians 4:16–17

> So when my latest breath
>   Shall rend the veil in twain,
> By death I shall escape from death,
>   And life eternal gain.
> That resurrection-word,
>   That shout of victory;
> Once more, 'For ever with the Lord!'
>   Amen, so let it be!

James Montgomery, 1771–1854

The full measure of Christ's love

It was just before the Passover Feast. Jesus knew that
the time had come for him to leave this world and go to
the Father. Having loved his own who were in the world,
he now showed them the full extent of his love.

The evening meal was being served, and the devil had
already prompted Judas Iscariot, son of Simon, to betray
Jesus. Jesus knew that the Father had put all things
under his power, and that he had come from God and
was returning to God; so he got up from the meal, took
off his outer clothing, and wrapped a towel around his
waist. After that, he poured water into a basin and
began to wash his disciples' feet, drying them with the
towel that was wrapped around him.

John 13:1—5

> He came from His blest throne,
>   Salvation to bestow:
> But men made strange, and none
>   The longed-for Christ would know.
> But O, my Friend!
>   My Friend indeed,
>   Who at my need
> His life did spend!

Samuel Crossman, 1624—83

A new commandment

When he [Jesus] had finished washing their feet, he put on his clothes and returned to his place. 'Do you understand what I have done for you?' he asked them. 'You call me "Teacher" and "Lord", and rightly so, for that is what I am. Now that I, your Lord and Teacher, have washed your feet, you also should wash one another's feet. I have set you an example that you should do as I have done for you. I tell you the truth, no servant is greater than his master, nor is a messenger greater than the one who sent him. Now that you know these things, you will be blessed if you do them.'

John 13:12–17

'A new command I give you: Love one another. As I have loved you, so you must love one another. By this all men will know that you are my disciples, if you love one another.'

John 13:34–35

> Beloved, let us love:
> Love is of God;
> In God alone hath love
> Its true abode.

Horatius Bonar, 1808–89

'You are not your own'

'Everything is permissible for me' – but not everything is beneficial. 'Everything is permissible for me' – but I will not be mastered by anything. 'Food for the stomach and the stomach for food' – but God will destroy them both. The body is not meant for sexual immorality, but for the Lord, and the Lord for the body. By his power God raised the Lord from the dead, and he will raise us also. Do you not know that your bodies are members of Christ himself? Shall I then take the members of Christ and unite them with a prostitute? Never! Do you not know that he who unites himself with a prostitute is one with her in body? For it is said, 'The two will become one flesh.' But he who unites himself with the Lord is one with him in spirit.

Flee from sexual immorality. All other sins a man commits are outside his body, but he who sins sexually sins against his own body. Do you not know that your body is a temple of the Holy Spirit, who is in you, whom you have received from God? You are not your own; you were bought at a price. Therefore honour God with your body.

1 Corinthians 6:12–20

All to Thee is yielded,
   I am not my own;
Blissful, glad surrender –
   I am Thine alone.

E. May Grimes 1868–1927

To every believer the promise of God

'You are Israel's teacher,' said Jesus, 'and do you not understand these things? I tell you the truth, we speak of what we know, and we testify to what we have seen, but still you people do not accept our testimony. I have spoken to you of earthly things and you do not believe; how then will you believe if I speak of heavenly things? No-one has ever gone into heaven except the one who came from heaven – the Son of Man. Just as Moses lifted up the snake in the desert, so the Son of Man must be lifted up, that everyone who believes in him may have eternal life.

'For God so loved the world that he gave his only begotten Son, that whoever believes in him shall not perish but have eternal life. For God did not send his Son into the world to condemn the world, but to save the world through him. Whoever believes in him is not condemned, but whoever does not believe stands condemned already because he has not believed in the name of God's only begotten Son.'

John 3:10–18

O perfect redemption, the purchase of blood!
To every believer the promise of God;
The vilest offender who truly believes,
That moment from Jesus a pardon receives.

Praise the Lord! praise the Lord! Let the earth hear His voice!
Praise the Lord! praise the Lord! Let the people rejoice!
O come to the Father through Jesus the Son:
And give Him the glory! great things He hath done!

Frances Jane Van Alstyne, 1820–1915

Jesus comforts his disciples

'Do not let your hearts be troubled. Trust in God; trust also in me. In my Father's house are many rooms; if it were not so, I would have told you. I am going there to prepare a place for you. And if I go and prepare a place for you, I will come back and take you to be with me that you also may be where I am. You know the way to the place where I am going.' Thomas said to him, 'Lord, we don't know where you are going, so how can we know the way?'

Jesus answered, 'I am the way and the truth and the life. No-one comes to the Father except through me. If you really knew me, you would know my Father as well. From now on, you do know him and have seen him.' Philip said, 'Lord, show us the Father and that will be enough for us.' Jesus answered: 'Don't you know me, Philip, even after I have been among you such a long time? Anyone who has seen me has seen the Father. How can you say, "Show us the Father"? Don't you believe that I am in the Father, and that the Father is in me? The words I say to you are not just my own. Rather, it is the Father, living in me, who is doing his work.'

John 14:1–10

Thou art gone up before us, Lord,
  To make for us a place,
That we may be where now Thou art,
  And look upon God's face.

Lift up our hearts, lift up our minds;
  Let Thy dear grace be given,
That, while we wander here below,
  Our treasure be in heaven.

Cecil Frances Alexander, 1818–95

Simply trusting thee, Lord Jesus

'I am the true vine, and my Father is the gardener. He cuts off every branch in me that bears no fruit, while every branch that does bear fruit he prunes so that it will be even more fruitful. You are already clean because of the word I have spoken to you. Remain in me, and I will remain in you. No branch can bear fruit by itself; it must remain in the vine. Neither can you bear fruit unless you remain in me.

'I am the vine; you are the branches. If a man remains in me and I in him, he will bear much fruit; apart from me you can do nothing. If anyone does not remain in me, he is like a branch that is thrown away and withers; such branches are picked up, thrown into the fire and burned. If you remain in me and my words remain in you, ask whatever you wish, and it will be given you. This is to my Father's glory, that you bear much fruit, showing yourselves to be my disciples.'

John 15:1–8

Jesus, I am resting, resting
In the joy of what Thou art;
I am finding out the greatness
Of Thy loving heart.
Thou hast bid me gaze upon Thee,
And Thy beauty fills my soul,
For by Thy transforming power
Thou hast made me whole.

Simply trusting Thee, Lord Jesus,
I behold Thee as Thou art,
And Thy love, so pure, so changeless,
Satisfies my heart;
Satisfies its deepest longings,
Meets, supplies its every need,
Compasseth me round with blessings;
Thine is love indeed!

Jean Sophia Pigott, 1845–82

The Shepherd of the sheep

Through Jesus, therefore, let us continually offer to God a sacrifice of praise – the fruit of lips that confess his name. And do not forget to do good and to share with others, for with such sacrifices God is pleased. Obey your leaders and submit to their authority. They keep watch over you as men who must give an account. Obey them so that their work will be a joy, not a burden, for that would be of no advantage to you.

Pray for us. We are sure that we have a clear conscience and desire to live honourably in every way. I particularly urge you to pray so that I may be restored to you soon. May the God of peace, who through the blood of the eternal covenant brought back from the dead our Lord Jesus, that great Shepherd of the sheep, equip you with everything good for doing his will, and may he work in us what is pleasing to him, through Jesus Christ, to whom be glory for ever and ever. Amen.

Hebrews 13:15–21

Now may He, who from the dead
   Brought the Shepherd of the sheep,
Jesus Christ, our King and Head,
   All our souls in safety keep.

May He teach us to fulfil
   What is pleasing in His sight,
Perfect us in all His will,
   And preserve us day and night.

To that dear Redeemer's praise,
   Who the covenant sealed with blood,
Let our hearts and voices raise
   Loud thanksgivings to our God.

John Newton, 1725–1807

Peace with God

Therefore, since we have been justified through faith, we have peace with God through our Lord Jesus Christ, through whom we have gained access by faith into this grace in which we now stand. And we rejoice in the hope of the glory of God. Not only so, but we also rejoice in our sufferings, because we know that suffering produces perseverance; perseverance, character; and character, hope. And hope does not disappoint us, because God has poured out his love into our hearts by the Holy Spirit, whom he has given us.

Romans 5:1–5

I hear the words of love,
  I gaze upon the blood,
I see the mighty sacrifice,
  And I have peace with God.

'Tis everlasting peace,
  Sure as Jehovah's Name;
'Tis stable as His steadfast throne,
  For evermore the same.

My love is oft-times low,
  My joy still ebbs and flows;
But peace with Him remains the same –
  No change Jehovah knows.

Horatius Bonar, 1808–89

The promise of the Spirit

'Believe me when I say that I am in the Father and the Father is in me; or at least believe on the evidence of the miracles themselves. I tell you the truth, anyone who has faith in me will do what I have been doing. He will do even greater things than these, because I am going to the Father. And I will do whatever you ask in my name, so that the Son may bring glory to the Father. You may ask me for anything in my name, and I will do it.

'If you love me, you will obey what I command. And I will ask the Father, and he will give you another Counsellor to be with you for ever – the Spirit of truth. The world cannot accept him, because it neither sees him nor knows him. But you know him, for he lives with you and will be in you. I will not leave you as orphans; I will come to you. Before long, the world will not see me any more, but you will see me. Because I live, you also will live. On that day you will realize that I am in my Father, and you are in me, and I am in you. Whoever has my commands and obeys them, he is the one who loves me. He who loves me will be loved by my Father, and I too will love him and show myself to him.'

John 14:11–21

And so the yearning strong,
With which the soul will long,
   Shall far outpass the power of human telling;
For none can guess its grace,
Till he become the place
   Wherein the Holy Spirit makes His dwelling.

Bianco da Siena, c. 1350–1434
tr. Richard Frederick Littledale, 1833–90

The way of faith

Now we know that if the earthly tent we live in is destroyed, we have a building from God, an eternal house in heaven, not built by human hands. Meanwhile we groan, longing to be clothed with our heavenly dwelling, because when we are clothed, we will not be found naked. For while we are in this tent, we groan and are burdened, because we do not wish to be unclothed but to be clothed with our heavenly dwelling, so that what is mortal may be swallowed up by life. Now it is God who has made us for this very purpose and has given us the Spirit as a deposit, guaranteeing what is to come.

Therefore we are always confident and know that as long as we are at home in the body we are away from the Lord. We live by faith, not by sight. We are confident, I say, and would prefer to be away from the body and at home with the Lord. So we make it our goal to please him, whether we are at home in the body or away from it. For we must all appear before the judgment seat of Christ, that each one may receive what is due to him for the things done while in the body, whether good or bad.

2 Corinthians 5:1–10

> Teach me Thy way, O Lord,
>   Teach me Thy way;
> Thy gracious aid afford,
>   Teach me Thy way;
> Help me to walk aright,
> More by faith, less by sight;
> Lead me with heavenly light:
>   Teach me Thy way.

Benjamin Mansell Ramsey, 1849–1923

God's precious word

The law of the Lord is perfect, reviving the soul. The statutes of the Lord are trustworthy, making wise the simple. The precepts of the Lord are right, giving joy to the heart. The commands of the Lord are radiant, giving light to the eyes. The fear of the Lord is pure, enduring for ever. The ordinances of the Lord are sure and altogether righteous. They are more precious than gold, than much pure gold; they are sweeter than honey, than honey from the comb. By them is your servant warned; in keeping them there is great reward.

Who can discern his errors? Forgive my hidden faults. Keep your servant also from wilful sins; may they not rule over me. Then will I be blameless, innocent of great transgression.

May the words of my mouth and the meditation of my heart be pleasing in your sight, O Lord, my Rock and my Redeemer.

Psalm 19:7–14

> Who can tell the pleasure,
> Who recount the treasure,
> By Thy Word imparted,
> To the simple-hearted?
>
> Word of mercy, giving
> Succour to the living;
> Word of life, supplying
> Comfort to the dying!

Henry Williams Baker, 1821–77

The great banquet

When one of those at the table with him heard this, he said to Jesus, 'Blessed is the man who will eat at the feast in the kingdom of God.' Jesus replied: 'A certain man was preparing a great banquet and invited many guests. At the time of the banquet he sent his servant to tell those who had been invited, "Come, for everything is now ready." But they all alike began to make excuses. The first said, "I have just bought a field, and I must go and see it. Please excuse me." Another said, "I have just bought five yoke of oxen, and I'm on my way to try them out. Please excuse me." Still another said, "I have just got married, so I can't come."

'The servant came back and reported this to his master. Then the owner of the house became angry and ordered his servant, "Go out quickly into the streets and alleys of the town and bring in the poor, the crippled, the blind and the lame." "Sir," the servant said, "what you ordered has been done, but there is still room." Then the master told his servant. "Go out to the roads and country lanes and make them come in, so that my house will be full. I tell you, not one of those men who were invited will get a taste of my banquet."'

Luke 14:15–24

Sent by my Lord, on you I call,
The invitation is to all:
Come, all the world; come, sinner, thou!
All things in Christ are ready now.

His love is mighty to compel;
His conquering love consent to feel,
Yield to His love's resistless power,
And fight against your God no more.

Charles Wesley, 1707–88

'Abba, Father'

You are all sons of God through faith in Christ Jesus, for all of you who were baptised into Christ have clothed yourselves with Christ. There is neither Jew nor Greek, slave nor free, male nor female, for you are all one in Christ Jesus. If you belong to Christ, then you are Abraham's seed, and heirs according to the promise.

What I am saying is that as long as the heir is a child, he is no different from a slave, although he owns the whole estate. He is subject to guardians and trustees until the time set by his father. So also, when we were children, we were in slavery under the basic principles of the world. But when the time had fully come, God sent his Son, born of a woman, born under law, to redeem those under law, that we might receive the full rights of sons. Because you are sons, God sent the Spirit of his Son into our hearts, the Spirit who calls out, 'Abba, Father.' So you are no longer a slave, but a son; and since you are a son, God has made you also an heir.

Galatians 3:26–4:7

> If in our Father's love
>   We share a filial part,
> Send down Thy Spirit like a dove
>   To rest upon each heart.
>
> We would no longer lie
>   Like slaves beneath Thy throne;
> Our faith shall 'Abba, Father' cry,
>   And Thou the kindred own.

Isaac Watts, 1674–1748

Work out your salvation

Therefore, my dear friends, as you have always obeyed – not only in my presence, but now much more in my absence – continue to work out your salvation with fear and trembling, for it is God who works in you to will and to act according to his good purpose.

Do everything without complaining or arguing, so that you may become blameless and pure, children of God without fault in a crooked and depraved generation, in which you shine like stars in the universe as you hold out the word of life – in order that I may boast on the day of Christ that I did not run or labour for nothing. But even if I am being poured out like a drink offering on the sacrifice and service coming from your faith, I am glad and rejoice with all of you. So you too should be glad and rejoice with me.

Philippians 2:12–18

Thou canst keep my feet from falling,
    Even my poor wayward feet –
Thou who dost present me faultless,
    In Thy righteousness complete;
Jesus, Lord, in knowing Thee,
O what strength and victory!

Make my life a bright outshining
    Of Thy life, that all may see
Thine own resurrection power
    Mightily put forth in me;
Ever let my heart become
Yet more consciously Thy home.

Jean Sophia Pigott, 1845–82

He will meet all our needs

I have learned to be content whatever the circumstances. I know what it is to be in need, and I know what it is to have plenty. I have learned the secret of being content in any and every situation, whether well fed or hungry, whether living in plenty or in want. I can do everything through him who gives me strength.

Yet it was good of you to share in my troubles. Moreover, as you Philippians know, in the early days of your acquaintance with the gospel, when I set out from Macedonia, not one church shared with me in the matter of giving and receiving, except you only; for even when I was in Thessalonica, you sent me aid again and again when I was in need. And my God will meet all your needs according to his glorious riches in Christ Jesus.

To our God and Father be glory for ever and ever. Amen.

Philippians 4:11–16, 19–20

My every need He richly will supply,
Nor will His mercy ever let me die;
In Him there dwells a treasure all divine,
And matchless grace has made that treasure mine.

William Gadsby, 1773–1844

Submitting to God

What causes fights and quarrels among you? Don't they come from your desires that battle within you? You want something but don't get it. You kill and covet, but you cannot have what you want. You quarrel and fight. You do not have, because you do not ask God. When you ask, you do not receive, because you ask with wrong motives, that you may spend what you get on your pleasures.

You adulterous people, don't you know that friendship with the world is hatred towards God? Anyone who chooses to be a friend of the world becomes an enemy of God. Or do you think Scripture says without reason that the spirit he caused to live in us envies intensely? But he gives us more grace. That is why Scripture says: 'God opposes the proud but gives grace to the humble.'

Submit yourselves, then, to God. Resist the devil, and he will flee from you. Come near to God and he will come near to you. Wash your hands, you sinners, and purify your hearts, you double-minded. Grieve, mourn and wail. Change your laughter to mourning and your joy to gloom. Humble yourselves before the Lord, and he will lift you up.

James 4:1–10

Here from the world we turn,
   Jesus to seek;
Here may His loving voice
   Tenderly speak.
Jesus, our dearest Friend,
While at Thy feet we bend,
O let Thy smile descend!
   'Tis Thee we seek.

Frances Jane Van Alstyne, 1820–1915

The mediator, the man Christ Jesus

I urge, then, first of all, that requests, prayers, intercession and thanksgiving be made for everyone – for kings and all those in authority, that we may live peaceful and quiet lives in all godliness and holiness. This is good, and pleases God our Saviour, who wants all men to be saved and to come to a knowledge of the truth. For there is one God and one mediator between God and men, the man Christ Jesus, who gave himself as a ransom for all men – the testimony given in its proper time. And for this purpose I was appointed a herald and an apostle – I am telling the truth, I am not lying – and a teacher of the true faith to the Gentiles.

1 Timothy 2:1–7

> For ever God, for ever Man,
> My Jesus shall endure;
> And fixed on Him, my hope remains
> Eternally secure.

Edward Caswall, 1814–78

You are my hiding-place

Therefore let everyone who is godly pray to you while you may be found; surely when the mighty waters rise, they will not reach him. You are my hiding-place; you will protect me from trouble and surround me with songs of deliverance.

I will instruct you and teach you in the way you should go; I will counsel you and watch over you. Do not be like the horse or the mule, which have no understanding but must be controlled by bit and bridle or they will not come to you. Many are the woes of the wicked, but the Lord's unfailing love surrounds the man who trusts in him.

Rejoice in the Lord and be glad, you righteous; sing, all you who are upright in heart!

Psalm 32:6–11

O safe to the Rock that is higher than I
My soul in its conflicts and sorrows would fly;
So sinful, so weary, Thine, Thine would I be;
Thou blest Rock of Ages, I'm hiding in Thee!

Hiding in Thee! hiding in Thee!
Thou blest Rock of Ages, I'm hiding in Thee!

William Orcutt Cushing, 1823–1903

Our gracious powerful God

Praise awaits you, O God, in Zion; to you our vows will be fulfilled. O you who hear prayer, to you all men will come. When we were overwhelmed by sins, you forgave our transgressions. Blessed are those you choose and bring near to live in your courts! We are filled with the good things of your house, of your holy temple.

You answer us with awesome deeds of righteousness, O God our Saviour, the hope of all the ends of the earth and of the farthest seas, who formed the mountains by your power, having armed yourself with strength, who stilled the roaring of the seas, the roaring of their waves, and the turmoil of the nations. Those living far away fear your wonders; where morning dawns and evening fades you call forth songs of joy.

Psalm 65:1–8

Praise, Lord, for Thee in Zion waits;
Prayer shall besiege Thy temple gates;
All flesh shall to Thy throne repair,
And find, through Christ, salvation there.

How blest Thy saints! how safely led!
How surely kept! how richly fed!
Saviour of all in earth and sea,
How happy they who rest in Thee!

Henry Francis Lyte, 1793–1847

Whom have I in heaven but you?

Yet I am always with you; you hold me by my right hand. You guide me with your counsel, and afterwards you will take me into glory. Whom have I in heaven but you? And earth has nothing I desire besides you. My flesh and my heart may fail, but God is the strength of my heart and my portion for ever.

Those who are far from you will perish; you destroy all who are unfaithful to you. But as for me, it is good to be near God. I have made the Sovereign Lord my refuge; I will tell of all your deeds.

Psalm 73:23–28

Whom have I on earth below?
Thee, and only Thee, I know;
Whom have I in heaven but Thee?
Thou art all in all to me.

All my treasure is above,
All my riches is Thy love:
Who the worth of love can tell?
Infinite, unsearchable.

Charles Wesley, 1707–88

Looking at Jesus

Therefore, since we are surrounded by such a great cloud of witnesses, let us throw off everything that hinders and the sin that so easily entangles, and let us run with perseverance the race marked out for us. Let us fix our eyes on Jesus, the author and perfecter of our faith, who for the joy set before him endured the cross, scorning its shame, and sat down at the right hand of the throne of God. Consider him who endured such opposition from sinful men, so that you will not grow weary and lose heart.

In your struggle against sin, you have not yet resisted to the point of shedding your blood. And you have forgotten that word of encouragement that addresses you as sons: 'My son, do not make light of the Lord's discipline, and do not lose heart when he rebukes you, because the Lord disciplines those he loves, and he punishes everyone he accepts as a son.'

Hebrews 12:1–6

Onward! Christian soldiers,
　　Marching as to war,
Looking unto Jesus,
　　Who is gone before:
Christ, the royal Master,
　　Leads against the foe;
Forward into battle,
　　See, His banners go!

Onward! Christian soldiers,
　　Marching as to war,
Looking unto Jesus,
　　Who is gone before.

Sabine Baring-Gould, 1834–1924

The choir of creation

Praise the Lord.

Praise the Lord from the heavens, praise him in the heights above. Praise him, all his angels, praise him, all his heavenly hosts. Praise him, sun and moon, praise him, all you shining stars. Praise him, you highest heavens and you waters above the skies. Let them praise the name of the Lord, for he commanded and they were created. He set them in place for ever and ever; he gave a decree that will never pass away.

Praise the Lord from the earth, you great sea creatures and all ocean depths, lightning and hail, snow and clouds, stormy winds that do his bidding, you mountains and all hills, fruit trees and all cedars, wild animals and all cattle, small creatures and flying birds, kings of the earth and all nations, you princes and all rulers on earth, young men and maidens, old men and children.

Psalm 148:1–12

> For the beauty of the earth,
>   For the beauty of the skies,
> For the love which from our birth
>   Over and around us lies:
>
> *Gracious God, to Thee we raise*
> *This our sacrifice of praise.*
>
> For each perfect gift of Thine
>   To our race so freely given,
> Graces human and divine,
>   Flowers of earth and buds of heaven:

Folliott Stanford Pierpoint, 1835–1917

Crowned with glory and honour

It is not to angels that he has subjected the world to come, about which we are speaking. But there is a place where someone has testified: 'What is man that you are mindful of him, the son of man that you care for him? You made him a little lower than the angels; you crowned him with glory and honour and put everything under his feet.' In putting everything under him, God left nothing that is not subject to him. Yet at present we do not see everything subject to him. But we see Jesus, who was made a little lower than the angels, now crowned with glory and honour because he suffered death, so that by the grace of God he might taste death for everyone.

In bringing many sons to glory, it was fitting that God, for whom and through whom everything exists, should make the author of their salvation perfect through suffering. Both the one who makes men holy and those who are made holy are of the same family. So Jesus is not ashamed to call them brothers.

Hebrews 2:5–11

Crown Him the Lord of years,
The Potentate of time,
Creator of the rolling spheres,
Ineffably sublime!
All hail, Redeemer, hail!
For Thou hast died for me:
Thy praise shall never, never fail
Throughout eternity.

Matthew Bridges, 1800–94
and Godfrey Thring, 1823–1903

NOVEMBER 17

The shedding of Christ's blood

For this reason Christ is the mediator of a new covenant, that those who are called may receive the promised eternal inheritance – now that he has died as a ransom to set them free from the sins committed under the first covenant.

In the case of a will, it is necessary to prove the death of the one who made it, because a will is in force only when somebody has died; it never takes effect while the one who made it is living. This is why even the first covenant was not put into effect without blood. When Moses had proclaimed every commandment of the law to all the people, he took the blood of calves, together with water, scarlet wool and branches of hyssop, and sprinkled the scroll and all the people. He said, 'This is the blood of the covenant, which God has commanded you to keep.' In the same way, he sprinkled with the blood both the tabernacle and everything used in its ceremonies. In fact, the law requires that nearly everything be cleansed with blood, and without the shedding of blood there is no forgiveness.

Hebrews 9:15–22

Christ is my peace; He died for me,
  For me He gave His blood;
And, as my wondrous sacrifice,
  Offered Himself to God.

John Mason, c. 1646–94

God's good gifts

Blessed is the man who perseveres under trial, because when he has stood the test, he will receive the crown of life that God has promised to those who love him.

When tempted, no-one should say, 'God is tempting me.' For God cannot be tempted by evil, nor does he tempt anyone; but each one is tempted when, by his own evil desire, he is dragged away and enticed. Then, after desire has conceived, it gives birth to sin; and sin, when it is full-grown, gives birth to death.

Don't be deceived, my dear brothers. Every good and perfect gift is from above, coming down from the Father of the heavenly lights, who does not change like shifting shadows. He chose to give us birth through the word of truth, that we might be a kind of firstfruits of all he created.

James 1:12–18

> *All good gifts around us*
> *Are sent from heaven above,*
> *Then thank the Lord, O thank the Lord,*
> *For all His love.*

Matthias Claudius, 1740–1815
tr. Jane Montgomery Campbell, 1817–78

What he says, we will do

My dear brothers, take note of this: Everyone should be quick to listen, slow to speak and slow to become angry, for man's anger does not bring about the righteous life that God desires. Therefore, get rid of all moral filth and the evil that is so prevalent, and humbly accept the word planted in you, which can save you.

Do not merely listen to the word, and so deceive yourselves. Do what it says. Anyone who listens to the word but does not do what it says is like a man who looks at his face in a mirror and, after looking at himself, goes away and immediately forgets what he looks like. But the man who looks intently into the perfect law that gives freedom, and continues to do this, not forgetting what he has heard, but doing it – he will be blessed in what he does.

James 1:19–25

Then in fellowship sweet
We will sit at His feet,
    Or we'll walk by His side in the way;
What He says we will do,
Where He sends we will go –
    Never fear, only trust and obey!

Trust and obey!
For there's no other way
    To be happy in Jesus
But to trust and obey.

John Henry Sammis, 1846–1919

Taming the tongue

The tongue is a small part of the body, but it makes great boasts. Consider what a great forest is set on fire by a small spark. The tongue also is a fire, a world of evil among the parts of the body. It corrupts the whole person, sets the whole course of his life on fire, and is itself set on fire by hell.

All kinds of animals, birds, reptiles and creatures of the sea are being tamed and have been tamed by man, but no man can tame the tongue. It is a restless evil, full of deadly poison.

With the tongue we praise our Lord and Father, and with it we curse men, who have been made in God's likeness. Out of the same mouth come praise and cursing. My brothers, this should not be.

James 3:5–10

> Take my voice, and let me sing
> Always, only for my King;
> Take my lips, and let them be
> Filled with messages from Thee.

Frances Ridley Havergal, 1836–79

Dead to sin

What shall we say, then? Shall we go on sinning, so that grace may increase? By no means! We died to sin, how can we live in it any longer? Or don't you know what all of us who were baptised into Christ Jesus were baptised into his death? We were therefore buried with him through baptism into death in order that, just as Christ was raised from the dead through the glory of the Father, we too may live a new life.

If we have been united with him like this in his death, we will certainly also be united with him in his resurrection. For we know that our old self was crucified with him so that the body of sin might be done away with, that we should no longer be slaves to sin – because anyone who has died has been freed from sin.

Now if we died with Christ, we believe that we will also live with him. For we know that since Christ was raised from the dead, he cannot die again; death no longer has mastery over him. The death he died, he died to sin once for all; but the life he lives, he lives to God.

In the same way, count yourselves dead to sin but alive to God in Christ Jesus.

Romans 6:1–11

As dead indeed to sin,
    From its dominion free,
Henceforth, as not our own, but Thine,
    We follow only Thee.

Baptised into Thy death,
    With Thee again we rise,
To newness of a life of faith,
    To new and endless joys.

Anonymous

The coming king

Endow the king with your justice, O God, the royal son with your righteousness. He will judge your people in righteousness, your afflicted ones with justice. The mountains will bring prosperity to the people, the hills the fruit of righteousness. He will defend the afflicted among the people and save the children of the needy; he will crush the oppressor.

He will endure as long as the sun, as long as the moon, through all generations. He will be like rain falling on a mown field, like showers watering the earth. In his days the righteous will flourish; prosperity will abound till the moon is no more. He will rule from sea to sea and from the River to the ends of the earth.

Psalm 72:1–8

Hail to the Lord's Anointed,
　　Great David's greater Son!
Hail, in the time appointed,
　　His reign on earth begun!
He comes to break oppression,
　　To set the captive free,
To take away transgression,
　　And rule in equity.

He shall come down like showers
　　Upon the fruitful earth,
And love, joy, hope, like flowers,
　　Spring in His path to birth:
Before Him on the mountains
　　Shall peace, the herald, go;
And righteousness, in fountains,
　　From hill to valley flow

James Montgomery, 1771–1854

'Stay with us'

As they approached the village to which they were going, Jesus acted as if he were going further. But they urged him strongly, 'Stay with us, for it is nearly evening; the day is almost over.' So he went in to stay with them.

When he was at the table with them, he took bread, gave thanks, broke it and began to give it to them. Then their eyes were opened and they recognized him, and he disappeared from their sight. They asked each other, 'Were not our hearts burning within us while he talked with us on the road and opened the Scriptures to us?'

They got up and returned at once to Jerusalem. There they found the Eleven and those with them, assembled together and saying, 'It is true! The Lord has risen and has appeared to Simon.' Then the two told what had happened on the way, and how Jesus was recognized by them when he broke the bread.

Luke 24:28–35

Our restless spirits yearn for Thee
  Where'er our changeful lot is cast;
Glad, when Thy gracious smile we see;
  Blest, when our faith can hold Thee fast.

O Jesus, ever with us stay;
  Make all our moments calm and bright;
Chase the dark night of sin away;
  Shed o'er our souls Thy holy light.

Latin, c. 11th century
tr. Ray Palmer, 1808–87

The world for the gospel

He [Jesus] said to them, 'This is what I told you while I was still with you: Everything must be fulfilled that is written about me in the Law of Moses, the Prophets and the Psalms.'

Then he opened their minds so they could understand the Scriptures. He told them, 'This is what is written: The Christ will suffer and rise from the dead on the third day, and repentance and forgiveness of sins will be preached in his name to all nations, beginning at Jerusalem. You are witnesses of these things. I am going to send you what my Father has promised; but stay in the city until you have been clothed with power from on high.'

When he had led them out to the vicinity of Bethany, he lifted up his hands and blessed them. While he was blessing them, he left them and was taken up into heaven. Then they worshipped him and returned to Jerusalem with great joy. And they stayed continually at the temple, praising God.

Luke 24:44–53

'For my sake and the gospel's, go
    And tell redemption's story';
His heralds answer, 'Be it so,
    And Thine, Lord, all the glory!'
They preach His birth, His life, His cross,
    The love of His atonement,
For whom they count the world but loss,
    His Easter, His enthronement.

Edward Henry Bickersteth, 1825–1906

God, our refuge

He who dwells in the shelter of the Most High will rest in the shadow of the Almighty. I will say of the Lord, 'He is my refuge and my fortress, my God, in whom I trust.'

Surely he will save you from the fowler's snare and from the deadly pestilence. He will cover you with his feathers, and under his wings you will find refuge; his faithfulness will be your shield and rampart. You will not fear the terror of night, nor the arrow that flies by day, nor the pestilence that stalks in the darkness, nor the plague that destroys at midday. A thousand may fall at your side, ten thousand at your right hand, but it will not come near you. You will only observe with your eyes and see the punishment of the wicked.

Psalm 91:1–8

Inspirer and Hearer of prayer,
    Thou Shepherd and Guardian of Thine,
My all to Thy covenant care
    I sleeping and waking resign.
If Thou art my Shield and my Sun,
    The night is no darkness to me;
And fast as my moments roll on,
    They bring me but nearer to Thee.

Augustus Montague Toplady, 1740–78

Continuing in prayer

Then Jesus told his disciples a parable to show them that they should always pray and not give up. He said: 'In a certain town there was a judge who neither feared God nor cared about men. And there was a widow in that town who kept coming to him with the plea, "Grant me justice against my adversary."

'For some time he refused. But finally he said to himself, "Even though I don't fear God or care about men, yet because this widow keeps bothering me, I will see that she gets justice, so that she won't eventually wear me out with her coming!"'

And the Lord said, 'Listen to what the unjust judge says. And will not God bring about justice for his chosen ones, who cry out to him day and night? Will he keep putting them off? I tell you, he will see that they get justice, and quickly. However, when the Son of Man comes, will he find faith on the earth?'

Luke 18:1–8

Prayer is the burden of a sigh,
  The falling of a tear;
The upward glancing of an eye,
  When none but God is near.

Prayer is the Christian's vital breath,
  The Christian's native air;
His watchword at the gates of death;
  He enters heaven with prayer.

James Montgomery, 1771–1854

Trusting in God

Some wandered in desert wastelands, finding no way to
a city where they could settle. They were hungry and
thirsty, and their lives ebbed away. Then they cried out
to the Lord in their trouble, and he delivered them from
their distress. He led them by a straight way to a city
where they could settle. Let them give thanks to the
Lord for his unfailing love and his wonderful deeds for
men, for he satisfies the thirsty and fills the hungry with
good things.

Psalm 107:4–9

He who fears the Lord has a secure fortress, and for his
children it will be a refuge.

The fear of the Lord is a fountain of life, turning a
man from the snares of death.

Proverbs 14:26–27

> Put thou thy trust in God,
>   In duty's path go on;
> Walk in His strength with faith and hope,
>   So shall thy work be done.
>
> Commit thy ways to Him,
>   Thy works into His hands,
> And rest on His unchanging word,
>   Who heaven and earth commands.
>
> Leave to His sovereign sway
>   To choose and to command;
> So shalt thou, wondering, own His way,
>   How wise, how strong, His hand.

Paul Gerhardt, 1607–76
tr. John Wesley, 1703–91

On life's journey

Remember your word to your servant, for you have given me hope. My comfort in my suffering is this: Your promise preserves my life. The arrogant mock me without restraint, but I do not turn from your law. I remember your ancient laws, O Lord, and I find comfort in them. Indignation grips me because of the wicked, who have forsaken your law. Your decrees are the theme of my song wherever I lodge. In the night I remember your name, O Lord, and I will keep your law. This has been my practice: I obey your precepts.

Psalm 119:49–56

Children of the heavenly King,
As ye journey, sweetly sing;
Sing your Saviour's worthy praise,
Glorious in His works and ways.

We are travelling home to God
In the way the fathers trod;
They are happy now, and we
Soon their happiness shall see.

Lord, obediently we go,
Gladly leaving all below:
Only Thou our Leader be,
And we still will follow Thee.

John Cennick, 1718–55

Jesus, our Lord

'I am the Alpha and the Omega,' says the Lord God, 'who is, and who was, and who is to come, the Almighty.'

I, John, your brother and companion in the suffering and kingdom and patient endurance that are ours in Jesus, was on the island of Patmos because of the word of God and the testimony of Jesus. On the Lord's Day I was in the Spirit, and I heard behind me a loud voice like a trumpet, which said: 'Write on a scroll what you see and send it to the seven churches: to Ephesus, Smyrna, Pergamum, Thyatira, Sardis, Philadelphia and Laodicea.'

Revelation 1:8–11

Love divine, all loves excelling,
    Joy of heaven, to earth come down,
Fix in us Thy humble dwelling,
    All Thy faithful mercies crown.
Jesus, Thou art all compassion,
    Pure, unbounded love Thou art;
Visit us with Thy salvation,
    Enter every trembling heart.

Breathe, O breathe Thy loving Spirit
    Into every troubled breast;
Let us all in Thee inherit,
    Let us find Thy promised rest.
Take away the love of sinning,
    Alpha and Omega be;
End of faith, as its beginning,
    Set our hearts at liberty.

Charles Wesley, 1707–88

He lives for ever!

I turned round to see the voice that was speaking to me. And when I turned I saw seven golden lampstands, and among the lampstands was someone 'like a son of man', dressed in a robe reaching down to his feet and with a golden sash round his chest. His head and hair were white like wool, as white as snow, and his eyes were like blazing fire. His feet were like bronze glowing in a furnace, and his voice was like the sound of rushing waters. In his right hand he held seven stars, and out of his mouth came a sharp double-edged sword. His face was like the sun shining in all its brilliance.

When I saw him, I fell at his feet as though dead. Then he placed his right hand on me and said: 'Do not be afraid. I am the First and the Last. I am the Living One; I was dead, and behold I am alive for ever and ever! And I hold the keys of death and Hades.'

Revelation 1:12–18

Rejoice and be glad! the Redeemer hath come:
Go, look on His cradle, His cross, and His tomb.

Sound His praises, tell the story of Him who was slain;
Sound His praises, tell with gladness He liveth again.

Rejoice and be glad! for the Lamb that was slain
O'er death is triumphant, and liveth again.

Horatius Bonar, 1808–89

My Lord and my God!

Now Thomas (called Didymus), one of the Twelve, was not with the disciples when Jesus came. So the other disciples told him, 'We have seen the Lord!'

But he said to them, 'Unless I see the nail marks in his hands and put my finger where the nails were, and put my hand into his side, I will not believe it.'

A week later his disciples were in the house again, and Thomas was with them. Though the doors were locked, Jesus came and stood among them and said, 'Peace be with you!' Then he said to Thomas, 'Put your finger here; see my hands. Reach out your hand and put it into my side. Stop doubting and believe.'

Thomas said to him, 'My Lord and my God!'

Then Jesus told him, 'Because you have seen me, you have believed; blessed are those who have not seen and yet have believed.'

John 20:24–29

Lord, in this blest and hallowed hour
Reveal Thy presence and Thy power;
Show to my faith Thy hands and side,
My Lord and God, the Crucified!

Josiah Conder, 1789–1855

The city of our God

In that day this song will be sung in the land of Judah:
We have a strong city; God makes salvation its walls
and ramparts. Open the gates that the righteous nation
may enter, the nation that keeps faith. You will keep
in perfect peace him whose mind is steadfast, because
he trusts in you. Trust in the Lord for ever, for the Lord,
the Lord, is the Rock eternal.

The path of the righteous is level; O upright One,
you make the way of the righteous smooth. Yes, Lord,
walking in the way of your laws, we wait for you; your
name and renown are the desire of our hearts. My soul
yearns for you in the night; in the morning my spirit
longs for you. When your judgments come upon the
earth, the people of the world learn righteousness.

Isaiah 26:1–4, 7–9

How glorious Zion's courts appear,
   The city of our God!
His throne He hath established here,
   Here fixed His loved abode.

Its walls, defended by His grace,
   No power shall e'er o'erthrow,
Salvation is its bulwark sure
   Against the assaulting foe.

Here shall ye taste unmingled joys,
   And dwell in perfect peace,
Ye, who have known Jehovah's Name,
   And trusted in His grace.

Scottish Paraphrases, 1781

'Turn to me and be saved'

'Turn to me and be saved, all you ends of the earth; for I am God, and there is no other. By myself I have sworn, my mouth has uttered in all integrity a word that will not be revoked: Before me every knee will bow; by me every tongue will swear. They will say of me, "In the Lord alone are righteousness and strength."' All who have raged against him will come to him and be put to shame. But in the Lord all the descendants of Israel will be found righteous and will exult.

Isaiah 45:22–25

For it is by grace you have been saved, through faith – and this not from yourselves, it is the gift of God – not by works, so that no-one can boast.

Ephesians 2:8–9

> Look unto Him, ye nations, own
> Your God, ye fallen race;
> Look, and be saved through faith alone,
> Be justified by grace.

Charles Wesley, 1707–88

The good news of peace

How beautiful on the mountains are the feet of those who bring good news, who proclaim peace, who bring good tidings, who proclaim salvation, who say to Zion, 'Your God reigns!' Listen! Your watchmen lift up their voices; together they shout for joy. When the Lord returns to Zion, they will see it with their own eyes. Burst into songs of joy together, you ruins of Jerusalem, for the Lord has comforted his people, he has redeemed Jerusalem. The Lord will lay bare his holy arm in the sight of all the nations, and all the ends of the earth will see the salvation of our God.

Isaiah 52:7–10

How beauteous are their feet
　　Who stand on Zion's hill,
Who bring salvation on their tongues
　　And words of peace reveal!

The Lord makes bare His arm
　　Through all the earth abroad;
Let every nation now behold
　　Their Saviour and their God.

Isaac Watts, 1674–1748

The triumph of grace

'Build up, build up, prepare the road! Remove the obstacles out of the way of my people.' For this is what the high and lofty One says – he who lives for ever, whose name is holy: 'I live in a high and holy place, but also with him who is contrite and lowly in spirit, to revive the spirit of the lowly and to revive the heart of the contrite. I will not accuse for ever, nor will I always be angry, for then the spirit of man would grow faint before me – the breath of man that I have created. I was enraged by his sinful greed; I punished him, and hid my face in anger, yet he kept on in his wilful ways. I have seen his ways, but I will heal him; I will guide him and restore comfort to him, creating praise on the lips of the mourners in Israel. Peace, peace, to those far and near,' says the Lord. 'And I will heal them.'

Isaiah 57:14–19

O how I fear Thee, living God,
　　With deepest, tenderest fears,
And worship Thee with trembling hope
　　And penitential tears!

Yet I may love Thee, too, O Lord,
　　Almighty as Thou art;
For Thou hast stooped to ask of me
　　The love of my poor heart.

Frederick William Faber, 1814–63

Coming to Christ

'Come to me, all you who are weary and burdened, and I will give you rest. Take my yoke upon you and learn from me, for I am gentle and humble in heart, and you will find rest for your souls. For my yoke is easy and my burden is light.'

Matthew 11:28–30

'For God so loved the world that he gave his only begotten Son, that whoever believes in him shall not perish but have eternal life.'

John 3:16

> Jesu, lover of my soul,
>   Let me to Thy bosom fly,
> While the nearer waters roll,
>   While the tempest still is high:
> Hide me, O my Saviour, hide,
>   Till the storm of life be past;
> Safe into the haven guide;
>   O receive my soul at last!
>
> Other refuge have I none;
>   Hangs my helpless soul on Thee;
> Leave, ah! leave me not alone,
>   Still support and comfort me:
> All my trust on Thee is stayed,
>   All my help from Thee I bring;
> Cover my defenceless head
>   With the shadow of Thy wing.

Charles Wesley, 1707–88

Our sovereign protector

If you make the Most High your dwelling – even the Lord, who is my refuge – then no harm will befall you, no disaster will come near your tent. For he will command his angels concerning you to guard you in all your ways; they will lift you up in their hands, so that you will not strike your foot against a stone. You will tread upon the lion and the cobra; you will trample the great lion and the serpent.

'Because he loves me,' says the Lord, 'I will rescue him; I will protect him, for he acknowledges my name. He will call upon me, and I will answer him; I will be with him in trouble, I will deliver him and honour him. With long life will I satisfy him and show him my salvation.'

Psalm 91:9–16

> A sovereign Protector I have,
>   Unseen, yet for ever at hand,
> Unchangeably faithful to save,
>   Almighty to rule and command.
> He smiles, and my comforts abound;
>   His grace as the dew shall descend;
> And walls of salvation surround
>   The soul He delights to defend.

Augustus Montague Toplady, 1740–78

Rejoice in the Lord!

Though the fig-tree does not bud and there are no grapes
on the vines, though the olive crop fails and the fields
produce no food, though there are no sheep in the pen
and no cattle in the stalls, yet I will rejoice in the Lord,
I will be joyful in God my Saviour.

The Sovereign Lord is my strength; he makes my feet
like the feet of a deer, he enables me to go on the heights.
Habakkuk 3:17–19

Rejoice in the Lord always. I will say it again: Rejoice!
Philippians 4:4

> Though vine nor fig-tree neither
> Their wonted fruit should bear,
> Though all the field should wither,
> Nor flocks nor herds be there,
> Yet God the same abiding,
> His praise shall tune my voice;
> For while in Him confiding,
> I cannot but rejoice.

William Cowper, 1731–1800

Christ in us

I have become its [the church's] servant by the commission God gave me to present to you the word of God in its fulness – the mystery that has been kept hidden for ages and generations, but is now disclosed to the saints. To them God has chosen to make known among the Gentiles the glorious riches of this mystery, which is Christ in you, the hope of glory.

We proclaim him, admonishing and teaching everyone with all wisdom, so that we may present everyone perfect in Christ. To this end I labour, struggling with all his energy, which so powerfully works in me.

I want you to know how much I am struggling for you and for those at Laodicea, and for all who have not met me personally. My purpose is that they may be encouraged in heart and united in love, so that they may have the full riches of complete understanding, in order that they may know the mystery of God, namely, Christ, in whom are hidden all the treasures of wisdom and knowledge. I tell you this so that no-one may deceive you by fine-sounding arguments. For though I am absent from you in body, I am present with you in spirit and delight to see how orderly you are and how firm your faith in Christ is.

Colossians 1:25 – 2:5

Jesus, Prince of Peace, be near us,
    Fix in all our hearts Thy home;
With Thy gracious presence cheer us,
    Let Thy sacred kingdom come.
Raise to heaven our expectation;
    Give our ransomed souls to prove
Glorious and complete salvation
    In the realms of bliss above.

Charles Wesley, 1707 – 88

Longing for home

How lovely is your dwelling-place, O Lord Almighty!
My soul yearns, even faints, for the courts of the Lord;
my heart and my flesh cry out for the living God

Even the sparrow has found a home, and the swallow
a nest for herself, where she may have her young – a
place near your altar, O Lord Almighty, my King and
my God. Blessed are those who dwell in your house; they
are ever praising you.

Blessed are those whose strength is in you, who have
set their hearts on pilgrimage. As they pass through the
Valley of Baca, they make it a place of springs; the
autumn rains also cover it with pools. They go from
strength to strength, till each appears before God in
Zion.

Psalm 84:1–7

> Pleasant are Thy courts above,
> In the land of light and love;
> Pleasant are Thy courts below,
> In this land of sin and woe.
> O! my spirit longs and faints
> For the converse of Thy saints,
> For the brightness of Thy face,
> For Thy fulness, God of grace!
>
> Happy souls! their praises flow
> Even in this vale of woe;
> Waters in the desert rise,
> Manna feeds them from the skies.
> On they go from strength to strength,
> Till they reach Thy throne at length,
> At Thy feet adoring fall,
> Who hast led them safe through all.

Henry Francis Lyte, 1793–1847

The greatness of Christ

Although I hope to come to you soon, I am writing you these instructions so that, if I am delayed, you will know how people ought to conduct themselves in God's household, which is the church of the living God, the pillar and foundation of the truth. Beyond all question, the mystery of godliness is great: He appeared in a body, was vindicated by the Spirit, was seen by angels, was preached among the nations, was believed on in the world, was taken up in glory.

1 Timothy 3:14–16

The Word became flesh and made his dwelling among us.

John 1:14

> Let earth and heaven combine,
>   Angels and men agree,
> To praise in songs divine,
>   The incarnate Deity,
> Our God contracted to a span,
> Incomprehensibly made man.
>
> Unsearchable the love
>   That hath the Saviour brought;
> The grace is far above
>   Or man or angel's thought:
> Suffice for us that God, we know,
> Our God, is manifest below.

Charles Wesley, 1707–88

The majestic king

The Lord announced the word, and great was the company of those who proclaimed it: 'Kings and armies flee in haste; in the camps men divide the plunder.'

The chariots of God are tens of thousands and thousands of thousands; the Lord has come from Sinai into his sanctuary. When you ascended on high, you led captives in your train; you received gifts from men, even from the rebellious – that you, O Lord God, might dwell there.

Praise be to the Lord, to God our Saviour, who daily bears our burdens.

Our God is a God who saves; from the Sovereign Lord comes escape from death.

Psalm 68:11–12, 17–20

> Songs of praise the angels sang,
> Heaven with hallelujahs rang,
> When creation was begun,
> When God spake and it was done.
>
> Songs of praise awoke the morn,
> When the Prince of Peace was born;
> Songs of praise arose, when He
> Captive led captivity.
>
> Heaven and earth must pass away,
> Songs of praise shall crown that day;
> God will make new heavens, new earth,
> Songs of praise shall hail their birth.

James Montgomery, 1771–1854

God helps us

In my anguish I cried to the Lord, and he answered by setting me free. The Lord is with me; I will not be afraid. What can man do to me? The Lord is with me; he is my helper. I will look in triumph on my enemies.

It is better to take refuge in the Lord than to trust in man. It is better to take refuge in the Lord than to trust in princes.

Psalm 118:5–9

And my God will meet all your needs according to his glorious riches in Christ Jesus.

Philippians 4:19

> Why should I fear the darkest hour,
> Or tremble at the tempter's power?
> Jesus vouchsafes to be my tower.
>
> Though hot the fight, why quit the field?
> Why must I either fly or yield,
> Since Jesus is my mighty shield?
>
> I know not what may soon betide,
> Or how my wants shall be supplied;
> But Jesus knows, and will provide.

John Newton, 1725–1807

Casting our cares on the Lord

Cast your cares on the Lord and he will sustain you; he
will never let the righteous fall.

Psalm 55:22

Do not be anxious about anything, but in everything,
by prayer and petition, with thanksgiving, present your
requests to God. And the peace of God, which transcends
all understanding, will guard your hearts and your
minds in Christ Jesus.

Finally, brothers, whatever is true, whatever is noble,
whatever is right, whatever is pure, whatever is lovely,
whatever is admirable – if anything is excellent or
praiseworthy – think about such things. Whatever you
have learned or received or heard from me, or seen in
me – put it into practice. And the God of peace will be
with you.

Philippians 4:6–9

How gentle God's commands,
How kind His precepts are!
Come, cast your burdens on the Lord,
And trust His constant care.

While providence supports,
Let saints securely dwell;
That hand which bears all Nature up
Shall guide His children well.

Why should this anxious load
Press down your weary mind?
Haste to your heavenly Father's throne,
And sweet refreshment find.

Philip Doddridge, 1702–51

Christ above all

So he [God's Son] became as much superior to the angels
as the name he has inherited is superior to theirs.

For to which of the angels did God ever say, 'You are
my Son; today I have begotten you'? Or again, 'I will be
his Father, and he will be my Son'? And again, when
God brings his firstborn into the world, he says, 'Let all
God's angels worship him.' In speaking of the angels he
says, 'He makes his angels winds, his servants flames
of fire.' But about the Son he says, 'Your throne, O God,
will last for ever and ever, and righteousness will be the
sceptre of your kingdom. You have loved righteousness
and hated wickedness; therefore God, your God, has set
you above your companions by anointing you with the
oil of joy.'

Hebrews 1:4–9

Name of Jesus! highest Name!
   Name that earth and heaven adore!
From the heart of God it came,
   Leads me to God's heart once more.

Only Jesus! fairest Name!
   Life, and rest, and peace, and bliss,
Jesus, evermore the same,
   He is mine, and I am His.

Gerhard Tersteegen, 1667–1769
tr. Emma Frances Bevan, 1827–1909

The final judgment

Then I saw a great white throne and him who was seated on it. Earth and sky fled from his presence, and there was no place for them. And I saw the dead, great and small, standing before the throne, and books were opened. Another book was opened, which is the book of life. The dead were judged according to what they had done as recorded in the books. The sea gave up the dead that were in it, and death and Hades gave up the dead that were in them, and each person was judged according to what he had done. Then death and Hades were thrown into the lake of fire. The lake of fire is the second death. If anyone's name was not found written in the book of life, he was thrown into the lake of fire.

Revelation 20:11–15

Behold! on flying clouds He comes,
   And all earth's nations then shall see
The glorious face of Him from whom
   Both heaven and earth away shall flee.

The unbelieving world shall wail,
   While we rejoice to see the day;
Come, Lord, nor let Thy promise fail,
   Nor let Thy chariots long delay!

Isaac Watts, 1674–1748

The new Jerusalem

Then I saw a new heaven and a new earth, for the first heaven and the first earth had passed away, and there was no longer any sea. I saw the Holy City, the new Jerusalem, coming down out of heaven from God, prepared as a bride beautifully dressed for her husband. And I heard a loud voice from the throne saying, 'Now the dwelling of God is with men, and he will live with them. They will be his people, and God himself will be with them and be their God. He will wipe every tear from their eyes. There will be no more death or mourning or crying or pain, for the old order of things has passed away.'

He who was seated on the throne said, 'I am making everything new!' Then he said, 'Write this down, for these words are trustworthy and true.'

He said to me: 'It is done. I am the Alpha and the Omega, the Beginning and the End. To him who is thirsty I will give to drink without cost from the spring of the water of life. He who overcomes will inherit all this, and I will be his God and he will be my son.'

Revelation 21:1–7

O Christ, He is the fountain,
  The deep, sweet well of love;
The streams on earth I've tasted,
  More deep I'll drink above;
There, to an ocean fulness,
  His mercy doth expand,
And glory, glory dwelleth
  In Immanuel's land.

Anne Ross Cousin, 1824–1906

DECEMBER 18

The river of life

Then the angel showed me the river of the water of life, as clear as crystal, flowing from the throne of God and of the Lamb down the middle of the great street of the city. On each side of the river stood the tree of life, bearing twelve crops of fruit, yielding its fruit every month. And the leaves of the tree are for the healing of the nations. No longer will there be any curse. The throne of God and of the Lamb will be in the city, and his servants will serve him. They will see his face, and his name will be on their foreheads. There will be no more night. They will not need the light of a lamp or the light of the sun, for the Lord God will give them light. And they will reign for ever and ever.

Revelation 22:1–5

There is a land of pure delight,
  Where saints immortal reign;
Infinite day excludes the night,
  And pleasures banish pain.

Isaac Watts, 1674–1748

The sign of Immanuel

Again the Lord spoke to Ahaz, 'Ask the Lord your God for a sign, whether in the deepest depths or in the highest heights.'

But Ahaz said, 'I will not ask; I will not put the Lord to the test.'

Then Isaiah said, 'Hear now, you house of David! Is it not enough to try the patience of men? Will you try the patience of my God also? Therefore the Lord himself will give you a sign: The virgin will be with child and will give birth to a son, and will call him Immanuel. He will eat curds and honey when he knows enough to reject the wrong and choose the right. But before the the boy knows enough to reject the wrong and choose the right, the land of the two kings you dread will be laid waste, the Lord will bring on you and on your people and on the house of your father a time unlike any since Ephraim broke away from Judah – he will bring the king of Assyria.'

Isaiah 7:10–17

Christ, by highest heaven adored,
Christ, the Everlasting Lord,
Late in time behold Him come,
Offspring of a virgin's womb.
Veiled in flesh the Godhead see!
Hail the incarnate Deity!
Pleased as Man with man to dwell,
Jesus, our Immanuel.

Hark! the herald angels sing
Glory to the new-born King.

Charles Wesley, 1707–88

The wonderful counsellor

The people walking in darkness have seen a great light; on those living in the land of the shadow of death a light has dawned. You have enlarged the nation and increased their joy; they rejoice before you as people rejoice at the harvest, as men rejoice when dividing the plunder. For as in the day of Midian's defeat, you have shattered the yoke that burdens them, the bar across their shoulders, the rod of their oppressor. Every warrior's boot used in battle and every garment rolled in blood will be destined for burning, will be fuel for the fire. For to us a child is born, to us a son is given, and the government will be on his shoulders. And he will be called Wonderful Counsellor, Mighty God, Everlasting Father, Prince of Peace. Of the increse of his government and peace there will be no end. He will reign on David's throne and over his kingdom, establishing and upholding it with justice and righteousness from that time on and for ever. The zeal of the Lord Almighty will accomplish this.

Isaiah 9:2−7

Thou whose Name is called Jesus,
　　Risen Lord of life and power,
O it is so sweet to trust Thee
　　Every day and every hour!
Of Thy wondrous grace I sing,
Saviour, Counsellor and King.

Jean Sophia Pigott, 1845−82

The ruler from Bethlehem

Marshal your troops, O city of troops, for a siege is laid against us. They will strike Israel's ruler on the cheek with a rod.

'But you, Bethlehem Ephrathah, though you are small among the clans of Judah, out of you come for me one who will be ruler over Israel, whose origins are from of old, from ancient times.'

Therefore Israel will be abandoned until the time when she who is in labour gives birth and the rest of his brothers return to join the Israelites.

He will stand and shepherd his flock in the strength of the Lord, in the majesty of the name of the Lord his God. And they will live securely, for then his greatness will reach to the ends of the earth. And he will be their peace.

Micah 5:1–5

Jesus was born in Bethlehem in Judea, during the time of King Herod.

Matthew 2:1

> O holy Child of Bethlehem,
>   Descend to us, we pray;
> Cast out our sin, and enter in;
>   Be born in us today.
> We hear the Christmas angels
>   The great glad tidings tell;
> O come to us, abide with us,
>   Our Lord Immanuel.

Phillips Brooks, 1835–93

Jesus' birth foretold

In the sixth month, God sent the angel Gabriel to Nazareth, a town in Galilee, to a virgin pledged to be married to a man named Joseph, a descendant of David. The virgin's name was Mary. The angel went to her and said, 'Greetings, you who are highly favoured! The Lord is with you.'

Mary was greatly troubled at his words and wondered what kind of greeting this might be. But the angel said to her, 'Do not be afraid, Mary, you have found favour with God. You will be with child and give birth to a son, and you are to give him the name Jesus. He will be great and will be called the Son of the Most High. The Lord God will give him the throne of his father David, and he will reign over the house of Jacob for ever; his kingdom will never end.'

'How will this be,' Mary asked the angel, 'since I am a virgin?' The angel answered, 'The Holy Spirit will come upon you, and the power of the Most High will overshadow you. So the holy one to be born will be called the Son of God. Even Elizabeth your relative is going to have a child in her old age, and she who was said to be barren is in her sixth month. For nothing is impossible with God.'

'I am the Lord's servant,' Mary answered. 'May it be to me as you have said.' Then the angel left her.

Luke 1:26–38

> Silent night! holy night!
> Son of God, love's pure light
> Radiant beams from Thy holy face,
> With the dawn of redeeming grace,
> Jesus, Lord, at Thy birth.

Joseph Mohr, 1792–1848

Zechariah's prophecy

Zechariah was filled with the Holy Spirit and prophesied: 'Praise be to the Lord, the God of Israel, because he has come and has redeemed his people. He has raised up a horn of salvation for us in the house of his servant David (as he said through his holy prophets of long ago), salvation from our enemies and from the hand of all who hate us – to show mercy to our fathers and to remember his holy covenant, the oath he swore to our father Abraham: to rescue us from the hand of our enemies, and to enable us to serve him without fear in holiness and righteousness before him all our days.'

Luke 1:67–75

O come, O come, Immanuel,
And ransom captive Israel,
That mourns in lonely exile here
Until the Son of God appear.

Rejoice! rejoice! Immanuel
Shall come to thee, O Israel!

Latin, 12th century
tr. John Mason Neale, 1818–66

O come let us adore him!

In the beginning was the Word, and the Word was with God, and the Word was God. He was with God in the beginning. Through him all things were made; without him nothing was made that has been made. In him was life, and that life was the light of men. The light shines in the darkness, but the darkness has not understood it.

There came a man who was sent from God; his name was John. He came as a witness to testify concerning that light, so that through him all men might believe. He himself was not the light; he came only as a witness to the light. The true light that gives light to every man was coming into the world.

The Word became flesh and made his dwelling among us. We have seen his glory, the glory of the Begotten, who came from the Father, full of grace and truth.

John 1:1–9, 14

O come, all ye faithful,
Joyful and triumphant,
O come ye, O come ye to Bethlehem;
Come and behold Him,
Born the King of angels:

O come, let us adore Him,
O come, let us adore Him,
O come, let us adore Him, Christ the Lord!

God of God,
Light of Light,
Lo, He abhors not the Virgin's womb;
Very God,
Begotten, not created.

Latin, 17th century
tr. Frederick Oakeley, 1802–80

The Saviour is born

In those days Caesar Augustus issued a decree that a census should be taken of the entire Roman world. (This was the first census that took place while Quirinius was governor of Syria.) And everyone went to his own town to register.

So Joseph also went up from the town of Nazareth in Galilee to Judea, to Bethlehem the town of David, because he belonged to the house and line of David. He went there to register with Mary, who was pledged to be married to him and was expecting a child. While they were there, the time came for the baby to be born, and she gave birth to her firstborn, a son. She wrapped him in cloths and placed him in a manger, because there was no room for them in the inn.

Luke 2:1–7

Once in royal David's city
  Stood a lowly cattle-shed,
Where a mother laid her Baby
  In a manger for His bed.
Mary was that mother mild,
Jesus Christ her little Child.

He came down to earth from heaven
  Who is God and Lord of all,
And His shelter was a stable,
  And His cradle was a stall.
With the poor, and mean, and lowly
Lived on earth our Saviour holy.

Cecil Frances Alexander, 1818–95

The shepherds and the angels

And there were shepherds living out in the fields near by, keeping watch over their flocks at night. An angel of the Lord appeared to them, and the glory of the Lord shone around them, and they were terrified. But the angel said to them, 'Do not be afraid. I bring you good news of great joy that will be for all the people. Today in the town of David a Saviour has been born to you; he is Christ the Lord. This will be a sign to you: You will find a baby wrapped in cloths and lying in a manger.'

Suddenly a great company of the heavenly host appeared with the angel, praising God and saying, 'Glory to God in the highest, and on earth peace to men on whom his favour rests.'

When the angels had left them and gone into heaven, the shepherds said to one another, 'Let's go to Bethlehem and see this thing that has happened, which the Lord has told us about.'

Luke 2:8–15

Then to the watchful shepherds it was told,
Who heard the angelic herald's voice, 'Behold,
I bring good tidings of a Saviour's birth
To you and all the nations upon earth;
This day hath God fulfilled His promised word,
This day is born a Saviour, Christ the Lord.'

He spake; and straightway the celestial choir
In hymns of joy unknown before conspire;
The praises of redeeming love they sang,
And heaven's whole orb with hallelujahs rang;
God's highest glory was their anthem still,
'Peace upon earth, and unto men goodwill.'

John Byrom, 1692–1768

The Magi worship Jesus

After Jesus was born in Bethlehem in Judea, during the time of King Herod, Magi from the east came to Jerusalem and asked, 'Where is the one who has been born king of the Jews? We saw his star in the east and have come to worship him.'

Then Herod called the Magi secretly and found out from them the exact time the star had appeared. He sent them to Bethlehem and said, 'Go and make a careful search for the child. As soon as you find him, report to me, so that I too may go and worship him.'

After they had heard the king, they went on their way, and the star they had seen in the east went ahead of them until it stopped over the place where the child was. When they saw the star, they were overjoyed. On coming to the house, they saw the child with his mother Mary, and they bowed down and worshipped him. Then they opened their treasures and presented him with gifts of gold and of incense and of myrrh. And having been warned in a dream not to go back to Herod, they returned to their country by another route.

Matthew 2:1–2, 7–12

Then entered in those wise men three
Full reverently on bended knee,
And offered there, in His presence,
Their gold, and myrrh, and frankincense.

Nowell, Nowell, Nowell, Nowell,
Born is the King of Israel.

Then let us all with one accord
Sing praises to our heavenly Lord,
That hath made heaven and earth of nought,
And with His blood mankind hath bought.

Traditional, c. 17th century

Jesus is kept safe

When they had gone, an angel of the Lord appeared to Joseph in a dream. 'Get up,' he said, 'take the child and his mother and escape to Egypt. Stay there until I tell you, for Herod is going to search for the child to kill him.' So he got up, took the child and his mother during the night and left for Egypt, where he stayed until the death of Herod. And so was fulfilled what the Lord had said through the prophet: 'Out of Egypt I called my son.'

When Herod realised that he had been outwitted by the Magi, he was furious, and he gave orders to kill all the boys in Bethlehem and its vicinity who were two years old and under, in accordance with the time he had learned from the Magi. Then what was said through the prophet Jeremiah was fulfilled: 'A voice is heard in Ramah, weeping and great mourning, Rachel weeping for her children and refusing to be comforted, because they are no more.'

Matthew 2:13–18

Unto us a Boy is born!
　King of all creation,
Came He to a world forlorn
　The Lord of every nation.

Herod then with fear was filled:
　'A Prince,' he said, 'in Jewry!'
All the little boys he killed
　At Bethlehem in his fury.

Now may Mary's Son, who came
　So long ago to love us,
Lead us all with hearts aflame
　Unto the joys above us.

German, 15th century
tr. Percy Dearmer, 1867–1936

The long-expected Jesus

Now there was a man in Jerusalem called Simeon, who was righteous and devout. He was waiting for the consolation of Israel, and the Holy Spirit was upon him. It had been revealed to him by the Holy Spirit that he would not die before he had seen the Lord's Christ. Moved by the Spirit, he went into the temple courts. When the parents brought in the child Jesus to do for him what the custom of the Law required, Simeon took him in his arms and praised God, saying: 'Sovereign Lord, as you have promised, you now dismiss your servant in peace. For my eyes have seen your salvation, which you have prepared in the sight of all people, a light for revelation to the Gentiles and for glory to your people Israel.'

Luke 2:25–32

Come, Thou long-expected Jesus,
    Born to set Thy people free;
From our fears and sins release us,
    Let us find our rest in Thee.

Israel's strength and consolation,
    Hope of all the earth Thou art;
Dear desire of every nation,
    Joy of every longing heart.

Charles Wesley, 1707–88

Hallelujah!

Praise the Lord.

Praise God in his sanctuary; praise him in his mighty heavens. Praise him for his acts of power; praise him for his surpassing greatness. Praise him with the sounding of the trumpet, praise him with the harp and lyre, praise him with tambourine and dancing, praise him with the strings and flute, praise him with the clash of cymbals, praise him with resounding cymbals. Let everything that has breath praise the Lord.

Praise the Lord.

Psalm 150:1–6

O praise ye the Lord!
　Praise Him in the height;
Rejoice in His Word,
　Ye angels of light;
Ye heavens, adore Him
　By whom ye were made,
And worship before Him,
　In brightness arrayed.

O praise ye the Lord!
　Thanksgiving and song
To Him be outpoured
　All ages along:
For love in creation,
　For heaven restored,
For grace of salvation
　O praise ye the Lord!

Henry Williams Baker, 1821–77

Come, Lord Jesus!

'I, Jesus, have sent my angel to give you this testimony for the churches. I am the Root and the Offspring of David, and the bright Morning Star.'

The Spirit and the bride say, 'Come!' And let him who hears say, 'Come!' Whoever is thirsty, let him come; and whoever wishes, let him take the free gift of the water of life.

I warn everyone who hears the words of the prophecy of this book: If anyone adds anything to them, God will add to him the plagues described in this book. And if anyone takes words away from this book of prophecy, God will take away from him his share in the tree of life and in the holy city, which are described in this book.

He who testifies to these things says, 'Yes, I am coming soon.' Amen. Come, Lord Jesus. The grace of the Lord Jesus be with God's people. Amen.

Revelation 22:16–21

> Yea, Amen! let all adore Thee,
>   High on Thine eternal throne!
> Saviour, take the power and glory;
>   Claim the kingdom for Thine own:
>   O come quickly!
>   Hallelujah, come, Lord, come!

John Cennick, 1718–55,
and Charles Wesley, 1707–88

COLLINS GEM

COLLINS GEM

Bestselling Collins Gem titles include:

Gem English Dictionary (£3.50)
Gem Calorie Counter (£2.99)
Gem Thesaurus (£2.99)
Gem French Dictionary (£3.50)
Gem German Dictionary (£3.50)
Gem Burns Anthology (£3.50)
Gem Birds (£3.50)
Gem Babies' Names (£3.50)
Gem Card Games (£3.50)
Gem World Atlas (£3.50)

All Collins Gems are available from your local bookseller or can be ordered direct from the publishers.

In the UK, contact Mail Order, Dept 2M, HarperCollins Publishers, Westerhill Rd, Bishopbriggs, Glasgow, G64 2QT, listing the titles required and enclosing a cheque or p.o. for the value of the books plus £1.00 for the first title and 25p for each additional title to cover p&p. Access and Visa cardholders can order on 041-772 2281 (24 hr).

In Australia, contact Customer Services, HarperCollins Distribution, Yarrawa Rd, Moss Vale 2577 (tel. [048] 68 0300). **In New Zealand**, contact Customer Services, HarperCollins Publishers, 31 View Rd, Glenfield, Auckland 10 (tel. [09] 444 3740). **In Canada**, contact your local bookshop.

All prices quoted are correct at time of going to press.